D1614183

Digital Watermarking
for Digital Media

Juergen Seitz
University of Cooperative Education Heidenheim, Germany

 Information Science Publishing

Hershey • London • Melbourne • Singapore

Acquisitions Editor:	Renée Davies
Development Editor:	Kristin Roth
Senior Managing Editor:	Amanda Appicello
Managing Editor:	Jennifer Neidig
Copy Editor:	Joyce Li
Typesetter:	Cindy Consonery
Cover Design:	Lisa Tosheff
Printed at:	Yurchak Printing Inc.

Published in the United States of America by
Information Science Publishing (an imprint of Idea Group Inc.)
701 E. Chocolate Avenue, Suite 200
Hershey PA 17033
Tel: 717-533-8845
Fax: 717-533-8661
E-mail: cust@idea-group.com
Web site: http://www.idea-group.com

and in the United Kingdom by
Information Science Publishing (an imprint of Idea Group Inc.)
3 Henrietta Street
Covent Garden
London WC2E 8LU
Tel: 44 20 7240 0856
Fax: 44 20 7379 3313
Web site: http://www.eurospan.co.uk

Library of Congress Cataloging-in-Publication Data

Digital watermarking for digital media / Juergen Seitz, editor.
     p. cm.
  Summary: "The book discusses new aspects of digital watermarking in a worldwide context"--Provided by publisher.
  Includes bibliographical references and index.
  ISBN 1-59140-518-1 (h/c) -- ISBN 1-59140-519-X (s/c) -- ISBN 1-59140-520-3 (ebook)
  1. Computer security. 2. Digital watermarking. 3. Multimedia systems--Security measures. 4. Intellectual property. I. Seitz, Juergen, 1968-
   QA76.9.A25D56 2005
   005.8'2--dc22
                                                  2004029852

British Cataloguing in Publication Data
A Cataloguing in Publication record for this book is available from the British Library.

All work contributed to this book is new, previously-unpublished material. The views expressed in this book are those of the authors, but not necessarily of the publisher.

zation (WIPO), political signals, which prove their importance, were set. Therefore, the features of the digital world lead to economical chances as well as to serious problems in simplifying unauthorized copying and distribution. Digital watermarking is a possibility to interface and close the gap between copyrights and digital distribution.

This book will take the reader through a series of discussions that describe, analyze, explain, and hypothesize about digital watermarking technology and its usage.

In Chapter I, *Digital Watermarking: An Introduction*, Tino Jahnke and I give an overview on the methodology of digital watermarking, as well as on requirements of applications, applications, and a categorization of attacks on digital watermarks. There is also a short summary of the historical development of digital watermarking technology. Activities, initiatives, and projects of different associations and interest groups are discussed.

The main focus of Chapter II, *Digital Watermarking Schemes for Multimedia Authentication*, written by Chang-Tsun Li, is on multimedia data authentication. The technical aspects of security, resolution of tamper localization, and embedding distortion are explained. Fragile, semi-fragile, and reversible schemes are the three main categories of watermarking approaches to the issues and challenges that are presented. Merits and limitations of the specific schemes are compared and discussed.

Dan Yu and Farook Sattar focus in Chapter III, *Digital Watermarking for Multimedia Transaction Tracking,* on the issue of transaction tracking in multimedia distribution applications through digital watermarking technology. An approach is proposed that can overcome the problems of existing watermarking schemes. In the absence of the original data, watermark, embedding locations, and strengths, the watermarking scheme is introduced for efficient watermark extraction with some side information. The robustness of the proposed scheme is discussed.

In Chapter IV, *A New Public-Key Algorithm for Watermarking of Digital Images*, Eberhard Stickel presents a two-dimensional public-key algorithm that is based on a one-time digital signature scheme in non-abelian groups. The public key is certified by a trusted third party. Authenticity may be verified by anybody who knows the certified public key. The approach is discussed in relation to images made by surveillance cameras of automatic teller machines (ATMs) in financial institutions.

Zhang Li and Sam Kwong present in Chapter V, *Geometric Distortions Correction Using Image Moment in Image Watermarking,* a method for detecting and recovering geometrical attacks, such as rotation, scaling, and translation, by using geometric moments of the original image. The moment information can be used as a preprocess of the extraction process. Different types of watermarking techniques are analyzed.

The main focus of Chapter VI, *Audio Watermarking: Requirements, Algorithms, and Benchmarking*, by Nedeljko Cvejic and Tapio Seppänen, is on the usage of digital watermarking for audio data. Audio watermarking algorithms are characterized. Signal modifications that are usually used to distort embedded watermarks and to prevent detection of hidden data are presented. Recently developed and future applications areas are listed.

Jong-Nam Kim and Byung-Ha Ahn introduce in Chapter VII, *MPEG Standards and Watermarking Technologies,* watermarking technologies of MPEG standards. A framework of watermarking technology for intellectual property protection is presented as well as an overview of MPEG-2/4, IPMP standard of MPEG-2/4, and watermarking technologies of MPEG-2/4 IPMP. The concept of IPMP and required technical items are summarized. MPEG-21 and its part 11, PAT (Persistent Association Technologies) methodologies, requirements, and evaluation methods are described. Future trends of MPEG-related watermarking technologies and requirements are discussed.

Ernst Leiss outlines in Chapter VIII, *Time-Variant Watermarks for Digital Videos: An MPEG-Based Approach,* an approach that permits a significant increase of the amount of information that can be accommodated in a watermark. The approach is formulated assuming the video is represented in an MPEG format. Implementation issues of time-variant watermarks are discussed with emphasis on defeating attacks using filtering, cropping, resizing, and other standard methods used to defeat watermarks, such as changing existing frames, as well as new attacks, such as removing, repeating, or permuting frames.

Finally, Alexander P. Pons and Hassan Aljifri present in Chapter IX, *Active Watermarking System: Protection of Digital Media,* a novel approach that combines the reactive rule-based scheme of an active database management system with the technology of digital watermarking to automatically protect digital data. The integration of these two technologies provides a powerful mechanism for protecting digital data in a consistent and formal manner.

References

Rosenblatt, B., Trippe, B., & Mooney, S. (2002). *Digital rights management— Business and technology*. New York: M&T Books.

SDMI. (n.d.). Retrieved June 4, 2004, from *http://www.sdmi.org*

VIVA. (n.d.). Retrieved June 4, 2004, from *http://www.intec.rug.ac.be/Research/Groups/hfhsdesign/viva/*

Acknowledgments

This book is the product of the collaborative efforts of many dedicated individuals. I would like to acknowledge the help of all involved in the collation and review process of the book, without whose support the project could not have been satisfactorily completed. Most of the authors of chapters included in this book also served as reviewers for articles written by other authors. Thanks to all those who provided constructive and comprehensive reviews.

The creation of this book has been a stimulating and enlightening experience and I hope that this book will be a useful addition to the literature on digital watermarking.

Dr. Juergen Seitz
University of Cooperative Education
Heidenheim, Germany
June 2004

Chapter I

Digital Watermarking:
An Introduction

Juergen Seitz
University of Cooperative Education Heidenheim, Germany

Tino Jahnke
University of Cooperative Education Heidenheim, Germany

Abstract

In order to solve intellectual property problems of the digital age, two basic procedures are used: "buy and drop," linked to the destruction of various peer-to-peer solutions and "subpoena and fear," as the creation of nonnatural social fear by specific legislations. Although customers around the world are willing to buy digital products over networks, the industry is still using conventional procedures to push such a decisive customer impulse back into existing and conventional markets. But digital media, like audio, video, images, and other multimedia documents, can be protected against copyright infringements with invisible, integrated patterns based on steganography and digital watermarking techniques. Digital watermarking is described as a possibility to interface and close the gap between copyright and digital distribution. It is based on steganographic techniques and enables useful rights protection mechanisms. Digital watermarks are mostly inserted as a plain-bit sample or a transformed digital signal into the source data using a key-based embedding algorithm and a pseudo noise pattern. The embedded information is hidden in low-value bits or least significant bits of picture pixels, frequency, or other value domains, and linked inseparably with the source of the data structure. For the optimal application of watermarking technology, a trade-off has to be made between competing criteria such as robustness, nonperceptibility, nondetectability, and security. Most watermarking algorithms are resistant to selected and application-specific attacks. Therefore, even friendly attacks in the form of usual file and data modifications can easily destroy the watermark or falsify it. This paper gives an overview of watermarking technologies, classification, methodology, application, and problems.

Limitations, Threads, and Impacts on the Digital Age

In this decade, the Internet, especially the World Wide Web—a global working network with worldwide broadcasting potential—has been successfully integrated into public and business domains. Recent surveys and public opinion polls have accented the value of the Internet. Traditional television and the Internet converge (Merz, 1999, p. 209). In addition, the growth and integration of broadband access points, wireless and mobile technologies and the progress towards one-in-a-box device proves the significance of developing a legitimate marketplace for entertainment and business activities. Digital networks and libraries, Internet services, and the disposition of nonbranded digital products within a global accessible network support lead to illegal copying, modification, and redistribution and the loss of high company sales and profits. Particularly, the music and entertainment industry have struggled with illegal distribution over peer-to-peer and other networks for years. The International Intellectual Property Alliance (IIPA) has estimated that the annual worldwide trade loss due to copyright piracy is up to $10.2 billion excluding Europe and the United States in 2002 (IIPA, 2004). In 2003, the IIPA (special 301 report) estimated $20 to $22 billion in annual losses for the copyright industry. While the copyright industry generates the highest foreign sales for the U.S. economy, the annual loss in 2002 can be estimated up to 15% worldwide by $88 billion foreign sales (Siwek, 2002).

However, digital media can be straightforwardly copied and illegally redistributed over various channels. Risk and capital loss will prevent further activities and investments until a legal and technical protection mechanism is available. These concerns are supported by the facts that digital mass-recording devices like MD, CD, and MP3 recorders, digital photo devices, and camcorders have impressively entered the market (Anderson & Petitcolas, 1999; Cox, Miller, & Bloom, 2000; Hanjalic, Langelaar, van Roosalen, Biemond, & Langendijk, 2000; Hartung & Kutter, 1999; Mintzer, Braudaway, & Yeung, 1997; Petitcolas, Anderson, & Kuhn, 1999; Swanson, Kobayashi, & Tewfik, 1998; Wu & Liu, 2002). The importance and the supposed economical thread for copyright holders can be clarified by initiatives of the entertainment industry, such as VIVA (Visual Identity Verification Auditor), a project of the European Communities (European Communities, n.d.; VIVA, n.d.), and SDMI (Secure Digital Music Initiative) (SDMI, n.d.). Distributors, such as Time Warner, Disney, Lucas film, and various professional companies like T-Systems, SCO, Yahoo!, and other Internet service and e-commerce providers, have already recognized the advantages of upcoming digital area and are on their way to establishing various on-demand services. Additionally, major technical steps have been made by designing consistent, working distribution methods and channels as well as developing cutting-edge equipment such as HDTV cinema projectors and digital radio and television (e.g., Rogers, 2000).

As a result, the features of the digital world lead to economic opportunities such as cheap distribution and also to serious risks in simplifying unauthorized copying and distribution (Rosenblatt, Trippe, & Mooney, 2002).

Steganography, Data Hiding, and Historical Watermarking

The core principles of watermarking and data hiding can be traced back approximately 4,000 years to Egypt and Greece. At this time, hidden packets of information had been transferred by special character adjustments or mutations (Hanjalic et al., 2000). Herodotus, the great Greek storyteller, often refers to the hidden information methodology transferred on wax tablets or smuggling secret messages tattooed on the skull of human messengers (Cox et al., 2002).

Figure 1. Tattoo messages on Roman slaves (Bail, n.d.)

In Roman times a slave would have his head shaved, then tattooed with an important message, and as the hair began growing, he made his way as instructed through enemy lines and indifferent countries, across water and inhospitable terrain, sleet and snow, mountain ranges, etc. finally reaching the reader who immediately had the head shaved, and eagerly scanned the message.

The most famous method is to mark the document with invisible secret ink, such as the juice of a lemon, and hide information. Another method is to mark selected characters within a document by pinholes and to generate a pattern or signature (Schneier, 1998). Such techniques are often referred to steganography. Steganography is a subdiscipline of data hiding and a part of cryptology. While the art of cryptography is about protecting the content of messages, steganography is about covering their existence. Steganography means "secret writing" and consists of the Greek words *steganos* and *graphia*. The main security of a steganographic system is based on a simple procedure. Because the steganographic message is integrated invisibly and covered inside other harmless sources, it is very difficult to detect the message without knowing its existence and its appropriate encoding scheme.

Plain watermarking instead is strongly related to the invention of papermaking in China. It was intensively used in the 18th century in America and Europe as a trademark and a method against counterfeiting books and money (Cox et al., 2002; Schneier, 1998). Such watermarks are electronically archived by the International Association of Paper Historians and clarify mainly the historical meaning (Dittmann, 2000). In recent years, simple, skillful, and aesthetic watermarks have been developed to prove authenticity, originality, and authorship, and to complicate the illegal redistribution process. The most famous watermark can be detected holding a bank note against the light. Its digital pendant, the digital watermark, considers the main principles and practices of its steganographic approach.

Digital Watermarking Methodology

"Digital watermarking" means embedding information into digital material in such a way that it is imperceptible to a human observer but easily detected by computer algorithm. A digital watermark is a transparent, invisible information pattern that is inserted into a suitable component of the data source by using a specific computer algorithm (e.g., Dittmann, 2000; Hartung & Kutter, 1999; Katzenbeisser & Petitcolas, 2000; Petitcolas, Anderson, & Kuhn, 1999). Digital watermarks are signals added to digital data (audio, video, or still images) that can be detected or extracted later to make an assertion about the data.

The digital watermarking research field is well demarcated and the first noteworthy publications can be traced back to 1982. Since 1995, the interest in digital watermarking has increased notably. This movement was supported by the first SPIE Information Hiding Workshop in 1996 and various conferences about digital watermarking and multimedia security. At the same time, organizations such as the Copy Protection Technical Working Group (CPTWG) and the Secure Digital Music Initiative (SDMI) were founded in order to industrialize, standardize, and evaluate the digital watermarking field. Supported projects, such as the Visual Identity Verification Auditor (VIVA) and the Tracing Authors Right Labeling Image Services and Monitoring Access Network (TALISMAN), are examples of working watermarking applications for monitoring broadcasting material. Since MPEG is an accepted standard, the International Organization for Standardization (ISO) has adopted digital watermarking in its specification draft. Such activities can be measured as proof of its technical and industrial relevance.

Digital Watermarking Associations

In order to protect copyrighted material from illegal duplication, two typical technologies have been developed. One approach uses key-based cryptographic methods and procedures to control the process of copying, manipulating, and distributing of media assets. Cryptography and encryption techniques enable the appropriate security during the transmission process, but once the encrypted data is decoded, the control of redistribution and its spread fails. To address the limitations of encryption, the main idea is to label a digital material with specific marks, which are called digital watermarks. Such technology can be used as ownership proof for distribution channel tracking and other applications in business and public domains. Furthermore, watermarking technology enables the owner to obtain the copyright status of certain documents and distributors can be made accountable for the content. Additionally, compatible media player technology, that is, DivX and DVD player, can detect distorted marks and refuse to play, display, or execute the media asset files.

The lack of such technologies has enforced the establishment of research in information science disciplines and the foundation of organizations, such as SDMI and the Tracing Authors' Rights by Labeling Image Services and Monitoring Access Network (TALISMAN) (Delaigle, 1996). Such initiatives focus especially on the development and progress of watermarking technology for different applications. In the future, portable consumer devices may be equipped with specific hardware detectors to protect business models and the rights of the owners. The SDMI portable device specification clarifies such approaches (SDMI, n.d.).

On the other hand, digital rights management (DRM) concepts are already integrated into the Microsoft Windows Media environment and will be intensively focused in the next generation of operation and hardware systems. The upcoming palladium operation system or NGSCB (Next-Generation Secure Computing Base) (Microsoft, n.d.) and TCPA (Trusted Computing Platform Association) constricts user rights and only allows the user to use certified software and material (Anderson, 2004; TCPA, n.d.). In this case, the duplication of content could be successfully permitted at the technical source. However, the implication on society, culture, markets, and economy could be enormous, and wide state and law regulations need to be established for a working system.

The importance of these techniques for the digital business world has been emphasized by the implementation of exclusively revised copyright laws and acts in the American and the European legislation.

Digital Watermarking Initiatives, Companies, and Projects

In the last few years, various activities in the digital watermarking field can be detected. A powerful and significant nonprofit organization, the SDMI Secure Music Initiative, was established in 1999 and consists of 161 companies in the music, entertainment, and computer industries. SDMI develops specifications that enable the protection of the playing, storing, and distributing of digital music. SDMI points out that a new market for digital music, led by the Recording Industry Association of America (RIAA), may emerge. The strategy of SDMI is to mark music data in such a way that the data are permanently attached and recognized by all specified devices (Sherman, n.d.). Actually, they are reacting to the popularity of MP3 and the introduction of portable consumer electronic devices that play unprotected files. The SDMI consortium wanted to have SDMI-compliant devices available for Christmas 1999 (Lacy, Snyder, & Mahler, 1997), but the plan was impaired by technological and political limitations.

The Copy Protection Technical Working Group (CPTWG) researches effective protection mechanism for DVD video. Additional state-supported projects have brought out industrialized results, for example, TALISMAN and VIVA, engaging the development of watermarking technology for broadcast monitoring. Additionally, commercial products, such as MusiCode for audio material, and VEIL II and MediaTraxx for video, exist in the high-end consumer market. Digimarc, one of the first established watermarking companies, has successfully integrated its third-party plug-in into Adobe's Photoshop Suite and other graphic software. Furthermore, a Mediasec cooperation has developed a fragile watermarking framework used by the airplane industry to prevent terrorist attacks and to enable an authenticity mechanism for marked plane designs and technical instructions.

Other Activities

In June 1989, the music industry initiatives, RIAA and IFIPA, and producers, for example, Mitsubishi, Grundig, Philips, and Sony, agreed on the integration of a copy control mechanism for the digital audiotape called Serial Copy Management System (SCMS). Since 1989, consumer DAT devices are equipped with a copy mechanism which prohibits copying a copy. The DVD, the standard storage medium for video, was kept back from the market because of its copy control limitations. In all, approximately 10 safety techniques have been integrated in DVD devices. The famous ones of which are Content Scrambling System (CSS), Macro Vision, Content Generation Management System (CGMS), Regional Code Playback Control, and digital watermarking. CSS was integrated into DVD devices by patent activities around 1996 and is based on an encryption and authenticity system. CSS video streams are encrypted and can be decoded by a CSS-compliant MPEG decoder. In 1999, the CSS procedure was hacked and software tools (DeCSS) were available for download on the Internet. CGMS embeds information in the source document, enabling a mechanism to control if video stream can be copied or not. One of the most effective copy control mechanism is the regional code. It is integrated into the DVD disk and DVD device. It disables the playback possibilities in specific geographic regions (Bechtold, 2002).

Watermarking Applications

Digital watermarking is described as a viable method for the protection of ownership rights of digital audio, image, video, and other data types. It can be applied to different applications including digital signatures, fingerprinting, broadcast and publication monitoring, authentication, copy control, and secret communication (Cox, Killian, Leighton, & Shamoon, 1997; Cox, Miller, & Boom, 2000; Cox et al., 2002; Katzenbeisser & Petitcolas, 2000). As a signature, the watermark identifies the owner of the content and can be used as a fingerprint to identify content consumers. For example, a specific watermarking technique is planned to be used to secure passports against counterfeiting in the United States (Digimarc, 2001). Broadcast and publication monitoring describes the area of computer systems which automatically monitors television and radio broadcast to track the appearance of distributed material. Several commercial systems already exist that make use of this technology. The MusiCode system provides broadcast audio monitoring (National Association of Broadcasters, 1998), VEIL 2 (Video Encoded Invisible Light), and MediaTrax provide broadcast monitoring of video (MediaTrax, n.d.; Veil Interactive Technologies, n.d.). In 1997, a European Communities project named VIVA (Visual Identity Verification Auditor), which engages the development of watermarking technology for broadcast monitoring, began (European Communities, n.d.; VIVA, n.d.). Watermarking technology can also be used to guarantee authenticity and can be applied as proof that the content has not been altered since insertion. The watermark is often designed in such a way that any alteration either destroys the watermark or creates a mismatch between the content and the watermark, which can easily be detected (Miller, Cox, Linnart, & Kalker, 1999). Furthermore, watermarking enables applications for copy control. Here, the embedded watermark information contains rules of usage and copying (Cox et al., 2002). Digital watermarking is linked to steganography and data hiding. The field of secure and covert communication derived from the past, as Herodotus, the great Greek storyteller, reports of hidden messages tattooed on skulls of slaves and wax tablets for secure communication (Petitcolas et al., 1999). This is the classical application of steganography—the art of hiding pieces of information within another. Digital watermarking can be used to transmit such secret information in images, audio streams, or any type of digital data, and it is reported that some communication activities of people or groups linked to the 9/11 tragedy are based on such data-hiding approaches.

Copyright Protection and Authentication

Digital watermarks are often mentioned as being used for copyright and intellectual property protection (Cox et al., 2002; Fridrich, 1998). In this case, the author or originator integrates a watermark containing his/her own intellectual property signature into the original document and delivers it as usual. By doing this, he/she can proof his/her intellectual creation later on, for instance, in a legal proceeding and has the possibility to assert entitlement to the restricted use. The "Lena Image" in Figure 2 is one of the standard reference pictures used in the scientific digital imaging area and was used in the first digital watermarking publication without real permission of the owner (Cox et al., 2002).

Fingerprinting and Digital "Signatures"

In order to explain fingerprinting with digital watermarking, the pay-per-view scenario in Fridrich (1998) is used. Customers are buying different media types, such as images, video, and audio over the Internet. Within a real-time

Figure 2. The "Lena Image"

watermarking framework, the digital goods are individually marked with the fingerprint of the customer. This could be a generated original equipment manufacturer (OEM) number or another useful pattern. In this case, crypto-graphic methods could increase the data security and can be combined with digital signatures. Although there seems to be a conflict of digital signature and digital watermarking, because watermarking differs from the idea of a public-key encryption, it could be interesting to combine both techniques. To identify those who make illegal copies or redistribute them, an automated agent scanning system can be used to track down the traitor. According to the popularity of DivX and screened copies of brand new movies, "screeners," cinema and film projectionists, could be traced enabling such illegal action. Because of analogue techniques used in cinemas worldwide, the digital watermark has to survive the change from the analogue to the digital domain. However, such watermarks could be easily integrated with more security and reliability by using digital projector and digital devices.

Copy Protection and Device Control

Digital watermarks can be used to enable copy control devices. In this combination, the recording device scans the digital data stream for an existing watermark and enables or disables the recording action for a specific movie or stream. Such technology could extend the pay-per-view concept and close the gap between the applied cryptographic approach and its usability. However, the implementation in consumer devices seems to be possible in using the same procedures applied when inserting the Macro Vision and CSS DVD copy mechanisms. By limiting available DVDs to CSS-compliant DVD players, manufacturers had to integrate new encoders that are secured by patent law regulations in their devices to maintain market position.

Broadcast Monitoring

The production cost of broadcasting material, such as news, shows, and movies, are enormous and can be $100,000 per hour and more. Therefore, it is important for production companies, for example, Warner Bros., Miramax, and Universal Pictures, to secure their intellectual property and not permit illegal rebroadcasting activities. In this case, digital watermarking can enable technical frameworks such as TALISMAN, which automatically monitor broadcasting streams at satellite nodes all over the world and identify illegally broadcasted material. Furthermore, TV stations can be monitored and the unlawful use could be tracked and debited individually. In 1997, two Asian broadcasting stations had been identified for intentionally overbooking their advertising time and making customers pay for unplayed broadcasting time (Cox et al., 2002). Computer systems can be used for tracking and monitoring advertisement activities on broadcasting channels and for examining advertisement deals. Nielsen Media Research and Competitive Media Reporting offer such computer systems.

Data Authentication

Digital watermarking is often used to prove the authenticity of a specific digital document. The digital watermark contains information that can be used to prove that the content has not been changed. Any such operation on the file destroys or changes the integrated watermark. If the watermark information can be extracted without errors, the authenticity can be proved. In order to design an effective watermarking algorithm, the watermarking data or procedure can be linked to the content of the digital document. Such watermarks are called fragile watermarks or vapormarks (Cox et al., 1999).

Further Applications

Though the main application of digital watermarking is to secure the intellectual property, it can also be used in the medical field. In using digital watermarks as container for information about patients and their diagnosis, medical images, for example, X-ray or nuclear magnetic resonance (NMR) tomography, could be automatically associated with the patient (Petitcolas et al., 1999). Furthermore, digital watermarking could be used to save context or meta-information in source documents. In using special watermarking agents, generic search machines are able to retrieve such information and can offer time-based media documents as a result.

Classification and Requirements

Digital watermarks can be classified and measured on the basis of certain characteristics and properties that depend on the type of application. These characteristics and properties include the difficulties of notice, the survival of common distortions and resistance to malicious attacks, the capacity of bit information, the coexistence with other watermarks, and the complexity of the watermarking method (Heileman, Pizano, & Abdallah, 1999). In general, they are described as fidelity, robustness, fragility, tamper resistance, data payload, complexity, and other restrictions. Digital watermarks must fulfill the following, often contradictory, requirements (Kutter & Hartung, 2000):

- **Robustness**: It may not be possible without knowledge of the procedure and the secret key to remove the watermark or to make it illegible. Robustness also means the resistance ability of the watermark information changes and modifications made to the original file. As modifications, resizing, file compression, rotation, and common operations will be particularly considered. Above all, commonly used operations such as lossy compression (JPEG, MPEG) should not destroy the digital watermark (Hanjalic et al., 2000). Further examples are linear and nonlinear filters, lossy compression, contrast adjustment, gamma correction, recoloring, resampling, scaling, rotation, small nonlinear deformations, noise adding, pixel permutations, and so forth. Robustness does not include attacks on the embedding scheme based on the knowledge of the algorithm or on the availability of the detector function. Robustness means resistance to common operations applied in the imaging, motion picture, or audio field (Fridrich, 1998).

- **Nonperceptibility**: It is important to recognize whether the brought bit sample of the watermark produces perceptible changes acoustically or optically. A perfect nonperceptible bit sample is present if data material marked with watermark and the original cannot be distinguished from each other. This classifier is based on the idea and properties of the human visual system (HVS) and human audio system (HAS). The watermark is nonperceptible or invisible if a normal human being is unable to distinguish between the original and the carrier.

- **Nondetectable**: The data material with the brought watermark information is not detectable if it is consistent with the origin data. In this case, an embedding algorithm could use for example, steganographically the noise components of the data source of a picture to hide the watermark information. Nondetectability cannot directly be linked to nonperceptibility that is based on the concepts of human perceptions. Nondetectability is related to the data source and its components. It describes the consistency with the original data (Fridrich, 1998).

- **Security**: It is assumed that the attackers have full knowledge about the applied watermark procedure; however, no secret key would be known. Therefore, an attacker will try to manipulate the data to destroy the watermark, or again print and scan to win the original material without a copyright-protection note. The complexity is also connected with the security, that is, the algorithm for bringing in and reading watermark information should work with enough long keys to discourage the search for the appropriate secret key. However, for certain applications and persons, the watermark must be also detectable. The problem of secure key exchange emerges.

- **Complexity**: Complexity describes the expenditure to detect and encode the watermark information. A measurement technique could be the amount of time (Dittmann, 2000). It is recommended to design the watermarking procedure and algorithm as complex as possible so that different watermarks can be integrated. Thus, "trial-and-error" attacks can be avoided (Voyatzis, Nikolaides, & Pitas, 1998).

- **Capacity**: Capacity refers to the amount of information that can be stored in a data source. In using digital watermarking for simple copy control applications, a capacity of one bit (one = allow/zero = deny) seems to be sufficient. On the other hand, intellectual property applications require about 60 to 70 bit information capacity to store data about copyright, author, limitations, or International Standard Book Number (ISBN), International Standard Recording Code (ISRC), or OEM numbers.

For the optimal watermarking application, a trade-off has to be accepted between the above-mentioned criteria. Robustness means, for example, that many information of a watermark must be embedded that are, however, then in case of an attack, more visible or detectable. On the other hand, if a watermark consists only of a minimal bit sample that covers only a small part of the picture, such a watermark is quickly lost as a result of the modifications of the data (Woda & Seitz, 2002). Finally the amount of watermarking information and the robustness could have significant effects on the quality of the data source and influences on the requirements. Therefore, a decision has to be made for the right application.

Digital Watermark Types

In the previous section, we classified watermarks on the basis of their requirements. However, digital watermarks and their techniques can be subdivided and segmented into various categories; for example, they can be classified according to the application, source type (image watermarks, video watermarks, audio watermarks, text watermarks), human perception, and technique used. As watermarks can be applied in the spatial or frequency domain, different concepts, such as discrete Fourier (DFT), discrete cosine (DCT), and wavelet transformation, or additionally, manipulations in the color domain and noise adding can be mentioned. Furthermore, digital watermarks can be subdivided on the basis of human perception. Digital watermarks can be invisible or visible. We see visible watermarks every day watching television, that is, TV station logos. They can be robust against operations or even fragile for use in copy control or authenticity applications. At least, digital watermarks can be subdivided into blind and nonblind detection techniques, which are strongly related to the decoding process.

Blind and Nonblind Techniques

In order to detect the watermark information, blind and nonblind techniques are used. If the detection of the digital watermark can be done without the original data, such techniques are called blind. Here, the source document is scanned and the watermark information is extracted. On the other hand, nonblind techniques use the original source to extract the watermark by simple comparison and correlation procedures. However, it turns out that blind techniques are more insecure than nonblind methods.

A General Watermarking Framework

In contrast to common techniques, including copyright information inside data headers or visible areas, digital watermarks are weaved into the core structure of the digital document in an invisible and unrecognizable way (e.g., Wu & Liu, 2003). The main goal of watermarking research is to develop digital watermarking methods that survive all known formats and conventional transformations, D/A (digital to analogue) and A/D (analogue to digital) conversions, and any other kind of data operations used in image and audio processing. The basic digital watermarking methods integrating information packages in digital data are based on steganography methods. Figure 3 explains this generic scheme and its steganographically derived watermarking scheme. Digital watermarks are inserted into pictures, video, and audio with different embedding schemes, concepts, and algorithms. Almost all watermarking procedures are based on the use of secret keys, which are applied in the integration and detection process to extract the watermark information properly and to enable basic security (Kutter & Hartung, 2000).

In contrast to traditional cryptographic methods, the watermark set does not change the main functionality of the file. Therefore, the watermark must be inserted into the data structure imperceptibly. Depending on the given data type, it should neither be visible, audible, and so forth, nor detectable to strangers or observers. Each watermark method consists of an embedding algorithm and an extracting algorithm. The embedding algorithm inserts the watermark information in the data and the extracting algorithm decodes the watermark information (for example, Wu & Liu, 2002). However, some methods extract the whole watermark information and others only determine its existence. Such methods can be used either as ownership proof or verification.

Figure 3. Generic digital watermarking scheme

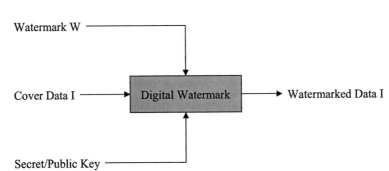

Figure 4. Watermark encoding example

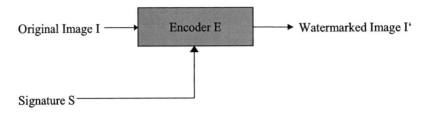

Watermark Encoding

In order to combine a watermark with a digital document, for example, images, you need an image (I), a signature (S = s_1, s_2, s_n) that contains the watermarking information, and an encoding algorithm (E) to create a watermarked image (I'). The encoder takes the signature and the cover document, and generates the watermarked image, that is described as a function: **E(I, S) = I'**. In this case, secret or public keys and other parameters can be used to extend the watermarking encoder.

Watermark Decoding

The watermark is extracted using a decoder function (see Figure 5). In this case, the decoder **D** loads the watermarked, normal or corrupted image I(w), and extracts the hidden signature **S**. Using nonblind watermarking techniques, the decoder **D** loads an additional image I, which is often the original image, to extract the watermarking information by correlation. Such methods are more robust against counterfeit attacks. The process can be described as **D(I, I (w)) = S**.

Figure 5. Watermark decoding example

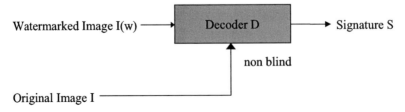

Watermarking Techniques

Why is it so difficult to find a needle in a haystack? Because of the size of the needle relative to the size of the haystack. Also, because once the needle falls out of your hand, it is not predictable where it will land in the haystack. Both principles—inconspicuousness and randomness—help conceal information in digital watermarks to protect intellectual property of multimedia documents. (Zhao, 1997)

Zhao clarifies the main principles for hiding information in digital documents. In using randomness and inconspicuousness to hide information, a reliable security level could be reached. Digital watermarking is a fairly new research area and combines studies and results from other research areas, such as digital signal processing, communications, compression, information theory, and cryptography (e.g., Pan, Wang, Jain, & Ichalkaranje, 2003; Yu & Sattar, 2002). Digital watermarking is based on different technical concepts and methods (Katzenbeisser & Petitcolas, 2000). Various watermarking methods have been developed and tested, but they are not reacting uniformly on methodical attacks (e.g., Le & Desmedt, 2003; Mihcak, Venkatesan, & Kesal, 2003; Voloshynovskiy, Pereira, Pun, Eggers, & Su, 2001). Primitive watermarking techniques, such as least significant bit techniques (Hanjalic et al., 2000), use existing digital noise pattern in any digital source to bind the watermarking information on its elementary binary structure. Other techniques generate pseudo noise patterns to integrate calculated bit information into different domains of the digital material. Further methods use fractal, vector, and time-variant approaches. Simple watermarking methods described in Kutter, Jordan, and Bossen (1997) modulate the blue channel of the images on a specific value. They use the limitation of the human visual system of recognizing minimal changes in the blue color spectrum. Additional methods use spread spectrum modulation and other techniques based on actual compression and multimedia methods, such as discrete cosine, fast Fourier, wavelet, and fractal transformations. In general, watermarking techniques can be divided into two main categories. The first category describes correlation-based methods; the second category comprises the noncorrelation-based techniques (Hanjalic et al., 2000). Algorithms of the first category embed digital watermarks by adding pseudo-random noise to the image components, which are detected by correlating the image noise with the components of the image.

The second category can be subdivided into least significant bit and geometrical relation techniques. Most commonly used watermarking methods are based on correlation techniques. The watermarking research area has produced a wide range of watermarking techniques which can be subdivided into various methodological complexity levels.

Noise pattern, either Gaussian or normal distributed, are excellent carrier signals for information brackets. Noise patterns are existent elements of life and often not predictable by human beings. Since natural noise patterns are linked to source material, it is not recognized in most cases. Therefore, we have to pay attention to the source material when designing the noise generator in order to integrate watermark information. Further techniques consider the transformation of the image and its specific domains. Most watermark techniques use the frequency or spatial domain in order to integrate the watermark information (Dittmann, 2000). Such algorithms are based on, for example, discrete Fourier, cosine, and wavelet transformations, or fractal approaches for digital images. On the other hand, time-variant materials, such as audio files or video streams, offer, sometimes in combination with DCT and DFT, other technical possibilities, for example, psychoacoustic transformations, phase modulations, echo-adding, and spread spectrum methods.

LSB Watermarking Technique

LSB watermarking describes a straightforward and basic way to integrate watermark information in digital documents. Considering a basic greyscale image, the pixel and its values can be sliced up into significant and irrelevant levels. Because the significant levels merely represent a digital noise pattern, it could be easily used for digital watermarking. In changing selected pixel values of the noise pattern using a special or key-based algorithm, the watermarking information can be easily integrated (Hanjalic et al., 2000). However, such technique is very insecure because the watermark can be easily destroyed. On the other hand, such technique can be useful in copy control and authenticity applications.

Spatial Domain Watermarking

Digital watermarking techniques in the spatial domain use the values of the color channels, luminance or brightness signals of a digital image (Dittmann, 2000).

One straightforward and rapid technique is based on the principle of generating a pseudo-generated noise pattern and integrates it into specific chrominance or luminance pixel values (Darmstaedter, Delaigle, Quisquater, & Macq, 1998). Such pseudo-random noise patterns consist of black (1), white (−1), and neutral values (0). The pseudo noise is generated with a "secret" key and algorithm. Additionally, the process could be adjusted to the image components or feature vectors to achieve a higher level of invisibility. In general, the watermark W(x, y) is integrated into the image components I(x, y) by a factor that allows amplification of the watermarking values in order to obtain the best results.

$$I_W(x, y) = I(x, y) + k * W(x, y)$$

The detection of the watermark is based on the principles of correlation. In this case, a specific detector compares the watermarked image $I_W(x, y)$ with the original image and automatically decides, based on a specific correlation level, whether a watermark exists (Hanjalic et al., 2000). Such techniques particularly enable the integration of one-bit watermark information. In integrating more information, various techniques have been invented. Such methods have the possibility to save up to 500 bits in one 512x512 image (Hanjalic et al., 2000). In order to clarify this main procedure, the original image will be subdivided into small blocks. Now, the selected blocks are watermarked or not and produce a bit sequence in the detection process. In this case, the watermarking detector scans the image and generates the bit sequence according to a specified correlation level. Using CRC method could improve the error tendency.

Frequency Domain Watermarking

The basic principles of adding or changing components of digital images and other digital documents can be transferred to other value domains. In order to integrate watermark information into frequency components, the document has to be transformed into its frequency components using discrete cosine, discrete Fourier, or Hadamard transformations (Dittmann, 2000; Hanjalic et al., 2000). As such transformations are used in lossy compression techniques, for example, MPEG and JPEG, the watermark appears to be very resistant to the usual attacks. Furthermore, in integrating watermarks in the most important frequency components improve security and resistance, because every change significantly reduces the quality of the image (Hanjalic et al., 2000). Therefore, it is important to identify the coefficients of the transformation that are less infected by the attack method. In most cases digital watermarks are integrated into the mid-band frequencies. Research has determined a specific sensibility of high-band frequencies against filter operations, lossy compression, and noise insertion whereas manipulating low frequencies seems to produce visible artifacts anytime (Hanjalic et al., 2000).

Spread Spectrum Watermarking

Spread spectrum techniques used in digital watermarking is borrowed from the communication field. The basic idea of spread spectrum is to spread the data across a large frequency band. In the case of audio, it is the entire audible spectrum; in the case of images, it is the whole visible spectrum. Spread spectrum is a military technology designed to handle interferences and disturbances. In most cases, signals that represent the information are modulated at low intensity across the source bandwidth. Spread spectrum communication is used in radar, navigation, and communication applications. The information is weaved into the source material using a secret key or an embedding procedure (Hanjalic et al., 2000).

Other Approaches

Further relevant watermarking methods for images use fractal transformation to integrate bit information into the structure of the document (Jacquin, 1992). Nevertheless, various procedures have yet been invented and used for diverse watermarking applications in the image, audio, or video field. In particular, watermarking for video data can profit by scientific findings of audio and image watermarking. Audio watermarking is based on psychoacoustic theories, amplitude modification, dithering techniques, echo integration, phase distortion, and spread spectrum techniques (Bassia & Pitas, 1999; Bender et al., 1996; Chen & Wornell, 1999; Cox et al., 1996; Gruhl, Lu, & Bender, 1996). Such techniques are usually based on the same concepts. In this case, watermarking using amplitude modification means embedding a pseudo-noise pattern in the least significant bit audio data by replacement or modification

(Bassia & Pitas, 1999). Other approaches, such as using echo signals to save the bit information, add a repeated adaptation of component with a small offset (delay time), initial amplitude, and decay rate to make it imperceptible (Chen & Wornell, 1999). Other applications, such as watermarking software code on the area of text watermarking and watermarking of notes in music score, complete the digital watermarking area.

Attacks on Digital Watermarks

Watermarking research has produced a wide range of watermarking techniques that can be subdivided into various methodological complexity levels. Each of these methods tries to reduce vulnerability in various attack scenarios. Attacks on digital watermarks can be mainly classified into two major groups: friendly and malicious attacks (Hanjalic et al., 2000; Hartung, Su, & Girod, 1999). Conventional image or data operations applied in the normal use of computer technology can destroy the watermark information. Different operation of the classical image processing field, such as scaling, color and gamma corrections, and so forth can be mentioned at this point. Today, compression techniques can be also be placed in the field of classical operations, but often separated as a single element in watermarking research. The friendly attack has two common features. It is generally described as an unintentional event where the user has no suppose and/or knowledge of the watermark and its embedded procedure. The second type of attack, the malicious attack, occurs with the intention of eliminating the information (Hanjalic et al., 2000). In order to test the robustness of watermarks, some applications have been developed. The powerful StirMark attack has been designed by a research group at the University of Cambridge (Anderson, Petitcolas, & Kuhn, 1999). The attack simulates image distortions that commonly occur when a picture is printed, photocopied, and rescanned. The image is slightly stretched and compressed by random amounts, a small amount of noise is added (Fridrich, 1998). Comparable applications are the mosaic and histogram attacks. The mosaic attack assembles and reassembles the watermarked image. The histogram attack describes attacks on simple watermarks methods. Finally, it is important to consider that partial knowledge of the watermark or the process of watermarking enables pirates to remove the entire watermark or to disturb it. A good model for classifying such attacks is given by Hartung, Su, and Girod (1999).

Simple Attacks

Simple watermark attacks try to wipe out the watermark information by manipulating the whole image and its components. The attack does not isolate or identify the specific watermark information. The attack is successful when the watermarking information cannot be extracted or recognized any longer and the usability has not been affected (Hanjalic et al., 2000). Examples are common signal processing operations, such as linear filtering, as in high-pass or low-pass filtering; nonlinear filtering, such as media filtering, color reduction, D/A–A/D conversions, resampling, requantization, and dithering distortion.

Detection Disabling Attacks

Detection disabling attacks directly destroy the watermarking information, for example, in disturbing the correlation process. Such a watermark attack usually is based on geometrical pixels or blocks shifting, or direct modifications. Examples are scaling, rotation, cropping, and inserting. One of the most famous attacks is based on the StirMark simulator, which destroys the watermark information by using randomly selected spatial modifications or a combination of other attacks.

Ambiguity and Removal Attacks

Ambiguity attacks disable the watermark by inserting a new, overlapping watermark in the source document. In inserting multiple watermarks, the use as mechanism for intellectual property applications can be hindered. Let us consider a document marked with Bob's and later on with Alice's watermark information. In this case, it is impossible to determine the originator of the document. Such attacks are related to the use of intellectual property application. Removal attacks analyze the watermark, estimate the technique or watermark, and attempt to extract the watermark in order to delete it. In this case, statistical applications are used to analyze the source material.

Problems of Digital Watermarking

Digital watermarking techniques are already effectively used in associated copy control applications and broadcast monitoring systems. In combination with digital rights management frameworks, they can solve the limitation of the intellectual property dilemma in audio- and image-related business areas. However, the main intellectual property problems cannot be solved by all existing watermarking methods. Watermarking techniques behave differently in different attack operations or applications. Simple, noncomplex methods described in Kutter, Jordan, and Bossen (1997) are not very resistant to JPEG and JPEG 2000 compression, but are resistant to normal image operations. Complex and difficult watermarking techniques based on discrete, fast Fourier, or wavelet transformations are, by contrast, very robust against compression techniques, but lack resistance in normal image operations. Today, most watermarking methods cannot reach the main approach. It is still a wide and attractive field for further research in which innovative methods and techniques may be established.

Conclusions

As a result, we summarize that watermarking technology is still at the beginning of its development. Most watermarking algorithms cannot tackle attacks. Even the friendly attacks in the form of usual file modifications can very easily destroy the watermarks or falsify them. Therefore, a desirable watermarking algorithm should not rely on a certain method, but it should insert watermarks repeatedly in different ways (using least significant bits, frequencies, or color and contrast relations) so that at least one of them survives an attack. After editing on the picture has taken place, a watermark should be refreshed automatically. The jurisdiction has to accept a digital watermark as permissible evidence of copyright infringement. Besides, organizational frameworks are necessary to put through an author's claim. Corresponding to this law and authorization problems, infrastructures are also demanded for the key management and time stamp services.

Meanwhile, several European Communities projects deal with copyright protection and its realization in the digital world: CITED (Copyright in Transmitted Electronic Documents) encloses access and user control (CITED,

1993). The system has exceptional flexibility; it accepts all widespread operating systems and can be applied for access over computer networks. COPEARMS provides a uniform standard to guarantee the copyright of digital documents (Scott, 1999). COPEARMS cooperates closely with another European Communities project named IMPRIMATUR (IMPRIMATUR, 1999). The project takes care of the secure transmission and payment of documents including the authentication. This year, in particular, a significant increase of activities can be determined. Microsoft is planning to develop its Palladium operating system; Apple Computer is successfully operating its music download platform; Yahoo! is trying to complement the same area with audio and video streams; RealNetworks and Microsoft (Windows Media Environment) are establishing digital rights management extension based partly on digital watermarking technology in their products. Such activities clarify the importance of digital watermarking, especially in combination with digital rights management, and offers chances for further interesting research. However, although the main argument for digital watermarking is linked to enabling and securing business activities, like distribution goods over networks, in the public and middle-class domains, it seems that digital watermarking is primarily supported by mighty international interest groups. Therefore, we suppose that digital watermarking is dominated by such initiatives and that running applications will be and are supported by them, before the public domain benefit from such a technology.

References

Anderson, R.J. (2004). Trusted computing. Frequently asked questions. Retrieved February 5, 2004, from *www.cl.cam.ac.uk/~rja14/tcpa-faq.html*

Anderson, R.J., & Petitcolas, F.A.P. (1999, August). Information hiding: An annotated bibliography. Retrieved November 21, 2003, from *www.petitcolas.net/fabien/steganography/bibliography/*

Bail, M. (n.d.). The Europeans. Retrieved August 19, 2003, from *www.brickmag.com*

Bassia, P., & Pitas, I. (1999). Robust audio watermarking in the time domain. *Proceedings of ICASSIP*.

Bechtold, S. (2002). *Vom Urheber- zum Informationsrecht – Implikationen des Digital Rights Managements*. Munich: Verlag C.H. Beck.

Bender, W. et al. (1996). Techniques for data hiding. *IBM Systems Journal*, 313–336.

Chen, B., & Wornell, G.W. (1999, January). Dither modulation: A new approach to digital watermarking and information embedding. *Proceedings of SPIE: Security and Watermarking of Multimedia Contents*, 342–353.

CITED (Copyright in Transmitted Electronic Documents). (1993, December). Retrieved August 19, 2003, from *www.newcastle.research.ec.org/esp-syn/text/5469.html*

COPEARMS. (n.d.). Retrieved August 19, 2003, from *www.nlc-bnc.ca/wapp/copearms/cop-surv.htm*

Cox, I.J. et al. (1996). Secure spread spectrum watermarking for images, audio and video. *International Conference on Image Processing*, 234–246.

Cox, I.J., Kilian, J., Leighton, F.T., & Shamoon, T. (1997). Secure spread spectrum watermarking for multimedia. *IEEE Transactions on Image Processing, 6*(12), 1673–1678.

Cox, I.J., Miller, M.L. & Bloom, J.A. (2000, March 27–29). Watermarking and their properties. *Proceedings of the International Conference on Information Technology: Coding and Computing, ITCC 2000*, Las Vegas, NV.

Cox, I.J., Miller, M.L., & Bloom, J.A. (2002). *Digital watermarking*. San Francisco: Morgan Kaufmann.

Cox, I.J., Miller, M.L., Linnartz, J.P.N.G., & Kalker, T. (1999). A review of watermarking principles and practices. In K. Parhi & T. Nishitani (Eds.), *Digital signal processing in multimedia systems* (pp. 461–485).

Darmstaedter, V., Delaigle, J.F., Quisquater, J.J., & Macq, B. (1998). Low cost spatial watermarking. *Computer & Graphics*, *22*(4), 417–424.

Delaigle, J.-F. (1996, September 27). TALISMAN. Retrieved November 21, 2003, from *www.tele.ucl.ac.be/TALISMAN/*

Digimarc. (2001). Secure ID solutions. Retrieved February 2, 2004, from *www.digimarc.com/DIDS/AboutIDSystems.asp*

Dittmann, J. (2000). *Digitale Wasserzeichen: Grundlagen, Verfahren, Anwendungsgebiete*. Berlin: Springer.

European Communities. (n.d.). Esprit programme. Retrieved November 21, 2003, from *www.cordis.lu/esprit/home.html*

Fridrich, J. (1998, November 4–6). Applications of data hiding in digital images. Tutorial of the *ISPACS '98 Conference*, Melbourne, Australia.

Gruhl, D., Lu, A., & Bender, W. (1996). Echo hiding. *Information Hiding First International Workshop Proceedings*, 295–315.

Hanjalic, A., Langelaar, G.C., van Roosmalen, P.M.G., Biemond, J., & Langendijk, R.L. (2000). *Image and video databases: Restauration, watermarking and retrieval.* Amsterdam: Elsevier.

Hartung, F., & Kutter, M. (1999). Multimedia watermarking techniques. *Proceedings of the IEEE, 87*(7), 1079–1107.

Hartung, F., Su, J.K., & Girod, B. (1999, January). Spread spectrum watermarking: Malicious attacks and counterattacks. *Proceedings of SPIE Electronic Imaging '99, Security and Watermarking of Multimedia Contents*, San Jose, CA.

Heileman, G.L., Pizano, C.E., & Abdallah, C.T. (1999, September). Performance measures for image watermarking schemes. *Proceedings of the Fifth Baiona Workshop on Emerging Technologies in Telecommunications*, Baiona, Spain. Retrieved February 14, 2004, from *www.eece. unm.edu/controls/papers/Hei_Piz_CTA.pdf*

IIPA (n.d.). International Intellectual Property Alliance, Country Reports. Retrieved February 3, 2004, from *www.iipa.com/countryreports.html*

IMPRIMATUR. (1999, January 15). Retrieved August 19, 2003, from *www.imprimatur.net/about.htm*

Jacquin, A.E. (1992). Image coding based on a fractal theory of iterated contractive image transformations. *IEEE Transactions on Image Processing, 2*(1), 18–30.

Katzenbeisser, S., & Petitcolas, F.A.P. (2000). *Information hiding: Techniques for steganography and digital watermarking.* Norwood, MA: Artech House Books.

Kutter, M., & Hartung, F. (2000). Introduction to watermarking techniques. In S. Katzenbeisser & F.A.P. Petitcolas (Eds.), *Information hiding techniques for steganography and digital watermarking.* Boston: Artech House.

Kutter, M., Jordan, F., & Bossen, F. (1997, February 13–14). Digital signature of color images using amplitude modulation. *Proceedings of*

SPIE Storage and Retrieval for Image and Video Databases, San Jose, CA.

Lacy, J., Snyder, J., & Mahler, D. (1997, July). Music on the internet and intellectual property protection problem. *Proceedings of ISIE*.

Le, T.V., & Desmedt, Y. (2003). Cryptoanalysis of UCLA watermarking schemes. In F.A.P. Petitcolas (Ed.), *Information hiding. 5th International Workshop, IH 2002, Noordwijkerhout, The Netherlands, October 2002* (pp. 213–225). Berlin: Springer.

MediaTrax. (n.d.). Retrieved November 21, 2003, from *www.mediatrax.com*

Merz, M. (1999). *Electronic commerce. Marktmodelle, Anwendungen und Technologien*. Heidelberg: dpunkt.verlag.

Microsoft (n.d.). NGSCB: Next-Generation Secure Computing Base. Retrieved November 21, 2003, from *www.microsoft.com/resources/ngscb/default.mspx*

Mihcak, M.K., Venkatesan, R., & Kesal, M. (2003). Cryptoanalysis of discrete-sequence spread spectrum watermarks. In F.A.P. Petitcolas (Ed.), *Information hiding. 5th International Workshop, IH 2002, Noordwijkerhout, The Netherlands, October 2002* (pp. 226–246). Berlin: Springer.

Miller, M., Cox, I., Linnart, J.P., & Kalker, T. (1999). A review of watermarking principles and practices. In K.K. Parhi & T. Nishitani (Eds.), *Digital signal processing in multimedia systems* (pp. 461–485). Marcel Dekker.

Mintzer, F., Braudaway, G.W., & Yeung, M.M. (1997, October). Effective and ineffective digital watermarks. *Proceedings of the IEEE International Conference on Image Processing (ICIP '97)*, Santa Barbara, CA.

National Association of Broadcasters. (1998, November 10). Electronic music copyright in a digital, web-centric, high-tech universe. Retrieved November 21, 2003, from *www.nab.org/Research/Reports/e-music_copyright.htm*

Pan, J.-S., Wang, F.-H., Jain, L., & Ichalkaranje, N. (2002, November). A multistage VQ based watermarking technique with fake watermarks. In F.A.P. Petitcolas & H.J. Kim, (Eds.), *Digital watermarking. First International Workshop, IWDW 2002, Seoul, Korea* (pp. 81–90). Berlin: Springer.

Petitcolas, F.A.P., Anderson, R.J., & Kuhn, M.G. (1999). Information hiding—A survey. *Proceedings of the IEEE, 87*(7), 1062–1078.

Rogers, G. (2000, July 26). HDTV and front protection systems. *CyberTheater™. The Internet Journal of Home Theater.* Retrieved February 14, 2004, from *www.cybertheater.com/Tech_Reports/ HD_Projectors/hd_projector.html*

Rosenblatt, B., Trippe, B., & Mooney, S. (2002). *Digital rights management—Business and technology.* New York: M&T Books.

Schneier, B. (1998). *Angewandte Kryptographie. Protokolle, Algorithmen und Sourcecode in C.* Bonn: Addison-Wesley.

Scott, M. (1999, February). Library-publisher relations in the next millennium. *The Library Perspective, 31*(2). Retrieved November 21, 2003, from *www.nlc-bnc.ca/publications/2/p2-9902-03-e.html*

SDMI. (n.d.). Retrieved November 21, 2003, from *www.sdmi.org*

Sherman, C. (n.d.). Presentations to SDMI Organizing Plenary. Retrieved from *www.sdmi.org/dscgi/ds.py/GetRepr/File-38/html*

Siwek, S.E. (2002). *Copyright industries in the U. S. economy: The 2002 report.* Washington, DC: International Intellectual Property Alliance.

Swanson, M.D., Kobayashi, M., & Tewfik, A.H. (1998). Multimedia data embedding and watermarking technologies. *Proceedings of IEEE, 86*(6), 1064–1087.

TCPA. (n.d.). Retrieved November 21, 2003, from *www.trustedcomputing.org/home/*

VEIL Interactive Technologies. (n.d.). Retrieved November 21, 2003, from *www.veilinteractive.com/2003/index.htm*

VIVA. (n.d.). Retrieved November 21, 2003, from *www.intec.rug.ac.be/ Research/Groups/hfhsdesign/viva/*

Voloshynovskiy, S., Pereira, S., Pun, T., Eggers, J.J., & Su, J.K. (2001). Attacks on digital watermarks: Classification, estimation-based attacks and benchmarks. *IEEE Communications Magazine, 39*(8), 118–127.

Voyatzis, G., Nikolaides, N., & Pitas, I. (1998, September 8–11). Digital watermarking—An overview. *Proceedings of IX European Signal Processing Conference (EUSIPCO),* Island of Rhodes, Greece.

Woda, K., & Seitz, J. (2002, April 24–25). The role of digital watermarking to the protection of rights for digital media assets. *Proceedings of the*

Fifth International Conference Business Information Systems BIS 2002, Poznan, Poland.

Wu, M., & Liu, B. (2003). *Multimedia data hiding*. New York: Springer.

Yu, D., & Sattar, F. (2002, November). A new blind watermarking technique based on independent component analysis. In F.A.P. Petitcolas & H.J. Kim (Eds.), *Digital watermarking. First International Workshop, IWDW 2002, Seoul, Korea* (pp. 51–63). Berlin: Springer.

Zhao, J. (1997, January). Digital watermarking is the best way to protect intellectual property from illicit copying. Retrieved August 19, 2003, from *www.byte.com/art/9701/sec18/art1.htm*

Chapter II

Digital Watermarking Schemes for Multimedia Authentication

Chang-Tsun Li
University of Warwick, UK

Abstract

As the interconnected networks for instant transaction prevail and the power of digital multimedia processing tools for perfect duplication and manipulation increases, forgery and impersonation become major concerns of the information era. This chapter is intended to disseminate the concept of digital watermarking for multimedia authentication. Issues and challenges, such as security, resolution of tamper localization, and embedding distortion, of this technical area are explained first. Three main categories of watermarking approaches, namely fragile, semi-fragile, *and* reversible *schemes, to the issues and challenges are then presented. Merits and limitations of specific schemes of each category are also reviewed and compared.*

Introduction

As the interconnected networks for instant transaction prevail and the power of digital multimedia processing tools for perfect duplication and manipulation increases, forgery and impersonation become major concerns of the information era. As a result, the importance of authentication and content verification became more apparent and acute. In response to these challenges, approaches conveying the authentication data in digital media have been proposed in the last decade. Applications for multimedia authentication can be found in many areas. For example:

- **Medical image archiving**: The authentication data of patients can be embedded at the time when their medical images are taken by the hospital to protect the patients' rights when medical malpractice happens and has to be resolved in court.

- **Imaging/sound recording of criminal events**: Authentic imaging or recording of legally essential event or conversation could lead to breakthrough in criminal cases while maliciously tampered imaging/recording, if not detected, could result in wrong ruling.

- **Accident scene capturing for insurance and forensic purposes**: Similar applications of the technique as mentioned above could be useful in protecting the rights of the parties including the insurance company involved in accidents or natural disasters.

- **Broadcasting**: During international crises, tampered or forged media could be used for propaganda and manipulating public opinion. Therefore, broadcasting is an area where multimedia authentication is applicable.

- **Military intelligence**: Multimedia authentication allows the military to authenticate whether the media they received do come from a legitimate source and to verify whether the content is original. Should the content be manipulated, an effective authentication scheme is expected to tell as much information about the manipulation as possible (e.g., location of tampering).

The aforementioned list is not intended to be exhaustive but just to identify some possible applications of multimedia authentication.

As Lou, Liu, and Li (2004) described, depending on the ways of conveying the authentication data for digital media, authentication techniques can be roughly divided into two categories: labeling-based techniques (Chen & Leiss, 1996; Friedman, 1993; Lin & Chang, 2001; Lou & Liu, 2000; Queluz, 2001; Schneider & Chang, 1996) and watermarking-based techniques (Hsieh, Li, & Wang, 2003; Li, Lou, & Chen, 2000; Li & Yang, 2003; Xie & Arce, 2001). The main difference between these two categories of techniques is that in labeling-based authentication, the authentication data or the signature of the medium is written into a separate file or a header that is separated from the raw data stored in the same file, while in watermarking-based authentication, the authentication data is embedded as watermark in the raw data itself.

Compared to watermarking-based techniques, labeling-based techniques potentially have the following advantages:

- The data-hiding capacity of labeling-based techniques is higher than that of watermarking.
- They can detect the change of every single bit of the image data if *strict* integrity has to be assured.

Given the above benefits, why would researchers propose watermarking approaches? The following are some of the issues regarding the use of labeling-based techniques:

- In labeling-based techniques, storing digital signatures in a separate file or in separate header segments of the file containing the raw data incurs significant maintenance overhead and may require extra transmission of the signature file.
- When the signed medium is manipulated, the embedded signature is not subjected to the same process of manipulation, which makes it difficult to infer what manipulation has been done and to pinpoint the temporal and spatial localities where tampering occurs.
- Traditional digital signatures used for labeling are not suitable for lossy or progressive transmission applications. For example, in light of network congestion in a progressive transmission scenario, low-priority layers of the medium (usually the high-frequency components or the details) are likely to be dropped, making the received data differ from the original. In this case, the received signature generated based on the original medium by the sender will

not match its counterpart generated according to the received medium by the recipient. As a result, the received medium will fail authentication.

- Transcoding or converting the format of media-protected with labeling-based techniques is not always possible. For example, converting a JPEG image with its authentication data/signature stored in the header to an image format without any header segments means that the signature has to be discarded, making authentication impossible at a later stage.

On the contrary, watermarking-based approaches embed the authentication data into the raw data of the host media directly, which will be subjected to the same possible transformation the host media would undergo. Therefore, fragile and semi-fragile digital watermarking schemes do not have the first two aforementioned problems. Moreover, by sensibly designing the embedding algorithm, semi-fragile watermarking schemes can also circumvent the last two problems mentioned above. Nevertheless, readers are reminded that no superiority of the semi-fragile schemes over the fragile schemes is implied here. In deciding whether to make the scheme fragile or semi-fragile, the designer has to take the nature of applications and scenario into account since no single optimal scheme is available for all applications. Because of their merits, the rest of this chapter will focus on the design of watermarking-based schemes.

Background

Various types of watermarking schemes have been proposed for different applications. For the purpose of copyright protection, embedded watermarks are expected to survive various kinds of manipulation to some extent, provided that the altered media is still valuable in terms of commercial significance or acceptable in terms of fidelity. Therefore, watermarking schemes for copyright protection are typically robust (Kutter, Voloshynovskiy, & Herrigel, 2000; Lu, Huang, Sze, & Liao, 2000; Trappe, Wu, & Liu, 2002; Wu & Liu, 2003), that is, they are trying to ignore or remain insensitive to the influence of malicious or unintentional attacks. On the other hand, in medical, forensic, broadcasting, and military applications where content verification and identity authentication are much more of a concern, more emphases are on the capability of the watermarking schemes to detect forgeries and impersonation. For example, the staff at a military headquarter always has to be sure that the digital images received come from the right people and that the contents are original. Therefore, this type of watermarks is usually fragile or semi-fragile and is expected to be sensitive to attacks (Li & Yang, 2003; van Leest, van der Veen & Bruekers, 2003; Winne, Knowles, Bull & Canagarajah, 2002; Wong & Memon, 2000; Xie & Arce, 2001). In addition to these two categories of schemes, some hybrid schemes incorporating a robust watermark and a fragile/semi-fragile watermark in attempt to provide copyright protection and authentication simultaneously have also been proposed (Deguillaume, Voloshynovskiy, & Pun, 2003).

This chapter deals with watermarking schemes for authentication purpose. A general authentication framework based on digital watermarking is illustrated in Figure 1. Usually, a secret key K available on both the embedding and authentication sides is used to generate a watermark to be embedded into the host media. The marked media is then delivered via the communication channel (e.g., Internet, satellite, etc.) or stored in a database. To authenticate the marked media, the same secret key is used to generate the original watermark so as to be used for extracting and comparing against the embedded version. The difference map, the output of the authentication system, tells the authenticity of the media.

Figure 1. A general authentication framework based on digital watermarking

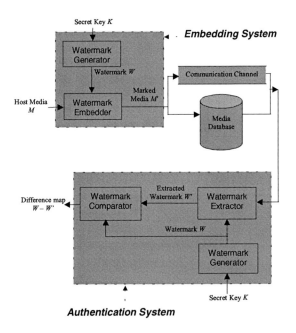

Authentication System

Fragile/semi-fragile digital watermarking is about embedding a small amount of information, the watermark, into the host media so that the watermark can be extracted later from the marked media to authenticate the identity of the embedder and to verify the content integrity of the media. The watermark can be an ID number of the embedder, a visually meaningful logo, or a sequence of random numbers generated with a secret key representing the embedder. The media can be text, audio, speech, image, video, multimedia, or a combination of them all.

When designing a watermarking scheme for digital media authentication, two categories of attacks have to be taken into consideration: content-targeting attacks and scheme-targeting attacks. Content-targeting attacks aim at manipulating the content of the media without taking into account the protection measures provided by the authentication algorithm. Common content-targeting attacks threatening digital media can be classified into two types:

- **Local tampering**: Typical examples of this type of tampering include removal of original objects/features and/or addition of new objects/features.

- **Global manipulations**: Typical examples of this type of manipulations include scaling, clipping, cropping, low-pass filtering, and histogram equalization.

Scheme-targeting attacks aim at defeating the security of the authentication scheme so that the scheme fails to detect malicious content manipulations. This type of attacks always goes along with content-targeting attacks because the ultimate goal of any malicious attacks is to tamper the content of the media. Typical examples of scheme-targeting attacks are as follows:

- Cover-up/cut-and-paste (Barreto, Kim, & Rijmen, 2002), which is an action of cutting one region/block of the image and pasting it somewhere else in the same or different image.

- Vector quantization attack (Wong & Memon, 2000) (also known as birthday attack [Barreto et al., 2002], the Holliman-Memon counterfeiting attack [Holliman & Memon, 2000], or collage attack [Fridrich, Goljan, & Memon, 2000]), which is devised on the basis of the so-called birthday paradox (Stallings, 1998, Appendix 8.A): *What is the minimum population size such that the probability that at least two of the people have the same birthday is greater than 0.5?* According to birthday paradox, using a hash function that produces a bit string of length l, the probability of finding at least two image blocks that hash to the same output is greater than 0.5 whenever roughly $2^{l/2}$ watermarked image blocks are available. The idea of the attack is to forge a new watermarked image (a collage) from a number of authenticated images watermarked with the same key and the same logo/watermark by combining portions of different authenticated images while preserving their relative positions in the image. Fridrich, Goljan and Memon (2000) showed that counterfeiting is possible even when the logo is unknown to the attacker provided that a larger number of images watermarked with the same key are available.

- Transplantation attacks derived by Barreto, Kim, and Rijmen (2002) work as follows. Let $I'_A \rightarrow I'_B$ denote that the hashing of image block I'_B involves the information about I'_A. Now, if images I' and I'' have blocks with following dependence relationships:

$$... \rightarrow I'_A \rightarrow I'_X \rightarrow I'_B \rightarrow I'_C \rightarrow ...$$
$$... \rightarrow I''_A \rightarrow I''_X \rightarrow I''_B \rightarrow I''_C \rightarrow ...$$

and block I'_A is identical to I''_A, I'_B is identical to I''_B, and I'_C is identical to I''_C, but I'_X is not identical to I''_X. Then the block pairs (I'_X, I'_B) and (I''_X, I''_B) are interchangeable without being detected by schemes adopting deterministic dependence (Li et al., 2000; Wong & Memon, 2000; Yeung & Minzter, 1997), that is, the information involved or dependent upon is deterministic. Barreto et al. (2002) further indicated that merely increasing the number of dependencies could not thwart the transplantation attack. For example, let $I_A \leftrightarrow I_B$ denote that the hashing of each block involves the information about the other. Now, if the following dependence relationships exist

$$\cdots \leftrightarrow I'_A \leftrightarrow I'_B \leftrightarrow I'_X \leftrightarrow I'_C \leftrightarrow I'_D \leftrightarrow \cdots$$
$$\cdots \leftrightarrow I''_A \leftrightarrow I''_B \leftrightarrow I''_X \leftrightarrow I''_C \leftrightarrow I''_D \leftrightarrow \cdots,$$

the triplet (I'_B, I'_X, I'_C) and (I''_B, I''_X, I''_C) are interchangeable if block I'_D is also identical to I''_D.

Based on the above discussions, it is clear that content-targeting attacks are naïve and can only succeed when the attacked media is *not* watermarked. Scheme-targeting attacks are more sophisticated and intended for making content-targeting attacks undetectable.

To be considered effective, a fragile/semi-fragile watermarking scheme must have the essential capabilities of detecting content-targeting attacks. Moreover, an effective fragile/semi-fragile watermarking scheme should show no security gaps to various kinds of scheme-targeting attacks such as cover-up, transplantation, and vector quantization attacks. Block-wise dependence is recognized as a key requirement to thwart vector quantization (Fridrich et al., 2000; Holliman & Memon, 2000; Li et al., 2000; Li & Yang, 2003; Wong & Memon, 2000). However, it is also proved that the dependency with deterministic context is susceptible to transplantation attack or even simple cover-up attack (Barreto et al., 2002). Nevertheless, Li and Yang (2003) pointed out that even nondeterministic block-wise dependency (i.e., the neighboring relationship among individual pixels in the block is nondeterministic) as adopted in Fridrich, Goljan, and Baldoza (2000) is still vulnerable to cropping attack.

Although spatial-domain approaches are effective for the applications where lossy compression is not acceptable (e.g., medical imaging), lossy compression standards such as JPEG and MPEG are commonly adopted for Internet transmission and multimedia storage in order to make efficient use of bandwidth and disk space. These two requirements make transform-domain approaches desirable. It is common in transform-domain schemes to watermark only a few selected transform coefficients in order to minimize embedding distortion. However, Hsieh, Li, and Wang (2003) pointed out that leaving most of the coefficients unmarked results in a wide-open security gap for attacks to be mounted on them. A solution Hsieh et al. (2003) proposed is to implicitly watermark all the coefficients by registering/blending the zero-valued coefficients in the watermark and involving the unembeddable coefficients during the process of embedding the embeddable ones.

However, fragile watermarking is intolerant not only to malicious attacks but also to content-preserving or incidental operations (e.g., further compression, transcoding, bit rate scaling, and frame rate conversion), which do not change the semantics or content of the media. Those content-preserving operations are sometimes necessary in many multimedia applications wherein fragile watermarking is not practical. Semi-fragile watermarking (Kundur & Hatzinakos, 1999; Xie & Arce, 2001) is the technique that allows those content-preserving operations while intolerant to malicious content-altering operations such as removal of original objects from the media.

In some applications, such as medical imaging and forensic image archiving, even imperceptible distortion due to watermark embedding is not acceptable. For example, in legal cases of medical malpractice, any distortion of an image, even if it is a result of watermark embedding itself, would cause serious debate in court. Therefore, the capability of recovering the original unwatermarked media from the authenticated watermarked version is of significant value for this type of application. A watermarking scheme with this capability is referred to as reversible (van Leest, van der Veen, & Bruekers, 2003), erasable (Cox, Miller, & Jeffrey, 2002). or invertible watermarking (Fridrich, Goljan, & Du, 2001).

In addition, it is more practical for a watermarking scheme to be able to verify the authenticity and integrity of the media without referring to the original versions. This characteristic is commonly called obliviousness or blind verification. In a more restrictive sense, obliviousness can also mean that no a priori knowledge (e.g., image index) about the image is required in the authentication process.

Low false-positive and false-negative rates are also important factors for effective schemes. False-positive rate is the occurrence rate that the watermark detector extracts a watermark that was *not* actually embedded. On the contrary, false-negative rate is the occurrence rate that the watermark detector fails to extract an embedded watermark. Low false-positive and false-negative rates are usually in conflict with low embedding distortion because reducing false-positive and false-negative rates usually means increasing the amount of watermark, which inevitably will inflict higher distortion on the quality of the watermarked media.

The aforementioned challenges and attacks do not constitute an exhaustive list since more new attacks are expected to be devised in the future. Nevertheless, at present, an effective watermarking scheme for authentication purpose should have the capability of thwarting known attacks.

Watermarking Approaches to Authentication

This section is intended to introduce some solutions to the problems posed previously. Several watermarking approaches will be discussed.

Fragile Watermarking Schemes

Among the proposed spatial-domain fragile watermarking techniques, the Yeung-Mintzer scheme (Yeung & Minzter, 1997) is one of the earliest and frequently cited. In Yeung and Minzter (1997), the watermark is a visually significant binary logo, which is much smaller than the image to be marked and is used to form a binary image as big as the image. Watermark embedding is conducted by scanning each pixel and performing the watermark extraction function based on a lookup table generated with a secret key. If the extracted watermark bit is equal to the authentic watermark bit, the pixel is left unchanged; otherwise, the gray scale of the pixel is adjusted until the extracted watermark bit is equal to the authentic one. Because of its pixel-wise scanning fashion, local tampering can be localized to pixel accuracy. The pixel-wise watermarking fashion is actually a special case of the block-wise style with block size equal to 1.

However, due to the lack of interrelationship among neighboring pixels during the watermarking process, their scheme is vulnerable to cover-up attacks when there are local features surrounded by a relatively larger smooth background. For example, without knowing the secret key, a handgun on the floor of a criminal scene can still be covered up by pasting a patch taken from the background. The scheme is also vulnerable to vector quantization attack (Fridrich et al., 2000; Holliman & Memon, 2000; Wong & Memon, 2000). Another attack derived by Fridrich et al. (2000) that can be mounted against the Yeung-Mintzer scheme is that the lookup table and the binary logo can be inferred when the same lookup table and logo are reused for multiple images.

Another well-known fragile watermarking technique is Wong's public-key scheme reported in Wong (1998). In this scheme, the gray scales of the least significant bits (LSBs) of the original image are first set to zero. Then the LSB-zeroed image is divided into blocks of the same size as that of a watermark block. The image size together with each LSB-zeroed image block is then provided as inputs to a hash function and the output together with the watermark block are subjected to an exclusive-or (XOR) operation. The result of the XOR operation is then encrypted using a private key of the RSA public-key cryptosystem and embedded in the LSBs of the original image. To verify the integrity of the received image, it is again divided into blocks and the encrypted data embedded in the LSBs of each block is then extracted and decrypted with a public key. Meanwhile, the LSB-zeroed version of each received image block together with the image size of the transmitted image are again taken as inputs to the same hash function as that used by the image sender. The output of the hash function and decrypted data are subjected to the XOR operation in order to reveal the watermark. The revealed watermark is then compared with the perfect watermark in the preestablished database at the receiver side. This scheme marries cryptography and watermarking elegantly and indeed works well in detecting cropping and scaling.

However, like the Yeung-Mintzer scheme, this method is also block-wise independent, and, therefore, vulnerable to cover-up and vector quantization attacks. Since the block size of Wong's scheme is 64, according to birthday paradox, given 2^{32} blocks, vector quantization attack can be successful with relatively high probability. This is possible in the applications of medical image archiving where large image database is maintained. Due to the lack of mutual dependence among neighboring blocks during the watermarking process, this scheme is also vulnerable to transplantation attacks. Moreover, the output length of the hash function sets the lower bound on the block size. Thus, the tampering localization accuracy is limited.

To thwart vector quantization attack, Wong and Memon (2000) proposed an improved scheme by adding an image index and a block index to the inputs of the hash function. With this new version, to forge each block, the choices for the attacker are now limited to only the blocks from all authenticated images with the same block index. Adding the image index is one step further to secure the scheme against vector quantization attack. In this case, the image index is just like a unique serial number of the image; therefore, vector quantization cannot succeed. However, this idea works at the expense of requiring the verifier to have the a priori knowledge about the image index, which limits its applicability to some extent. For example, an intelligence agent in a hostile territory has to send the index of the image he/she wants to transmit through a secure channel to the verifier.

Recognizing the importance of establishing dependence among neighboring pixels or blocks, Li, Lou, and Chen (2000) proposed a scheme that uses a binary feature map extracted from the underlying image as watermark. The watermark is then divided into blocks of size 32×16 pixels. Block-wise dependence is established by blending the neighboring blocks before encrypting and embedding into LSBs of the image. This method is effectively resistant to vector quantization and cover-up attacks and requires no a priori knowledge of the original image. However, the accuracy of localization is limited by the block size. Moreover, like Wong's (1998) scheme, this scheme is also vulnerable to transplantation attacks because the contextual dependence is established based on deterministic information. To circumvent these draw-backs, Li and Yang (2003) further proposed a scheme that is immune to transplantation attacks and is significantly accurate in locating tampering. To watermark the underlying image, the scheme adjusts the gray scale of each pixel by an imperceptible quantity according to the consistency between a key-dependent binary watermark bit and the parity of a bit stream converted from the gray scales of a secret neighborhood. The members of the secret neighbor-hood are selected according to the watermark sequence generated with the secret key, and therefore cannot be deterministically reestablished by the attacker. However, it is a spatial-domain approach, which is not suitable for transform-domain applications.

Although there are some transform-domain schemes reported in the literature, a common security gap inherent in many of them (Winne, Knowles, Bull, & Canagarajah, 2002; Wu & Liu, 1998; Xie & Arce, 2001) is that they neither explicitly nor implicitly watermark all the transform coefficients. As a result, manipulation of those unwatermarked coefficients will go unnoticed. For example, in the wavelet transform-domain approach proposed by Winne, Knowles, Bull, and Canagarajah (2002), to minimize embedding distortion and maintain high localization accuracy, only the coefficients of the high frequency subbands at the finest scale of the luminance component are watermarked. All the other coefficients and components are neither watermarked nor involved during the watermarking process of the embeddable coefficients. In Xie and Arce (2001), to make the scheme semi-fragile, only the LL component of the coarsest scale (i.e., the approximate of the original image) is involved in generating the signature, which is then used as the watermark. To minimize embedding distortion, only the coefficients of the finest scale are watermarked. Consequently, tampering the coefficients in other subbands and scales will certainly go undetected. For example, locally tampering the three unwatermarked high-frequency subbands at the coarsest scale that are not involved in gener-ating the signature is highly likely to change or at least destroy the semantic meaning of the watermarked image without raising alarm.

Given the limitations of the reviewed schemes, Hsieh, Li, and Wang (2003) designed a transform-domain scheme, which is immune to the aforementioned attacks and provides protection for *all* the transform coefficients without explicitly watermarking all of them. To embed the watermark, the target image X is first DCT transformed and quantized. A binary image A as big as X is generated with a secret key. A second binary image, B, is then created so that all of its pixels corresponding to the nonzero-valued coefficients are set to 1 and the others set to 0. *B* is intended to serve the purpose of registering the positions of the zero-valued coefficients. A binary watermark *W* is then created by taking the result of XOR operation on the binary images *A* and *B*. Like *X*, *W* is also divided into blocks of 8×8 pixels. For each DCT block X_i, four nonzero coefficients $X_i(h), X_i(h-1), X_i(h-2)$, and $X_i(h-3)$ with their frequencies lower than or equal to a middle frequency *h* are identified as watermarkable. The four selected coefficients $X_i(j), j \in [h-3, h]$, are modulated based on their corresponding watermark bits $W_i(j)$ and a secret sum $S_i(j)$ such that Equation (1) is satisfied.

$$Parity\ (S_i(j) © X_i(j)) = W_i(j) \tag{1}$$

where *Parity*(×) is a function which returns 1 or 0 as output to indicate that the number of '1' bits of its argument is *odd* or *even*. © is an operator that concatenates $S_i(j)$ and $X_i(j)$ expressed in two's complement format. The secret sum $S_i(j)$ is the sum of the nonzero unwatermarkable coefficients selected according to their corresponding watermark bits and $W_i(j)$ from a neighborhood $N_i(j)$ consisting of the DCT block X_i and its eight closest neighboring blocks. It can be expressed as

$$S_i(j) = \sum_{m \in N_i(j)} \sum_{n \in [h-3,h]} (W_m(n) \oplus W_i(j)) \cdot X_m(n) \tag{2}$$

The watermarking process repeats until all the blocks are marked. To authenticate and verify the received image, the verifier performs the same operations as applied on the embedding side in the reversed order to extract the embedded watermark and compares it with the original watermark generated in the same manner as that adopted by the embedder. A set of experimental results of this scheme is shown in Figure 2. Figure 2(a) is the original image while Figure 2(b) is the watermarked image. These two images show that the embedding distortion is invisible to human visual system (HVS). Figure 2(c) shows that the doorknob between the twins' heads has been removed (compare the difference between Figure 2(b) and 2(c)). This is a typical example of localized attack. Detected by the authentication scheme, the shaded block between the twins' head indicates that the image has been locally tampered with. These two figures show that the scheme is capable of localizing tampering to high accuracy.

Figure 2. (a) Original image. (b) Watermarked image. (c) Attacked image. The doorknob between the twins' heads in the watermarked image has been masked. (d) Authentication result. The shaded block between the twins' heads indicates that the received image has been locally tampered with.

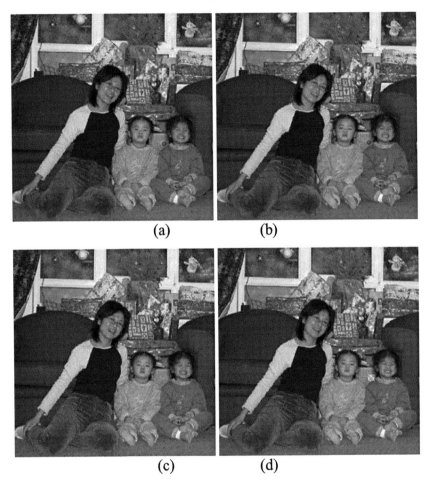

(a)　　　　(b)

(c)　　　　(d)

Semi-Fragile Watermarking Schemes

One characteristic of the aforementioned fragile watermarking scheme is its zero tolerance to any types of changes no matter how small they are. This characteristic makes the fragile scheme unsuitable in many applications where content-preserving manipulation is necessary. In order to make efficient use of bandwidth and storage, media is often transmitted or stored in compressed formats according to some specific standards such as JPEG and MPEG.

Transcoding is also a common practice to convert media from one format to another (e.g., from JPEG to TIFF). Compression and transcoding are deemed acceptable in many Internet and multimedia applications as they preserve the content. However, fragile watermarking schemes do not differentiate content-preserving operations from malicious tampering. Therefore, to meet the needs for authenticating the compressed or transcoded watermarked media, it is desirable to have semi-fragile schemes that are sensitive to malicious manipulations while tolerant to content-preserving operations.

Kundur and Hatzinakos (1999) developed a semi-fragile watermarking scheme for image authentication, which embeds the watermark by quantizing the wavelet coefficients to a predetermined degree. The scheme works as follows. They defined a quantization function $Q(f)$ as

$$Q(f) = \begin{cases} 0, & \text{if } \left\lfloor \dfrac{f}{\delta 2^l} \right\rfloor \text{ is even} \\[3mm] 1, & \text{if } \left\lfloor \dfrac{f}{\delta 2^l} \right\rfloor \text{ is odd} \end{cases} \tag{3}$$

where f stands for any coefficient, $\lfloor \cdot \rfloor$ is the floor function which returns the largest integer smaller than or equal to its argument, l is the index of the decomposition level, and d, the quantization step, is a positive integer. To watermark the image, the L-level Haar wavelet transform is performed first. Then for all the coefficients except the ones of the approximation of the image (i.e., the coefficients of the lowest-frequency subband) are subjected to the selection by using a secret key $ckey$. For each selected coefficient $f(i)$, if Equation 4 does not hold, the coefficient is adjusted according to Equation 5. Equations 4 and 5 are defined as follows:

$$Q(f(i)) = w(i) \oplus qkey\,(i) \tag{4}$$

where $w(i)$ is the ith bit of the watermark sequence, $qkey(i)$ is a function of the local component of the image around pixel i which returns either value 0 or 1 and is intended for increasing the security of the scheme, and $\oplus$ is the XOR operator,

$$f(i) := \begin{cases} f(i) - \delta 2^l, & \text{if } f(i) > 0 \\ \\ f(i) + \delta 2^l, & \text{if } f(i) \leq 0 \end{cases} \tag{5}$$

where the operator := stands for assignment. After the watermarking process as described above is finished, inverse Haar wavelet transform is performed on the watermarked coefficients to create the watermarked image.

As most of the existing digital image formats require that the gray level of the pixels must be an integer; when the inverse wavelet transform is applied to the watermarked coefficients, the resulting gray level of the watermarked image pixel must be rounded to integer values. However, the rounding operation may result in changing the watermark because of this tiny numerical modification. To solve this problem, Kundur and Hatzinakos (1999) chose Haar wavelet transform, exploiting the property that the coefficients at each decomposition level l are rational numbers of the form $r/2^l$ where r is an integer value. Watermarking the coefficients by using Equation 3 and adjusting the coefficients by a multiple of 2^l according to Equation 5, the gray levels of the inverse wavelet transform are guaranteed to be integers. We can also see from Equations 3 and 5 that the quantization step δ determines the degree of distortion and sensitivity of the scheme to changes in the image. A smaller value of d inflicts less significant distortion on the visual quality of the image while making the scheme less tolerant to changes.

Depending on the applications, the watermarked image may be subjected to some kind of content-preserving operations (e.g., lossy compression) before the image is transmitted through the communication channel or stored in the database. Therefore, to verify its authenticity, the received or retrieved watermarked image has to be transformed or decoded back to its spatial domain wherein the watermark extraction described as follows can take place. To extract the embedded watermark, the L-level Haar wavelet transform exactly as carried out in the embedding process is performed first. Then for all the coefficients except the ones of the approximation of the image are subjected to the selection by using a secret key *ckey*. For each selected coefficient $f(i)$, the corresponding watermark bit $\tilde{w}(i)$ is extracted according to

$$\tilde{w}(i) = Q(f(i)) \oplus qkey(i) \tag{6}$$

A tamper assessment function (TAF) is then calculated according to

$$TAF(\widetilde{w}, w) = \frac{1}{N_w} \sum_{i=1}^{N_w} w(i) \oplus \widetilde{w}(i) \qquad (7)$$

where w and $\widetilde{w}$ are the original and extracted watermark sequences, respectively, and N_w is the length of the watermark sequences. The received/retrieved image is deemed authentic if the value of TAF $(\widetilde{w}, w) < T$, where $0 \le T \le 1$ is a user-defined threshold. Otherwise, the changes to the image are considered content preserving and acceptable. The value of T is application dependent. We can see that the higher its value is, the more sensitive the scheme becomes. Experiments conducted by Kundur and Hatzinakos (1999) suggest that a value of approximately 0.15 for T allows the scheme to be robust against high-quality JPEG compression and be able to detect additional tampering.

Although desirable, it is difficult to draw a clear boundary between acceptable and malicious manipulations. The designer has to bear in mind what the application is so that he/she can differentiate acceptable distortions from malicious ones.

Reversible Watermarking Schemes

One limitation of watermarking-based authentication schemes is the distortion inflicted on the host media by the embedding process. Although the distortion is often insignificant, it may not be acceptable for some applications, especially in the areas of medical imaging. Therefore, watermarking scheme capable of removing the distortion and recovering the original media after passing the authentication is desirable. Schemes with this capability are often referred to as reversible watermarking schemes (also known as invertible [Fridrich et al., 2001] or erasable watermarking [Cox et al., 2002]). None of the algorithms mentioned previously are reversible. Usually, a reversible scheme performs some type of lossless compression operation on the host media in order to make space for hiding the compressed data and the Message Authentication Code (MAC) (e.g., hash, signature, or some other feature derived from the media) used as the watermark. To authenticate the received media, the hidden information is extracted and the compressed data is decompressed to reveal the possible original media. MAC is then derived from the possible original media. If the newly derived MAC matches the extracted one, the possible original media is deemed authentic/original. Two interesting reversible schemes are introduced as follows.

For the scheme proposed by Fridrich et al. (2001), first, the 128-bit hash of all the DCT coefficients is calculated. A number of middle-frequency coefficients are then selected from each DCT block. The least significant bits of the selected coefficients are losslessly compressed when the coefficients are scanned in a secretly determined order. The lossless compression stops when enough space has been created for embedding the hash. The compressed bit stream and the hash are then concatenated and replace the LSBs of the selected coefficients. To verify the authenticity, the verifier follows the same protocol to select the same middle-frequency coefficients in order to extract the compressed bit stream and hidden hash H from their LSBs. The extracted compressed bit stream is then decompressed and used to replace LSBs of those selected middle-frequency coefficients. The same hash function is applied to all the coefficients to obtain H'. If H' equals H, the received image is deemed authentic and the LSBs of the received image are replaced with the decompressed bit stream to yield the original. Despite its simplicity, the hash output conveys only global information about the image, that is, the signature of the image, with no local information. When a local attack is launched against the coefficients, their algorithm can only tell that the image is not authentic without being able to locate the position where the tampering occurs.

Van Leest, van der Veen, and Bruekers (2003) proposed another reversible watermarking scheme based on a transformation function that introduces "gaps" in the image histogram of image blocks. The transformation function maps the gray level of the input pixel to a unique output value so that one or two values in the range are not used, thus leaving one or two "gaps." The gaps are then used to hide the watermark. For example, a possible transformation function is one that maps the domain of $[0, 1, 2, ..., x, x+1, x+2, x+3, ..., x']$ to the range of $[0, 1, 2, ..., x, x+2, x+3, x+4, ..., x'+1]$, leaving value $x+1$ unmapped in the range. The scheme then embeds a "1" watermark bit by increasing the gray level of any pixel with a gray level of x by 1 to make it equal to $x+1$ and a "0" by not changing anything. We can see that after the embedding process is done, the gaps corresponding to gray level $x+1$ is partially filled and the embedding capacity is determined by the occurrences of gray level x. By allowing more gaps, higher embedding capacity can be gained at the expense of greater distortion to the visual quality. Along with some overhead information indicating the whereabouts of the gaps, the watermark verifier can extract the information and restore the original image in a bit-exact manner. Experiments demonstrated that embedding rates of approximately 0.06–0.60 bits per pixel could be achieved at PSNR levels of 45–50 dB. One drawback of this scheme is its need for the overhead information and the protocol to be hidden in the image. Moreover, a potential security loophole in the scheme is that given the fact that the computational cost for extracting the watermark is insignificant; an attacker can defeat the scheme by exhausting all the 256 possible gray level assuming that the gray level being tried is the gap.

Conclusions

This chapter is about the use of digital watermarking for multimedia authentication. The first section discussed the pressing needs for authenticating digital media in this information era and the two main categories of authentication techniques employed to meet these needs, namely labeling-based techniques and watermarking-based techniques. Characteristics of these two categories of techniques were compared and the reasons why watermarking is preferred in some applications were presented.

The second section identified some common attacks and classified them into content-targeting attacks and scheme-targeting attacks. How the attacks could be mounted on the media and what requirements have to be met in order to thwart those attacks were also explained.

In the third section, depending on the properties of the watermarking schemes and the desirable requirements of applications, digital watermarking schemes were broadly classified into three categories, namely fragile, semi-fragile, and reversible. Some existing schemes of each category were described in detail.

Based on the discussions made in the previous sections, it is observed that no single universal solution to all problems currently exist and is unlikely to be found in the future. The solutions are more likely to remain application dependent and the trade-offs between the conflicting requirements of low distortion, low false-positive and negative rates, and robustness to acceptable manipulations still have to be made. The authors expect that the future trends in this field are increasing the localization accuracy, identifying the type of tampering, and restoring the original media.

References

Barreto, P.S.L.M., Kim, H.Y., & Rijmen, V. (2002). Toward secure public-key blockwise fragile authentication watermarking. *IEE Proceedings— Vision, Image and Signal Processing, 148*(2), 57–62.

Chen, F., & Leiss, E.L. (1996). Authentication for multimedia documents. *Proceedings of Conferencia Latinoamérica de Informática*, 613–624.

Cox, I., Miller, M., & Jeffrey, B. (2002). *Digital watermarking: Principles and practice*. Morgan Kaufmann.

Deguillaume, F., Voloshynovskiy, S., & Pun, T. (2003). Secure hybrid robust watermarking resistant against tampering and copy-attack. *Signal Processing, 83*(10), 2133–2170.

Fridrich, J., Goljan, M., & Baldoza, A.C. (2000). New fragile authentication watermark for images. *Proceeding of the IEEE International Conference on Image Processing, I*, 446–449.

Fridrich, J., Goljan, M., & Du, R. (2001). Invertible authentication watermark for JPEG images. *Proceeding of the IEEE International Conference on Information Technology*, 223–227.

Fridrich, J., Goljan, M., & Memon, N. (2000). Further attack on Yeung-Mintzer watermarking scheme. *Proceeding of the SPIE Conference on Security and Watermarking of Multimedia Content, II*, 428–437.

Friedman, G.L. (1993). The trustworthy digital camera: Restoring credibility to the photographic image. *IEEE Transactions on Consumer Electronics, 39*(4), 905–910.

Holliman, M., & Memon, N. (2000). Counterfeiting attacks on oblivious block-wise independent invisible watermarking schemes. *IEEE Transactions on Image Processing, 9*(3), 432–441.

Hsieh, T.-H., Li, C.-T., & Wang, S. (2003). Watermarking scheme for authentication of compressed image. *Proceeding of the SPIE International Conference on Multimedia Systems and Applications, VI*, 1–9.

Kundur, D., & Hatzinakos, D. (1999). Digital watermarking for telltale tamper proofing and authentication. *Proceedings of IEEE, 87*(7), 1167–1180.

Kutter, , Voloshynovskiy, S., & Herrigel, A. (2000). Watermark copy attack. *Proceeding of the SPIE International Conference on Security and Watermarking of Multimedia Content, II*, 371–380.

Li, C.-T., & Yang, F.-M. (2003). One-dimensional neighbourhood forming strategy for fragile watermarking. *Journal of Electronic Imaging, 12*(2), 284–291.

Lin, C.-Y., & Chang, S.-F. (2001). A robust image authentication method distinguishing JPEG compression from malicious manipulation. *IEEE Transactions on Circuits and Systems of Video Technology, 11*(2), 153–168.

Li, C.-T., Lou, D.-C., & Chen, T.-H. (2000). Image authentication via content-based watermarks and a public key cryptosystem. *Proceedings of the IEEE International Conference on Image Processing, III*, 694–697.

Lou, D.-C., & Liu, J.-L. (2000). Fault resilient and compression tolerant digital signature for image authentication. *IEEE Transactions on Consumer Electronics, 46*(1), 31–39.

Lou, D.-C., Liu, J.-L., & Li, C.-T. (2004). Digital signature-based image authentication. In C.S. Lu (Ed.), *Multimedia security: Steganography and digital watermarking techniques for protection of intellectual property*. Hershey, PA: Idea Group.

Lu, C.S., Huang, S.K., Sze, C.J., & Liao, H.Y. (2000). Cocktail watermarking for digital image protection. *IEEE Transactions on Multimedia, 2*(4), 209–224.

Queluz, M.P. (2001). Authentication of digital images and video: Generic models and a new contribution. *Signal Processing: Image Communication, 16*, 461–475.

Schneider, M., & Chang, S.-F. (1996). Robust content based digital signature for image authentication. *Proceedings of the IEEE International Conference on Image Processing, III*, 227–230.

Stallings, W. (1998). *Cryptography and network security: Principles and practice*. Prentice Hall.

Trappe, W., Wu, M., & Liu, K.J. (2002). Collusion-resistant fingerprinting for multimedia. *Proceedings of the IEEE International Conference on Acoustics, Speech, and Signal Processing*, 3309–3312.

van Leest, A., van der Veen, M., & Bruekers, F. (2003). Reversible image watermarking. *Proceedings of the IEEE International Conference on Image Processing, II*, 731–734.

Winne, D.A., Knowles, H.D., Bull, D.R., & Canagarajah, C.N. (2002). Digital watermarking in wavelet domain with predistortion for authenticity verification and localization. *Proceeding of the SPIE Conference on Security and Watermarking of Multimedia Contents, IV,* 349–356.

Wong, P.-W. (1998). A public key watermark for image verification and authentication. *Proceeding of the IEEE International Conference on Image Processing, I,* 455–459.

Wong, P.-W., & Memon, N. (2000). Secret and public key authentication watermarking schemes that resist vector quantization attack. *Proceeding of the SPIE Conference on Security and Watermarking of Multimedia Contents, II,* 417–427.

Wu, M., & Liu, B. (1998). Watermarking for image authentication. *Proceeding of the IEEE International Conference on Image Processing, II,* 437–441.

Wu, M., & Liu, B. (2003). Data hiding in image and video: 1. Fundamental issues and solutions. *IEEE Transactions on Image Processing, 12*(6), 685–695.

Xie, L., & Arce, G.R. (2001). A class of authentication digital watermarks for secure multimedia communication. *IEEE Transactions on Image Processing, 10*(11), 1754–1764.

Yeung, M., & Minzter, F. (1997). An invisible watermarking technique for image verification. *Proceeding on the IEEE International Conference on Image Processing, I,* 680–683.

Chapter III

Digital Watermarking for Multimedia Transaction Tracking

Dan Yu
Nanyang Technological University, Singapore

Farook Sattar
Nanyang Technological University, Singapore

Abstract

This chapter focuses on the issue of transaction tracking in multimedia distribution applications through digital watermarking terminology. The existing watermarking schemes are summarized and their assumptions as well as the limitations for tracking are analyzed. In particular, an Independent Component Analysis (ICA)-based watermarking scheme is proposed, which can overcome the problems of the existing watermarking schemes. Multiple watermarking technique is exploited—one watermark to identify the rightful owner of the work and the other one to identify the legal user of a copy of the work. In the absence of original data, watermark, embedding locations and strengths, the ICA-based watermarking scheme is introduced for efficient watermark extraction with some side information. The robustness of the proposed scheme against some common signal-processing attacks as well as the related future work are also presented. Finally, some challenging issues in multimedia transaction tracking through digital watermarking are discussed.

Introduction

We are now in a digital information age. Digital information technology has changed our society as well as our lives. The information revolution takes place in the following two forms

* Data/information retrieval/representation
* Data/information dissemination/communication

Digital presentation of data allows information recorded in a digital format, and thus, it brings easy access to generate and replicate the information. It is such an easy access that provides the novelty in the current phase of the information revolution. Digital technology allows primarily use with the new physical communications media, such as satellite and fiber-optic transmission. Therefore, PCs, e-mail, MPCs, LANs, WANs, MANs, intranets, and the Internet have been evolving rapidly since the 1980s. The Internet has a worldwide broadcasting capability, a mechanism for information distribution, and a medium for collaboration and interaction between individuals and their computers regardless of geographic location. This allows researchers and professionals to share relevant data and information with each other.

As image, audio, video, and other works become available in digital form, perfect copies can be easily made. The widespread use of computer networks and the global reach of the World Wide Web have added substantially an astonishing abundance of information in digital form, as well as offering unprecedented ease of access to it. Creating, publishing, distributing, using, and reusing information have become many times easier and faster in the past decade. The good news is the enrichment that this explosive growth in information brings to society as a whole. The bad news is that it can also bring to those who take advantage of the properties of digital information and the Web to copy, distribute, and use information illegally. The Web is an information resource of extraordinary size and depth, yet it is also an information reproduction and dissemination facility of great demand and capability. Therefore, there is currently a significant amount of research in intellectual property protection issues involving multimedia content distribution via the Internet.

Thus the objective of this chapter is to present multimedia transaction tracking through digital watermarking terminology. The Independent Component Analysis (ICA) technique is employed efficiently for watermark extraction in order to verify the recipient of the distributed content, and hence, to trace illegal transaction of the work to be protected.

Multimedia Distribution Framework Through Digital Watermarking

The rapid growth of networked multimedia systems has increased the need for the protection and enforcement of intellectual property (IP) rights of digital media. IP protection is becoming increasingly important nowadays. The tasks to achieve IP protection for multimedia distribution on the Internet can be classified as follows:

- **Ownership identification**: The owner of the original work must be able to provide the trustful proof that he/she is the rightful owner of the content.
- **Transaction tracking**: The owner must be able to track the distributions of the work, so that he/she is able to find the person who is responsible for the illegal replication and redistribution.
- **Content authentication**: The owner should be able to detect any illegal attempts to alter the work.

This chapter concentrates on the task of transaction tracking for multimedia distribution applications. Let us consider the scenario when an owner wants to sell or distribute the work to registered users only. To enforce IP rights, two primary problems have to be solved. First of all, the owner must be able to prove that he/she is the legal owner of the distributed content. Second, if the data have been subsequently copied and redistributed illegally, the owner must be able to find the person who is responsible for the illegal copying and redistribution of the data (see Figure 1).

Figure 1. A multimedia distribution system where the digital content could be illegally redistributed to an illegal user

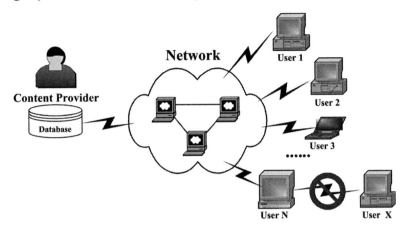

The first technology adopted to enforce protection of IP rights is cryptography. Cryptographic technology (Schneier, 1995) provides an effective tool to secure the distribution process and control the legal uses of the contents that have been received by a user. The contents to be delivered over the Internet are encrypted, and only legal users who hold the decryption key are able to use the encrypted data, whereas the data stream would be useless to a pirate without the appropriate decryption key. However, for an error-free transmission through a network, the contents after the decryption in the cryptography will be exactly the same as the original data. The data contents can be replicated perfectly many times and the user can also manipulate the contents.

Researchers and scientists are then turned to search for other technologies to counter copyright piracy on global networks that are not solvable by cryptography. In this context, recently digital watermarking technology (Cox, Miller, & Bloom, 2002) has drawn much attention. In digital watermarking, the information is transparently embedded into the work, rather than a specific media format, such as the header of a file that could be lost during transmission or file format transformation. Digital watermarking technique thus provides an efficient means for transaction tracking of illegal copying as well as redistribution of multimedia information. For a typical transaction-tracking application, the watermark identifies the first legal recipient of the work. If it is subsequently found that the work has been illegally redistributed, the watermark can then help to identify the person who is responsible for it.

Figure 2 presents a multimedia distribution framework to enforce IP rights through a technique of multiple watermarking. Multiple watermarking (Lu & Mark, 2001; Mintzer & Braudaway, 1999; Sheppard, Safavi-Naini, & Ogunbona, 2001), as suggested by the name, refers to embedding different types of watermarks into single multimedia content to accomplish different goals. For example, one of the watermarks could be used to verify ownership, the second one is to identify the recipient, and the third one is to authenticate content integrity.

For the Internet distribution application, the users first send a request to the content provider whenever they are interested for the multimedia contents. The owner can then distribute the work by signing a watermark to a registered user to uniquely identify the recipient of the work, as shown in Figure 2. All data sent to a registered user are embedded with an assigned watermark as well as the owner's watermark, while maintaining a good perceptual visual quality of the marked content. In this presented framework, the IP rights of the distributed works are enforced from the two following aspects by employing a multiple watermarking technique:

Figure 2. The multimedia distribution framework by inserting an owner's watermark to identify the ownership of the work and a unique user's watermark to identify each unique legal user

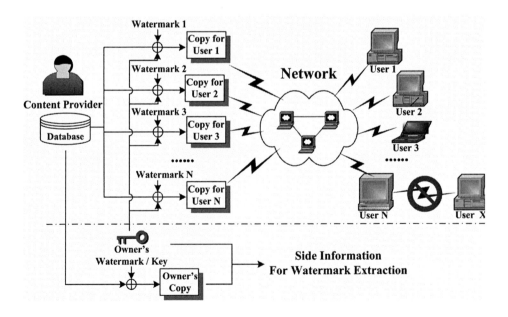

- Every copy of the work contains the owner's watermark to identify the rightful ownership of the work.

- The owner or an authorized representative can uniquely identify the recipient or the legal user of a particular copy of the multimedia content according to the embedded user's unique watermark.

Consider the case when the owner needs to prove the rightful ownership of the content. The owner can present his/her original data (without any marks) of the work as well as his/her watermark as evidence. The two embedded watermarks, including one owner's watermark and one user's watermark, are therefore able to extract by a simple subtraction method (Cox, Miller, & Bloom, 2002; Cox, Leighton, & Shamoon, 1997). One extracted watermark, that is, the owner's watermark, is matched with the previously presented owner's watermark. The rightful ownership of the content is thus verified. It is an essential prerequisite for IP protection to embed the owner's watermark into every copy of the work to be distributed over the Internet. The more difficult and challenging task, as discussed in this chapter, is to identify the legal users efficiently in the absence of the original data, and hence to trace the transactions of a particular copy of the multimedia content. For the purpose of security in multimedia, the original data are always kept in secret and should not be known to the public during watermark extraction. In some real applications, the owner needs the authorized representatives or service providers to perform the transaction-tracking tasks. For security reasons, the owner also cannot provide the original data to those representatives. Therefore, there arises a challenging issue how to extract the user's watermark in the absence of the original data. This is the main problem in transaction tracking through digital watermarking, which has been discussed in this chapter.

The Limitations of the Current Watermarking Schemes and Solutions

A wide range of watermarking algorithms has been proposed. In terms of various applications, the watermarking techniques can be classified into two categories:

1. **Robust copyright marking**: to provide evidence for proving the rightful ownership of the protected digital media

2. **Authenticate marking**: to authenticate any possible alteration in the protected digital media

Robust marks can verify the ownership of the digital data, whereas the authenticate marks are used to prove whether an object has been "touched" or manipulated. This chapter focuses on robust watermarking. Robust watermarking, as opposed to authentication marking, requires the embedded watermark to be robust against all types of attacks so that it should be able to survive against attacks before the quality of the watermarked image is drastically degraded.

The major research studies on current robust watermarking techniques include the following key technical points (Barni, Bartolini, Cappellini, & Piva, 1998; Cox et al., 1997; Delaigle, Vleeschouwer, & Macq, 1998; Hartung & Kutter, 1999; Katzenbeisser & Petitcolas, 2000; Nikolaidis, & Pitas, 1998; Parhi & Nishitani, 1999):

- The choice of a work space to perform the hiding operation, mainly a spatial domain (Nikolaidis & Pitas, 1998), or a transform domain such as full-frame Discrete Cosine Transform (full DCT) (Barni et al., 1998; Cox et al., 1997; Piva, Barni, Bartoloni, & Cappellini, 1997), block DCT (Benham, Memon, Yeo, & Yeung, 1997; Hartung & Girod, 1996; Koch & Zhao, 1995; Langelaar, Lubbe, & Lagendijk, 1997; Podilchuk & Zeng, 1997; Xia, Boncelet, & Arce, 1997), Fourier Transform (FT) (Ruanaidh, Dowling, & Boland, 1996), Mellin-Fourier (Ruanaidh & Pun, 1997, 1998), or wavelet (Dugad, Ratakonda, & Ahuja, 1998; Inoue, Miyazaki, Yamamoto, & Katsura, 1998; Kundur & Hatzinakos, 1998; Wang, Su, & Kuo, 1998; Xie & Arce, 1998)

- The study of optimal watermark embedding locations based on the human visual system (Delaigle et al., 1998; Kankanhalli, Rajmohan, & Ramakrishnan, 1998; Liu, Kong, Kong, & Liu, 2001; Voloshynovskiy, Herrigel, Baumgaertner, & Pun, 1999)

- The signal embedding techniques by addition, signal-adaptive addition, or modulation methods (Cox et al., 1997; Piva et al., 1997)

- The watermark detection and extraction algorithms either in blind (Piva et al., 1997) or nonblind manner (Cox et al., 1997)

Watermark recovery is usually more robust if its original, unwatermarked data are available. For example, a simple subtraction method (Cox et al., 1997) is used for watermark extraction at the locations where watermark is embedded. The presence of the watermark is determined by cross-correlation of the original and the recovered watermark. In Piva, Barni, Bartolini, and Cappellini's method (1997), the selected DCT coefficients, where the watermark is embedded, are directly matched with all the possible watermarks stored in the database. As a result, the original data are not required for watermark detection. However, a predefined threshold is still needed to determine the presence of the watermark.

From the viewpoint of the presence of a given watermark at the extraction or verification stage, there are two different types of watermarking systems found in the literature (Katzenbeisser & Petitcolas, 2000). The first type is to embed a specific watermark or information. Most watermarking techniques for copyright protection belong to this watermarking category, where it is assumed that the embedded watermark is previously known. The objective of this type of watermarking scheme is to verify the existence of the previously known watermark with or without the help of this watermark. The second type refers to embedding arbitrary information, which is, for example, useful for tracking the unique receipt of a copy of the distributed data. In such scenario, the watermark embedded in an image copy is previously unknown, therefore, no prior information regarding embedded watermark is available for watermark extraction. It makes the transaction tracking more difficult.

Assumptions as well as limitations for most of the existing watermarking schemes that can cause difficulties and ineffectiveness to apply in multimedia transaction tracking are summarized in the following:

(a) In some watermarking algorithms, watermark detection and extraction requires the presence of the original content. This is not desirable since the original data should always be kept secret and should not be shown to the public, or sometimes the original data are even not available immediately. Therefore, blind watermarking techniques are of great interest and concern nowadays.

(b) Most of the existing watermarking schemes (Cox et al., 1997; Cox et al., 2002; Katzenbeisser & Petitcolas, 2000) are based on some assumptions about watermark detection and extraction, such as the previous knowledge of watermark locations, strengths, or some threshold. However, in order to ensure the robustness and invisibility of the watermark, the optimum embedding locations as well as the embedding strengths are generally different for different images. For a large image database, it could be a disadvantage if it requires watermark locations and strengths information for detection and extraction of the watermark. As a result, a large amount of side information needs to be stored.

(c)   As explained previously, Figure 2 shows a framework to prevent illegal redistribution of the data by a legal user. In such scenario, the current watermark detection and extraction algorithms requiring information of the watermark locations and strengths, or even the original watermark, could fail because no one knows which watermark exists in the received copy of the work.

(d)   Moreover, the general watermark detection algorithm is based on a match filter finding the maximum correlation of the recovered watermark with the stored watermarks in the database containing the watermarks used to identify all possible users. It is a rather time-consuming and inefficient process, especially when a large database is needed for distribution among a large number of users.

In this chapter, an Independent Component Analysis (ICA)-based technique is proposed for watermark extraction (Yu, Sattar, & Ma, 2002). The proposed ICA-based blind watermarking scheme (Yu & Sattar, 2003) can overcome the problems of the current watermarking scheme for multimedia tracking as mentioned above. No a priori knowledge of watermark locations, strengths, threshold setting, or the original watermark is required for watermark extraction. This watermarking algorithm is found to be very effective in the application of legal data tracking compared to other watermarking algorithms. Therefore, by adopting this ICA-based watermarking approach, an efficient multimedia distribution framework for copyright protection can be accomplished.

A New ICA-Based Watermarking Scheme for Multimedia Transaction Tracking

This section presents an ICA-based wavelet-domain watermarking scheme. Two watermarks are to be embedded into two selected wavelet subbands of the original image. One is the owner's watermark (or the key of the watermarking system), and the other is a unique watermark assigned to a unique legal user. The ICA technique is applied for extraction of the user's watermark with the help of side information. The proposed scheme is described in the context of watermarking in grayscale images, but this technique can be extended to color images and other digital media such as audio and video.

Proposed Watermark Embedding Scheme

Figure 3 shows a second-level wavelet decomposition of the Lena image into four bands—low-frequency band (LL), high-frequency band (HH), low-high frequency band (LH), and high-low frequency band (HL). Subbands LL and HH are not suitable for watermark embedding among these four subbands. The image quality can be degraded if the watermark is embedding in LL subband since it contains the most important information of an image. Subband HH is insignificant compared to LH and HL subbands, and watermark embedding in such subband find it difficult to survive attacks, such as lossy JPEG compression. Watermark embedding in the two subbands (e.g., LH2 and HL2 of the second-level wavelet decomposition) consisting the middle-frequency pair is to be demonstrated.

Some digital signature/pattern or company logo (S), for example, a text image in Figure 4(b), can be used to generate the watermark (W) to be embedded. This type of recognizable image pattern is more intuitive and unique than the

Figure 3. Second-level wavelet decomposition of the Lena image

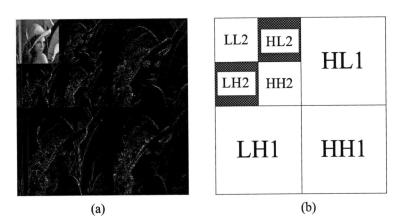

(a)   (b)

Figure 4. (a) An NVF masking function, (b) a text signature (64×64 pixels), (c) the modified text watermark based on the visual mask shown in (a), (d) an owner's watermark or key of watermarking system, (e) the modified key based on (a), (f) original Lena image (256×256 pixels), and (g) a watermarked Lena image (PSNR = 45.50dB)

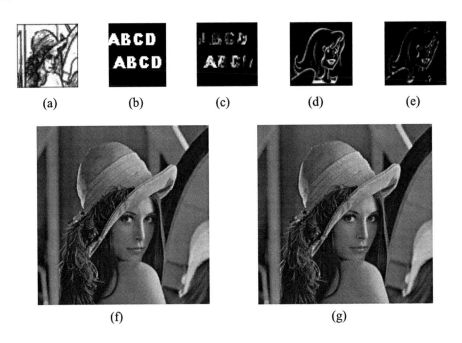

random sequence to identify the ownership of the work. By using grayscale watermark, our method is found to be more robust against various attacks because the grayscale images can always preserve a certain level of structural information, which are meaningful and recognizable and also can be much more easily verified by human eyes rather than some objective similarity measurements. A masking function—Noise Visibility Function (NVF) (Voloshynovskiy et al., 1999)—is applied to characterize the local image properties, identifying the textured and edge regions where the information can be more strongly embedded. Such high-activity regions are generally highly insensitive to distortion. With the visual mask, the watermark strength can be reasonably increased without visually degrading the image quality.

In the next section, the watermark generation and the detailed embedding algorithm are demonstrated, followed by the generation of side information for watermark extraction.

Watermark Embedding Algorithm

Figure 5 illustrates the watermark embedding procedure using second-level decomposed middle-frequency pair (LH2 and HL2):

Step 1: Perform the second-level discrete wavelet decomposition of the original image **I**. Subbands LH2 and HL2 are selected for the watermark insertion.

Step 2: The NVF masking function (Voloshynovskiy et al., 1999), **M**, of the original image is generated. Figure 4(a) shows an NVF mask for the Lena image. For the homogeneous region, NVF approaches 1 (white color), and the strength of the embedded watermark approaches 0. The watermark should be embedded in highly textured regions containing edges instead of homogeneous regions. The original signature image, **S**, is modified according to the generated NVF masking function to ensure the imperceptibility of the watermark embedded. The final watermark is quantized into 0–7 gray levels. The expression for watermark generation is given as

Figure 5. The proposed watermark embedding algorithm (for second-level wavelet decomposition)

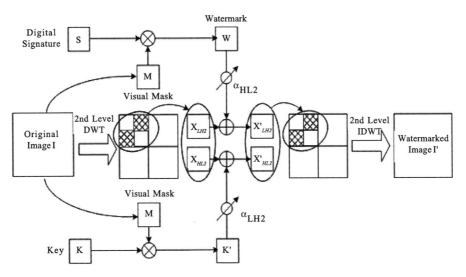

$$W = Q_8 [(1 - M) . S],\qquad(1)$$

where Q_8 denotes the quantization operator with 8 gray levels. Figure 4(c) shows a text watermark generated using the NVF masking function shown in Figure 4(a).

Step 3: The key **K,** which is also the owner's watermark, is preprocessed by multiplying the same visual mask **M** as

$$K' = Q_8 [(1 - M) . K],\qquad(2)$$

where Q_8 denotes the quantization operator with 8 gray levels. Figure 4(d) gives a key image for ownership authentication. Figure 4(e) shows the modified key after preprocessing by using the NVF masking function in Figure 4(a).

Step 4: The watermark **W** and the modified key **K′** are inserted into the LH2 and HL2 subband, respectively, in the following way:

$$\mathbf{X}'_{LH2} = \mathbf{X}_{LH2} + \alpha_{LH2} \cdot \mathbf{W} = \mathbf{X}_{LH2} + \alpha_{\mathbf{x}} \cdot \mu (|\,\mathbf{X}_{LH2}\,|) \cdot \mathbf{W};$$
$$\mathbf{X}'_{HL2} = \mathbf{X}_{HL2} + \alpha_{HL2} \cdot \mathbf{K2} = \mathbf{X}_{HL2} + \alpha_{\mathbf{x}} \cdot \mu (|\,\mathbf{X}_{HL2}\,|) \cdot \mathbf{K}',\qquad(3)$$

where **X** and **X′** are the wavelet transform coefficients of the original and the watermarked image, respectively. In Equation 3, α_{LH2} and α_{HL2} denote the weighting coefficients of the watermark embedding in subbands LH2 and HL2, respectively, while $\mu (|\ |)$ denotes the mean of the absolute value. A common control parameter $\alpha_{\mathbf{x}}$ in Equation 3 is used to adjust the watermark embedding strength to preserve a satisfactory quality of the final watermarked image (Peter, 2001).

Table 1. PSNR (in dB) of the watermarked image with respect to α_x

α_x	0.01	0.05	0.10	0.15	0.20	0.25	0.30
PSNR (dB)	67.50	53.52	47.50	43.98	41.48	39.54	37.96

Step 5: The watermarked image **I′** is obtained by the inverse discrete wavelet transform.

Step 6: Steps 4 and 5 are repeated until the quality of the final watermarked image is satisfactory, for instance, the PSNR (peak signal-to-noise ratio) measure is within the range of 40–50dB. Particularly the parameter α_x is tuned to adjust the watermark strength to obtain the desired embedding result. Decreasing the magnitude of α_x results in a better quality of the final marked image and vice versa. Figure 4(e) shows a watermarked Lena image with PSNR 45.50dB. Table 1 shows the quality of watermarked image (in dB) with respect to the control parameter α_x.

Side Information for Watermark Extraction

As discussed earlier, the original data may be unavailable in many real applications for security purposes. In order to identify legal users, some side information is necessary to extract the users' watermarks in the absence of the original data. The proposed method allows the owner to create a copy of the data set by embedding only the owner's watermark following the same procedure shown in Figure 5. The owner's watermark is, in fact, the key of the watermarking system that is used for watermark extraction. Using only the owner's copy **I′$_0$** and the key **K**, the owner is able to identify the recipient of any distributed image by ICA methods. This will be elaborated in the next subsection.

Figure 6 illustrates an owner's copy of the Lena image, embedded with the owner's watermark shown in Figure 4(d). The owner's copy is then obtained by embedding the modified key **K′** in the wavelet domain as follows:

$$\mathbf{X'}_{0LH2} = \mathbf{X}_{LH2} + \alpha_{LH2} \cdot \mathbf{K'} = \mathbf{X}_{LH2} + \alpha_{x0} \cdot \mu\,(\,|\,\mathbf{X}_{0LH2}\,|\,) \cdot \mathbf{K'};$$

$$\mathbf{X'}_{0HL2} = \mathbf{X}_{HL2} + \alpha_{HL2} \cdot \mathbf{K'} = \mathbf{X}_{HL2} + \alpha_{x0} \cdot \mu\,(\,|\,\mathbf{X}_{0HL2}\,|\,) \cdot \mathbf{K'}, \qquad (4)$$

where $\mathbf{X}_0$ and $\mathbf{X'}_0$ are respectively the wavelet transform coefficients of the original image and the watermarked channel, and α_{x0} is a control parameter for the visual quality of the watermarked image **I′$_0$**.

Figure 6. The owner's copy of the Lena image (256×256 pixels and PSNR = 46.72dB)

Suppose an owner wants to authorize a third party, called appointed representative, to do the tracing task. In such case, the owner should also assign a unique watermark to the appointed representative. This representative's watermark would then replace the owner's watermark embedded in the HL2 wavelet subband. It would also be used as the key during watermark extraction. However, at the same time, for ownership verification, the owner's watermark still needs to be embedded in the wavelet subband selected other than the LH2 and HL2 subbands.

Proposed Watermark Extraction Scheme Using the ICA Method

In this section, the concept of ICA is briefly introduced. Then a blind watermark extraction scheme is proposed. The ICA technique is employed for watermark extraction successfully, without knowing the original image and any prior information on the embedded watermark, embedding locations, and strengths.

Independent Component Analysis (ICA)

Independent Component Analysis (ICA) is one of the most widely used methods for performing blind source separation (BSS). It is a very general-purpose statistical technique to recover the independent sources given only sensor observations that are linear mixtures of independent source signals

(Hyvärinen, 1999b; Hyvärinen & Oja, 1999; Lee, 1998). ICA has been widely applied in many areas such as audio processing, biomedical signal processing, and telecommunications. In this paper, ICA is further applied in watermarking for blind watermark extraction.

The ICA model consists of two parts: the mixing process and unmixing process. In the mixing process (Hyvärinen, 1999b; Hyvärinen & Oja, 1999; Lee, 1998), the observed linear mixtures $x_1, \dots, x_m$ of n number of independent components are defined as

$$x_j = a_{j1}s_1 + a_{j2}s_2 + \dots + a_{jn}s_n; \ 1 \le j \le m, \tag{5}$$

where $\{s_k, k = 1, \dots, n\}$ denote the source variables, that is, the independent components, and $\{a_{jk}, j = 1, \dots, m; k = 1, \dots, n\}$ are the mixing coefficients. In vector-matrix form, the above mixing model can be expressed as

$$\mathbf{x} = \mathbf{As}, \tag{6}$$

where

$$\mathbf{A} = \begin{pmatrix} a_{11} & a_{12} & \dots & a_{1n} \\ a_{21} & a_{22} & \dots & a_{2n} \\ \vdots & \vdots & \ddots & \vdots \\ a_{m1} & a_{m2} & \dots & a_{mn} \end{pmatrix}$$

is the mixing matrix (Hyvärinen, 1999b; Hyvärinen & Oja, 1999; Lee, 1998), $\mathbf{x} = [x_1 \, x_2 \dots x_m]^T$, $\mathbf{s} = [s_1 \, s_2 \dots s_n]^T$, and T is the transpose operator. For the unmixing process (Hyvärinen, 1999b; Hyvärinen & Oja, 1999; Lee, 1998), after estimating the matrix $\mathbf{A}$, one can compute its inverse—the unmixing matrix $\mathbf{B}$ and the independent components are obtained as

$$\mathbf{s} = \mathbf{Bx}. \tag{7}$$

To ensure the identifiability of the ICA model, the following fundamental restrictions are imposed (Hyvärinen, 1999b; Hyvärinen & Oja, 1999):

- The source signals in the mixing process should be principally statistically independent.
- All independent components s_k, with the possible exception of one component, must be non-Gaussian.
- The number of observed linear mixtures m must be at least as large as the number of independent components n, that is, $m \geq n$.
- The matrix **A** must be of full column rank.

There are many ICA algorithms that have been proposed recently. Some popular ICA methods include Bell and Sejnowski's Infomax (1995), Hyvärinen and Oja's FastICA (1999), Cichocki and Barros' RICA (Robust batch ICA) (1999), Cardoso's JADE (Joint Approximate Diagonalization of Eigen-matrices) (1999), and so on. From the stability standpoint, it is more appropriate to choose RICA or JADE algorithms than Infomax and FastICA algorithms for our watermark extraction process. Both Infomax algorithm and FastICA algorithm require that the values of the mixing coefficients for the sources not be very close (Bell & Sejnowski, 1995; Hyvärinen, 1999a). However, both the watermark and the key are embedded by multiplication with small weighting coefficients to make them invisible. Therefore, the extraction of such weak watermark signals could fail by using Infomax or FastICA algorithm. The extraction results using FastICA algorithm also very much depend on the initial guess of the weighting coefficients (Hyvärinen, 1999a).

Cichocki and Barro's RICA algorithm is an effective blind source separation approach particularly for the temporally correlated sources, since it models the signal as an autoregressive (AR) process (Cichocki & Barros, 1999). The RICA algorithm thus can achieve the best extraction results when both the embedding and extraction are performed in the spatial domain. This is because, generally speaking, the natural images are spatially correlated and can be effectively modeled as temporally correlated sequences. However, for the proposed watermarking scheme described in this chapter, the watermark is embedded in the wavelet domain instead of the spatial domain. The experimental results show that the JADE algorithm (Cardoso, 1999) outperforms the other ICA algorithms for watermark extraction in our proposed watermarking scheme. This could be due to the use of higher-order statistical parameters in the JADE algorithm, such as fourth-order cumulant, which can model the statistical behavior of the wavelet coefficients more effectively. Therefore, the JADE algorithm is employed to elaborate the watermark extraction process in our proposed watermarking scheme, which will be described next.

Proposed Blind Watermark Extraction Scheme

This section proposes the ICA-based blind watermark extraction scheme. Instead of using the original image, only an owner's copy of the original image is required for watermark extraction. The new useful feature of the proposed scheme is that the proposed method does not require previous knowledge of the original watermark, embedding locations, and watermark strengths for extraction. The main idea is to consider two subbands $(\mathbf{X'_R})$ of the watermarked image to have a mixture image of the wavelet transformed image $(\mathbf{X_R})$ of the original image $(\mathbf{I})$, the watermark image $(\mathbf{W})$, and the modified key $(\mathbf{K'})$. Figure 7 shows the proposed blind watermark extraction scheme. Let us denote the received watermarked image as $\tilde{\mathbf{I}}'$. The symbol ($\sim$) is to indicate that the received data may or may not be the same as its original watermarked data due to transmission errors or possibly pirate attacks. This symbol ($\sim$) is removed in the following for simplicity.

Figure 7. Proposed blind watermark extraction scheme (using the second-level decomposition)

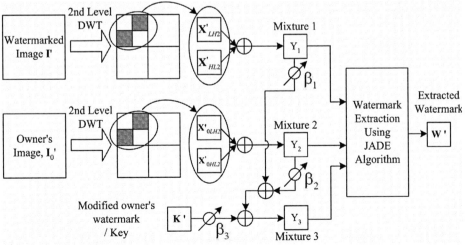

Step 1: Perform the second-level discrete wavelet decomposition of the watermarked image $\mathbf{I}'$ in order to obtain the wavelet coefficients $\mathbf{X}'_{LH2}$ and $\mathbf{X}'_{HL2}$ for the two selected subbands of LH2 and HL2.

Step 2: The first mixture signal $\mathbf{Y}_1$ is obtained by

$$\mathbf{Y}_1 = \mathbf{X}'_{LH2} + \mathbf{X}'_{HL2}. \tag{8}$$

From Equation 3, $\mathbf{X}'_R$ ($\mathbf{R} \in [LH2, HL2]$) are the mixture observations of the wavelet transform of the original image ($\mathbf{X}_R$), the watermark ($\mathbf{W}$), and the modified key ($\mathbf{K}'$), therefore, Equation 8 can be rewritten as

$$\mathbf{Y}_1 = \mathbf{X} + \alpha_1 \mathbf{W} + \alpha_2 \mathbf{K}', \tag{9}$$

where $\mathbf{X} = \mathbf{X}_{LH2} + \mathbf{X}_{HL2}$, $\alpha_1 = \alpha_x \cdot \mu(|\mathbf{X}_{LH2}|)$ and $\alpha_2 = \alpha_x \cdot \mu(|\mathbf{X}_{HL2}|)$. It is found that the first mixture signal is a linear mixture of the three independent sources, that is, $\mathbf{X}$, $\mathbf{W}$ and $\mathbf{K}'$.

Step 3: Repeat the procedure in Steps 1 and 2 for the owner's image $\mathbf{I}'_0$. The second mixture $\mathbf{Y}_2$ is obtained by

$$\mathbf{Y}_2 = \mathbf{X}'_{0LH2} + \mathbf{X}'_{0HL2}. \tag{10}$$

Similarly $\mathbf{Y}_2$ is also a linear mixture of the wavelet transform of the original image ($\mathbf{X}_R$, $\mathbf{R} \in [LH2, HL2]$) and the key/owner's watermark ($\mathbf{K}$). It can be written as

$$\mathbf{Y}_2 = \mathbf{X} + \alpha_3 \mathbf{K}', \tag{11}$$

where $\alpha_3 = \alpha_{x0} \cdot [\mu(|X_{0LH2}|) + \mu(|X_{0HL2}|)]$.

Step 4: From Equations 8 and 10, two mixture images can be obtained containing three sources or independent components in the observations—X, the modified key K', and the watermark W. As was pointed out earlier, to exploit ICA methods for watermark extraction, it is required that the number of observed linear mixture inputs is at least equal to or larger than the number of independent sources in order to ensure the identifiability of the ICA model (Hyvärinen, 1999b; Hyvärinen & Oja, 1999; Lee, 1998). Therefore, another linear mixture of the three independent sources is needed. The third mixture Y_3 can then be generated by linear superposition of Y_1, Y_2 and K':

$$Y_3 = \beta_1 Y_1 + \beta_2 Y_2 + \beta_3 K', \tag{12}$$

where β_1 and β_2 are arbitrary real numbers, and b_3 is a nonzero arbitrary real number. Either β_1 or β_2 can be set to zero to efficiently reduce the computational load of ICA. Note that the modified key K' can be easily obtained by regenerating the NVF visual mask and multiplying it to the original owner's watermark K.

Step 5: The three mixtures input into the JADE ICA algorithm (Cardoso, 1999) and the watermark image W' is extracted. The user of any image copy can be uniquely identified from the signature of the extracted watermark. Figure 8 shows the extracted watermark from the watermarked image shown in Figure 4(g).

Figure 8. The extraction result for the user's watermark image (normalized correlation coefficient, r = 0.9790), using JADE ICA method

Performance Evaluation

The robustness results of the proposed watermarking scheme are shown in this section using the Lena image of size 256×256 when the simulations are performed in the MATLAB 6.5 software environment. A watermarked image (PSNR = 45.50 dB) in Figure 4(g) is generated by setting the watermark strength control parameter α_x as 0.15. In the experiments of watermark extraction, the parameters β_1, β_2, and β_3 are set as 0, 1, 1, respectively, to simplify the computational load of the ICA processing, and Daubechies-1 (Haar) orthogonal filters are employed for wavelet decomposition. In order to investigate the robustness of the watermark, the watermarked image is manipulated by various signal processing techniques, such as JPEG compression and JPEG2000 compression, quantization, cropping, and geometric distortions. The watermark extraction is performed for the distorted watermarked image and the extracted watermark is compared to the original.

The Performance Index

The performance of the blind watermark extraction result is evaluated in terms of normalized correlation coefficient, r, of the extracted watermark $\mathbf{W'}$ and the original watermark $\mathbf{W}$ as

$$r = \frac{\mathbf{W} \cdot \mathbf{W'}}{\sqrt{\mathbf{W}^2 \cdot \mathbf{W'}^2}} . \tag{13}$$

The magnitude range of r is [-1, 1], and the unity holds if the matching between the extracted image and the original image is perfect.

Robustness Against Compression and Quantization Attacks

In the following, the robustness of the proposed watermarking scheme is compared with some other blind wavelet-domain watermarking schemes (Peter, 2001) in terms of normalized correlation coefficient r as shown in

Equation 13. These techniques include Wang, Su, and Kuo's algorithm (1998), Inoue, Miyazaki, Yamamoto, and Katsura's blind algorithm (based on manipulating insignificant coefficients) (1998), Dugad, Ratakonda, and Ahuja's algorithm (1998), Kundur and Hatzinakos' algorithm (1998), and Xie and Arce's algorithm (1998).

Wang et al. (1998) have proposed an adaptive watermarking method to embed watermarks into selected significant subband wavelet coefficients. A blind watermark retrieval technique has been proposed by truncating selected significant coefficients to some specific value. Inoue et al. (1998) have classified insignificant and significant wavelet coefficients using the embedded zerotree wavelet (EZW) algorithm. Thereby, two types of embedding algorithms have been developed in respect to the locations of significant or insignificant coefficients. Information data are detected using the position of the zerotree's root and the threshold value after decomposition of the watermarked image. Dugad et al. (1998) have added the watermark in selected coefficients having significant energy in the transform domain to ensure nonerasability of the watermark. During watermark detection, all the high-pass coefficients above the threshold are chosen and are correlated with the original copy of the watermark. Kundur and Hatzinakos (1998) have presented a novel technique for the digital watermarking of still images based on the concept of multiresolution wavelet fusion, which is robust to a variety of signal distortions. Xie and Arce (1998) have developed a blind watermarking digital signature for the purpose of authentication. The signature algorithm is first implemented in the wavelet-transform domain and is coupled within the SPIHT (Set Partitioning in Hierarchical Trees) compression algorithm.

Figure 9 shows the comparison results in terms of performance index against the JPEG compression. For the proposed scheme, the extracted watermark's correlation decreases gradually with the compression quality factor. The image quality (in PSNR) has degraded significantly to 27 dB when the compression quality becomes quite low to 10%. In such a difficult case, the watermark can still be extracted with the value of r equal to 0.2553 for watermark embedding in second-level wavelet decomposition. According to Figure 9, the presented method can perform better than the Wang et al.'s and the Kundur and Hatzinakos' methods, while performing much better than the Inoue et al.'s method in terms of robustness against JPEG compression attack at a very low compression quality factor.

Figure 10 is the extraction comparison against the JPEG2000 compression attacks. The robustness of the proposed scheme is demonstrated up to the

Figure 9. Comparison of results against JPEG compression attacks

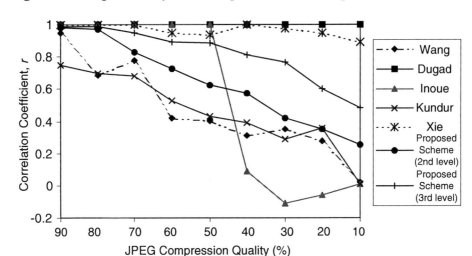

Figure 10. Comparison of results against JPEG2000 compression attacks

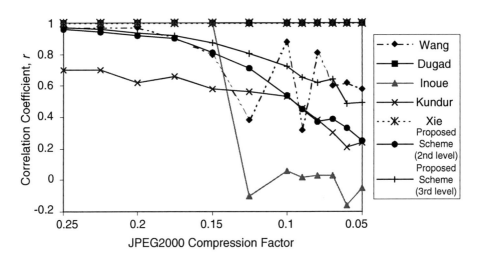

compression factor 0.05 or compression rate 0.4 bpp (bit per pixel). The proposed scheme gives better performance than Kundur and Hatzinakos' method, and comparable performance to the Wang et al.'s method. The extraction performance of the Inoue et al.'s method drops sharply when the JPEG2000 compression factor decreases to 0.125. Embedding in the subbands of higher wavelet decomposition level (see curves for third-level decomposition in Figures 9 and 10) can improve significantly the robustness of the proposed scheme against compression attacks.

Figure 11 shows the extraction results against quantization from gray level 256 to gray level 4 per pixel. The proposed scheme has very good robustness result against quantization. The performance of the proposed scheme is comparable to that of the Xie and Arce's method, and much better than the other methods.

From Figures 9 and 10, it is found that Xie and Arce's and Dugad et al.'s methods have excellent robustness performance against JPEG and JPEG2000 compression. In Xie and Arce's algorithm, the watermark is embedded solely in the approximation image (LL subband) of the host image (Xie & Arce, 1998). Although LL subband embedding is robust against compression attacks, the image quality could be degraded visually because the coefficients of this portion always contain the most important information of an image (Peter, 2001). It is claimed that the robustness of Xie and Arce's method very much depends on the number of decomposition levels. Very good robustness result can be obtained by employing a five-level wavelet decomposition using Daubechies-7/9 bi-orthogonal filters (Peter, 2001; Xie & Arce, 1998). On the other hand, in the Dugad et al.'s method, the watermark is embedded in the significant coefficients of all detail subbands (Dugad et al., 1998); therefore, it is more resistant to compression. During the watermark detection using Dugad et al.'s method, the original watermark is required to compute the correlation for the high-pass coefficients with the values above a threshold (Dugad et al., 1998). The presence of the watermark is determined by comparing this correlation with a threshold setting. It is not as general as our proposed scheme

Figure 11. Comparison of results against quantization

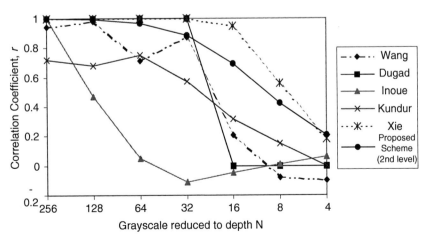

where the original watermark and the threshold are not required for watermark extraction.

The experimental results show that the proposed scheme has good robustness against the most prominent attacks such as JPEG and JPEG2000 compression, quantization, and can be comparable to existing blind wavelet-domain watermarking schemes. Experimental results also show that unlike the Xie and Arce's method (Peter, 2001; Xie & Arce, 1998), the choice of the wavelet transform is not critical concerning the robustness issue of the proposed watermarking method (the corresponding results are not included here).

Robustness Against Cropping and Geometric Distortions

Many watermarking techniques cannot survive geometric transformations such as rotation, scaling, and translation (RST) and sometimes cropping attack as well due to the loss of the synchronization of the watermark detector. A solution to such geometric attacks is to apply a resynchronization process (blind or nonblind) before performing the watermark extraction. Nonblind solution requires the presence of the original data, or at least some knowledge of the image features (Dugelay & Petitcolas, 2000). Davoine, Bas, Hébert, and Chassery (1999) have proposed a nonblind solution by splitting the original image into a set of triangular patches. This mesh serves as a reference mesh and is kept in the memory for synchronization preprocessing. This proposed method, however, is only efficient in the case of involving minor deformations. Johnson, Duric, and Jajodia (1999) have proposed a method to invert affine transformations by estimating the difference in the least square sense between the salient image feature points in the original and transformed images. Kutter (1998) has proposed alternative methods to retrieve the watermark from geometrically distorted image without using the original data. The first method is to preset a part of the watermark to some known values and to use them for spatial resynchronization. This approach decreases the hiding capacity of the useful information, and is also computationally very expensive. The second method proposed by Kutter (1998) is to use self-reference systems that embed the watermark several times at the shifted locations.

Generally speaking, the tuning process can be easier, more accurate and requires less computational load when the original data or reference feature points are available, although it may need extra memory to store the reference data. In our proposed watermarking scheme, original data are not available during the extraction process; however, an owner's or a representative's copy of the data is available. This image copy would be very similar to the original data, thus it is convenient to use it directly as a reference for synchronization of geometric distorted or cropped data. By simple comparisons, the tampered data can be adjusted back to original size and position rapidly and accurately. In the following, the watermark extraction results against attacks of cropping and RST are shown. The effectiveness of employing synchronization preprocessing is demonstrated by showing the significant improvements of extraction results with and without the synchronization.

As shown in Figure 12(a), the face portion of a marked Lena image is cropped. By comparison with the owner's Lena image copy, it can be easily detected that the pixels within a square area, with row index from 121 to 180 and column index from 121 to 180, are corrupted. The absence of the watermark information in this corrupted region (by considering both rows and columns from 31 ($\lceil 121/4 \rceil$) to 45 ($\lceil 180/4 \rceil$) results in an undesired overbrightness effect for the extracted watermark due to its high values in the corrupted region. This makes both the subjective and the objective verification measurements quite poor (see Figure 12(b)). One simple solution is to discard the corresponding undesired high-valued pixels from the extracted watermark and

Figure 12. (a) A cropped Lena image, (b) the extracted watermark (r = 0.2706), and (c) the extracted watermark after improving the contrast of (b) (r = 0.9036)

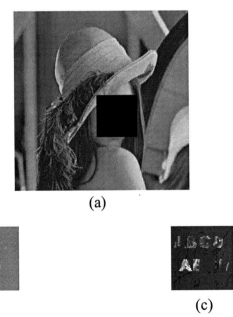

(a)

(b)   (c)

replace them with zero-valued pixels. In this way, according to Figure 12(c), the extracted watermark can be recovered mostly with some information loss in the corrupted region. Therefore, the normalized correlation coefficient r is found to increase from 0.2706 to 0.9036, showing the recovery of the low-contrast watermark (compare Figures 12(b) and 12(c)).

The watermark extraction of the geometrically distorted image may fail due to the loss of synchronization. A resynchronization preprocessing of the received data is necessary to tune it back to the right positions or sizes before input in the watermark decoder. However, the side information in the proposed watermarking scheme—the owner's or the representative's copy of the original image—provides a good reference to assist the synchronization process, and the watermark extraction performance is consequently improved. Figures 13(b), 13(d), and 13(f) show the extraction results under attacks of rotation, scaling, and translation (RST), respectively, after the synchronization process. The watermark extraction results are satisfactory in terms of both the subjective visualization and the objective similarity measurement.

Figure 13. (a) Lena image rotated by 10°, and (b) the corresponding extracted watermark (r = 0.5847); (c) Lena image downsized by reducing the number of rows and columns by 1/4, and (d) the corresponding extracted watermark (r = 0.4970); (e) Lena image translated to the left and downward by 10 and 36 lines, respectively, and (f) the corresponding extracted watermark (r = 0.5356)

(a)   (c)   (e)

(b)   (d)   (f)

Discussions

Watermarking versus Fingerprinting

To enforce IP rights for multimedia distribution over the Internet, it requires not only verification of the legal recipient, but also proof of the rightful ownership of the original work. The term *fingerprinting* (Katzenbeisser & Petitcolas, 2000; Arnold et al., 2003; Trappe, Wu, Wang, & Liu, 2003) is closely related to watermarking in the context of traitor tracking problem. Fingerprinting technique involves the embedding of different watermarks into each distributed copy of the work. The purpose of fingerprinting is to identify the legal recipient rather than the source of digital data. Thus, using the fingerprinting technique alone is not sufficient to enforce IP rights protection in multimedia distribution systems, as the owner cannot provide trustful evidence for proving the ownership. This chapter presents a multiple digital watermarking framework that can achieve the above two demands, that is, identifying the owner and the recipient of the distributed content.

Moreover, fingerprinting has another distinct interpretation, which does not involve the concept of digital watermarking at all. It refers to the extraction of unique features, such as semantically relevant or characteristic features from multimedia signals, in order to distinguish itself from other similar objects (Katzenbeisser & Petitcolas, 2000; Arnold et al., 2003). The extracted features are normally stored separately as signatures for authentication of the content rather than inserting them into the content as watermarks. This concept falls out of scope of this chapter.

Summary and Future Work of the Proposed Watermarking Scheme

The proposed ICA-based watermarking scheme shows its main advantage in terms of generality. Unlike other methods, no a priori information about the original watermark, embedding locations, strengths, as well as the threshold is needed for our blind watermark extraction scheme. Therefore, it is possible to extract the watermark from any copy of the watermarked image, where the embedded watermark is previously unknown. The other advantage of the proposed ICA-based method is that without using a pre-defined threshold, the extracted watermark could simply be verified from visual inspection instead of using the correlation-based matching technique with a threshold setting. This is possible because the embedded watermark used in our scheme is a readable digital signature image or a logo image. The generality of the proposed scheme implicates this method to be a quite useful tool for the transaction tracking in the application of Internet distribution. The only disadvantage to achieving the generality using ICA-based technique could be the complexity of the ICA itself. In this chapter, this has been compromised by the use of JADE algorithm, which is simple and computationally efficient. Furthermore, there are only three mixing sources (i.e., the original data, the key, and the watermark) involved in the presented watermarking scheme, which enables our ICA-based extraction processing to be fast.

In the future, more experiments need to be carried out in order to evaluate the resilience of this scheme against other types of attacks. For example, the collusion attacks and the possible counterattacks for multimedia distribution systems are to be investigated to improve the present scheme. The issue on the generation of a better perceptual mask as used to simulate the human visual system should also be studied to improve the visual quality of the watermarked data.

Concluding Remarks and Future Trends

This chapter investigates the multimedia transaction tracking issue by means of digital watermarking. One feasible solution of using an ICA-based watermarking technique is presented to perform ownership verification and traitor tracking for multimedia distribution through public networks. Two watermarks consisting of an owner's watermark for ownership identification and a user's watermark for unique recipient identification are embedded. Watermark is obtained by modification of the signature image with a visual mask in order to prevent the perceptual quality degradation of the watermarked image. The watermarks are inserted in the two middle frequency subband pair at the higher wavelet decomposition level (say second/third decomposition level) of the original image. Without requiring any information such as original watermark, embedding locations, and strengths, our proposed scheme can extract the user's watermark with the help of an owner's copy of the image and the owner's watermark/key. Experimental results show that the proposed watermarking scheme can provide good resistance to attacks of image compression, quantization, cropping, and geometric transformations.

It has been elaborated in this chapter that the ICA-based watermarking scheme can be employed as an efficient tool to trace the recipient of the distributed content. From the general perspective, the challenging issues of digital watermarking in the applications of transaction tracking for the Internet distribution include the following criteria:

- The original data are not available during extraction of the recipient's watermark. Thus the watermarking technique should be blind.

- No prior information about the embedded watermark and the corresponding locations is available for watermark extraction.

- In order to present as trustful evidence in the court to litigate the pirate, a highly robust watermarking scheme against common signal possessing attacks as well as collusion attacks is needed.

- For some applications, for example, searching for the pirated watermarked image using Web crawlers, it is required that the watermarking scheme is able to extract the watermark easily and with low complexity.

There is no doubt that transaction tracking is a more difficult task than copyright protection by means of digital watermarking. More general watermarking techniques are desired such that no original data and prior watermark information is needed for extraction, while providing the methods to be reliable, robust, and computationally efficient.

Another requirement to enforce the IP rights of the distributed work could be such that the owner should be able to detect any illegal attempts manipulating the content. Fragile watermark should be inserted as well in order to protect the integrity of the content. The authentication watermark should be then very sensitive to various attacks and, therefore, able to locate possible modifications. In such scenario, three watermarks would be hidden in the work in order to verify the owner, to identify the user, and to authenticate the content. Since the information-hiding capacity of the cover media is limited, we have further challenges to investigate, for example, how to compromise the three demands including the information-hiding capacity and the imperceptibility and robustness of the hidden watermark.

There has been no rush yet to embrace any of the current watermarking schemes for IP rights protection in multimedia distribution application. In fact, time is still needed for thorough inspection and appraisal to find solutions for better digital watermarking schemes. Before that, scientists and researchers have to fully understand the practical requirements associated with the real problems. In the meantime, the main challenge for researchers is to develop even more transparent and decodable schemes for robust or fragile watermarking, or perhaps to meet more demands required for a practical multimedia distribution system.

Acknowledgments

The authors would like to thank Professor N.G. Kingsbury for his valuable suggestions and comments that helped to improve the proposed watermarking scheme for transaction tracking in multimedia distribution applications. They are also thankful to Professor K.-K. Ma for contributing useful discussion regarding the use of ICA in image watermarking.

References

Arnold, M., Schmucker, M., & Wolthusen, S.D. (2003). *Techniques and applications of digital watermarking and content protection.* Boston: Artech House.

Barni, M., Bartolini, F., Cappellini, V., & Piva, A. (1998). A DCT-domain system for robust image watermarking. *Signal Processing, 66,* 357–372.

Barni, M., Bartolini, F., Cappellini, V., Piva, A., & Rigacci, F. (1998). A M.A.P. identification criterion for DCT-based watermarking. *Proc. Europ. Signal Processing Conf. (EUSIPCO'98)*, Rhodes, Greece.

Bell, A., & Sejnowski, T. (1995). An information-maximization approach to blind separation and blind deconvolution. *Neural Compt., 7,* 1129–1159.

Benham, D., Memon, N., Yeo, B.-L., & Yeung, M. (1997). Fast watermarking of DCT-based compressed images. *Proc. Int. Conf. Image Science, System, and Technology (CISST'97)*, Las Vegas, NV.

Cardoso, J.-F. (1999). High-order contrasts for independent component analysis. *Neural Computer, 11,* 157–192.

Cichocki, A., & Barros, A.K. (1999). Robust batch algorithm for sequential blind extraction of noisy biomedical signals. *Proc. ISSPA '99, 1,* 363–366.

Cox, I.J., Leighton, F.T., & Shamoon, T. (1997). Secure spread spectrum watermarking for multimedia. *IEEE Trans. on Image Processing, 6,* 1673–1687.

Cox, I.J., Miller, M.L., & Bloom, J.A. (2002). *Digital watermarking.* Morgan Kaufmann.

Davoine, F., Bas, P., Hébert, P.-A., & Chassery, J.-M. (1999). Watermarking et résistance aux déformations géométriques. *Cinquièmes journées d'études et d'échanges sur la compression et la représentation des signaux audiovisuels (CORESA '99),* Sophia-Antiplis, France.

Delaigle, J.F., Vleeschouwer, C.D., & Macq, B. (1998). Watermarking algorithm based on a human visual model. *Signal Processing, 66,* 319–335.

Dugad, R., Ratakonda, K., & Ahuja, N. (1998). A new wavelet-based scheme for watermarking images. *Proc. Int. Conf. Image Processing (ICIP).*

Dugelay, J.-L., & Petitcolas, F.A.P. (2000). Possible counter-attacks against random geometric distortions. *Proc. SPIE Security and Watermarking of Multimedia Contents II,* CA.

Hartung, F., & Girod, B. (1996). Digital watermarking of raw and compressed video. *Proc. SPIE digital compression technologies and systems for video commun., 2952,* 205–213.

Hartung, F., & Kutter, M. (1999). Multimedia watermarking technique. *Proc. IEEE, 8*(7), 1079–1106.

Hyvärinen, A. (1999a). Fast and robust fixed-point algorithms for independent component analysis. *IEEE Trans. Neural Networks, 10,* 626–634.

Hyvärinen, A. (1999b). Survey on independent component analysis. *Neural Computing Surveys, 2,* 94–128.

Hyvärinen, A., & Oja, E. (1999). Independent component analysis: a tutorial. Retrieved from *www.cis.hut.fi/projects/ica/*

Inoue, H., Miyazaki, A., Yamamoto, A., & Katsura, T. (1998). A digital watermark based on the wavelet transform and its robustness on image compression. *Proc. Int. Conf. Image Processing (ICIP).*

Johnson, N.F., Duric, Z., & Jajodia, S. (1999). Recovery of watermarks from distorted images. *Preliminary Proc. of the Third Int. Information Hiding Workshop*, 361–375.

Kankanhalli, M.S., Rajmohan, & Ramakrishnan, K.R. (1998). Content based watermarking of images. *Proc. of the Sixth ACM International Multimedia Conference.*

Katzenbeisser, S., & Petitcolas, F.A.P. (2000). *Information hiding techniques for steganography and digital watermarking.* Boston: Artech House.

Koch, E., & Zhao, J. (1995). Towards robust and hidden image copyright labeling. *Proc. Workshop Nonlinear Signal and Image Processing.*

Kundur, D., & Hatzinakos, D. (1998). Digital watermarking using multiresolution wavelet decomposition. *Proc. of the Int. Conference on Acoustics, Speech, and Signal Processing, 5*, 2969–2972.

Kutter, M. (1998). Watermarking resisting to translation, rotation and scaling. *Proc. of SPIE Int. Symposium on Voice, Video, and Data Communications—Multimedia Systems and Applications, 3528*, 423–431.

Langelaar, C., Lubbe, J.C.A., & Lagendijk, R.L. (1997). Robust labeling methods for copy protection of images. *Proc. Electronic Imaging, 3022*, 298–309.

Lee, T.-W. (1998). *Independent component analysis: Theory and applications.* Kluwer Academic.

Liu, H., Kong, X.-W., Kong, X.-D., & Liu, Y. (2001). Content based color image adaptive watermarking scheme. *Proc. of IEEE International Symposium on Circuits and Systems, 2*, 41–44.

Lu, C.-S., & Mark, Liao H.-Y. (2001). Multipurpose watermarking for image authentication and protection. *IEEE Transaction on Image Processing, 10.*

Mintzer, F., & Braudaway, G. (1999). If one watermark is good, are more better? *Proc. of the International Conference on Acoustics, Speech, and Signal Processing, 4.*

Nikolaidis, N., & Pitas, I. (1998). Robust image watermarking in the spatial domain. *Signal Processing, 66*, 385–403.

Parhi, K.K., & Nishitani, T. (1999). *Digital signal processing for multimedia systems.* New York: Marcel Dekker.

Peter, P. (2001). *Digital image watermarking in the wavelet transform domain.* Unpublished master's thesis.

Piva, A., Barni, M., Bartoloni, E., & Cappellini, V. (1997). DCT-based watermark recovering without resorting to the uncorrupted original image. *Proc. IEEE Int. Conf. Image Processing (ICIP), 1.*

Podilchuk, C., & Zeng, W. (1997). Watermarking of the JPEG bitstream. *Proc. Int. Conf. Imaging Science, Systems, and Applications (CISST'97),* 253–260.

Ruanaidh, J.J.K.Ó, & Pun, T. (1997). Rotation, scale and translation invariant digital watermarking. *Proc. IEEE Int. Conf. Image Processing (ICIP'97), 1,* 536–539.

Ruanaidh, J.J.K.Ó, & Pun, T. (1998). Rotation, scale and translation invariant digital watermarking. *Signal Processing, 66*(3), 303–318.

Ruanaidh, J.J.K.Ó, Dowling, W.J., & Boland, F.M. (1996). Phase watermarking of digital images. *Proc. Int. Conf. Image Processing (ICIP'96), 3,* 239–242.

Schneier, B. (1995). *Applied cryptography* (2nd ed.). John Wiley and Sons.

Sheppard, N.P., Safavi-Naini, R., & Ogunbona, P. (2001). On multiple watermarking. *Proc. of ACM Multimedia 2001.*

Trappe, W., Wu, M., Wang, J., & Liu, K.J.R. (2003). Anti-collusion fingerprinting for multimedia. *IEEE Trans. on Signal Processing, 51*(4), 1069–1087.

Voloshynovskiy, S., Herrigel, A., Baumgaertner, N., & Pun, T. (1999). A stochastic approach to content adaptive digital image watermarking. *Proc. of Int. Workshop on Information Hiding.*

Wang, H.-J.M., Su, P.-C., & Kuo, C.-C.J. (1998). Wavelet-based digital image watermarking. *Optics Express, 3*(12), 491–496.

Xia, X., Boncelet, C., & Arce, G. (1997). A multiresolution watermark for digital images. *Proc. Int. Conf. Image Processing (ICIP'97), 1,* 548–551.

Xie, L., & Arce, G.R. (1998). Joint wavelet compression and authentication watermarking. *Proc. Int. Conf. Image Processing (ICIP'98).*

Yu, D., & Sattar, F. (2003). A new blind image watermarking technique based on independent component analysis. *Springer-Verlag Lecture Notes in Computer Science, 2613,* 51–63.

Yu, D., Sattar, F., & Ma, K.-K. (2002). Watermark detection and extraction using independent component analysis method. *EURASIP Journal on Applied Signal Processing—Special Issue on Nonlinear Signal and Image Processing (Part II)*.

Chapter IV

A New Public-Key Algorithm for Watermarking of Digital Images

Eberhard Stickel
Hochschule der Sparkassen-Finanzgruppe,
University of Applied Sciences Bonn GmbH, Germany

Abstract

Conventional photographs may easily be used in court as evidence. The complete negative may be inspected. Subsequent numbers are a reliable proof that sequences of pictures have been generated. Modifications are usually quickly detected without major technical efforts. This is not true anymore for digital images, since they may easily be manipulated. This poses a problem, for example, for surveillance cameras of automatic teller machines in financial institutions. Digital watermarking techniques have been proposed to address this problem. In this chapter, a new public-key watermarking system will be presented. In contrast to digital signatures and other public-key watermarking techniques, it is two-dimensional and, hence, especially well-suited for applications involving digital images.

Introduction

Multimedia digital data play an increasingly important role in today's business. This is also true for the banking industry; in particular, surveillance cameras in teller machines, as well as archive systems rely on digital pictures or videos.

Conventional photographs may easily be used in court as evidence. The complete negative may be inspected. Subsequent numbers are a reliable proof that sequences of pictures have been generated. Modifications are usually quickly detected without major technical efforts.

The use of digital photographs and digital video sequences is not possible in the same manner. Courts did not trust such digital images since they can be manipulated more easily. The use of simple image-processing software allows even nonexpert users to modify images in every possible way. Also, in digital videos, there is no equivalent to sequential image numbers in analogous videos. Therefore, digital video sequences may have gaps or may consist of different parts pasted together in a suitable way.

According to internal documents of the German banking industry, in around 50% of all cases, digital images (without watermarks) could not be used as evidence in court. On the other hand, the use of hardware, producing digital images is much cheaper than conventional analogous technology. Digital watermarks were suggested as a solution to this problem. Such a watermark is included in the digital image and basically guarantees its authenticity. The digital image obtains the watermark as soon as it is read out of the archive or camera system. Within the system, manipulations of images are not possible. If modification is attempted on a watermarked digital image, the watermark is either destroyed or the watermark suitable for the post-image does not match the watermark that was originally constructed for the pre-image.

Various digital watermarks are discussed in the literature (Kutter & Hartung, 2000, p. 97). One approach relies on public-key methods widely used in cryptographic applications. In particular, conventional digital signatures are suggested. Digital images are stored in files. The content of such a file, or more commonly a suitable hash digest of the file content, may be signed using a digital signature algorithm. If the image is modified, another hash digest results. Consequently, the verification of the signature fails. The use of digital signatures has the drawback that which parts of a digital image have been corrupted cannot be checked. The same argument applies to Message Authentication Codes (MAC) (for details, see Cox, Miller, & Bloom, 2002, p. 365).

Other watermarking techniques add information to the pixels of a digital image. An example is the use of the least significant bit of an image to store watermarking information. Generally, modifications of the least significant bit cannot be realized when visually inspecting the image (Katzenbeisser, 2000, p. 26).

The security of such watermarks refers to its ability to resist intentional tampering. It should be detected if the watermarked image is modified or the watermark itself is removed or changed.

Since it would be quite easy to modify an image and then to add a suitable watermark, special crypto techniques to "secure" the process of watermarking need to be applied (Dugelay & Roche, 2000, p. 121). Therefore, it seems reasonable to compute the watermarking information from the digital image. Then, there is an encryption step that secures the watermark. Here, public-key techniques are especially useful. The private key of the encrypting device is used for this purpose. Finally, the watermark is embedded into the image.

In order to verify an image, the watermark is extracted. Then it is decrypted using the public key of the device above. Parallel to this, the watermark is recomputed from the image under investigation. If both watermarks are identical, the image is considered to be original. The process is illustrated in Figures 1 (watermarking) and 2 (verification).

Note that this process cannot be used to prove ownership of an image since this watermark can be easily destroyed. For digital rights issues, more complex techniques need to be applied. A summary of the problems involved may be found in Johnson, Duric, and Jajoda (2001) and Wayner (2002).

In the next section, the basics of the new methodology will be presented. The third section discusses the details of the implementation. The paper concludes

Figure 1. Process of watermarking

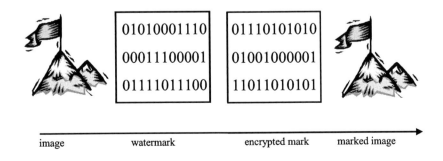

| image | watermark | encrypted mark | marked image |

Figure 2. Process of verification

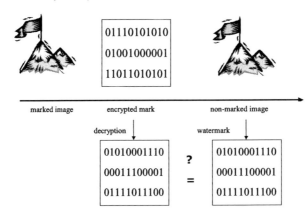

with an outlook indicating possible directions of improvement and future research.

Presentation of Methodolgy

Preliminaries

Public-key cryptography uses two keys: a private key known only to the owner and a public key which is usually published (Koblitz, 1994). To encrypt a message, the public key of the receiver is used. Decryption requires the private key, which is known to the receiver only. Private and public keys are inverse to each other in a certain sense. Public-key methods are based on so-called one-way functions with trapdoor: f is called a one-way function if it is easy to compute $f(x)$ from the argument x, but it is difficult to compute x, if only $f(x)$ is known, except when a so-called trapdoor—the private key—exists. It is not clear until now if such one-way functions exist. There are certain candidates, namely, factoring of integers and discrete logarithm problems. No algorithms with polynomial runtime are known for these problems today. They are considered computationally hard problems (Koblitz, 1994, p. 85).

Many popular public-key encryption systems are based on such number-theoretic problems such as factoring of integers or finding discrete logarithms (Discrete Logarithm Problem, DLP) (see Koblitz, 1994, for details). Factoring large numbers into prime factors generally is a hard problem in the sense that computing time increases exponentially with the size of the integer for all known algorithms. RSA, for example, is based on the problem to factor the product of two large primes (e.g., 512, 1024, 2048, or 4096 bit prime numbers [Koblitz, 1994, p. 92]). The discrete logarithm problem may be characterized as follows (Menezes, van Oorschot, & Vanstone, 1997, p. 103). Let $b = a^x$ mod n be given. The numbers b, a, and n are known, x is called the discrete logarithm of b to the basis a. All computations are done modulo n: b is divided by n, the rest thus obtained is called b mod n.

Logarithms generally are easy to compute. However, discrete logarithms modulo n, where n is a large prime or the product of two large primes, usually is a hard problem in the sense of the explanations above. Diffie-Hellman methods are an example of cryptographic primitives based on the discrete logarithm problem (DLP). For more details, see Koblitz (1994).

A problem related to factoring integers and computing discrete logarithms is the rapid development of better algorithms to solve the underlying computational problem, as well as technological progress in computing power. This requires permanent enlargement of the size of the keys used. RSA, for example, is no longer considered highly secure for a key length less than 1024 bit (512 bit primes) (Menezes et al., 1997, p. 287).

The underlying algebraic structures used in common public-key methods usually are abelian groups (cf. Rotman, 1994). There has been some research in using non-abelian groups for public-key encryption algorithms (cf. Lee & Park, 2003, p. 477). Most methods discussed require a great deal of implementation effort and are far from practical usability. Generally, non-abelian groups are much more complex than abelian groups. In the following section, a public-key method will be presented that generalizes the Diffie-Hellman approach to non-abelian groups. Techniques to compute discrete logarithms in abelian groups may not be applied in this setting. Moreover, the method presented is very easy to implement and is especially well suited for watermarking images, as discussed in the first section. The next section briefly sketches the classic Diffie-Hellman approach.

Diffie-Hellman Problem

The original method proposed by Diffie and Hellman (1976) was used to exchange secret keys over an insecure channel (e.g., the Internet).

Let p be a large prime or the power of a large prime. Let g be a number with $1<g<p$. g and p are publicly known. The Diffie-Hellman problem is as follows (cf. Menezes et al., 1997, p. 113)

- Given $g^a \bmod p$ and $g^b \bmod p$, compute $g^{ab} \bmod p$.

To exchange keys between users, Alice and Bob, the following protocol may be used

- Suppose Alice has published p, g and $g^a \bmod p$ as her public key. a is kept secret as private key.
- Bob chooses b which is kept secret, forms $g^b \bmod p$ and $(g^a)^b \bmod p$ and submits the latter number to Alice.
- Alice computes $(g^{ab})^{1/a} = g^b \bmod p$. This is the secret key exchanged.

In order to break this system, which means determining the exponent b, discrete logarithms mod p need to be computed. This is a computationally hard problem and may be considered unfeasible for large p.

More details and variants may be found in Menezes et al. (1997, p. 515). Variants are used to establish authentication and signature schemes. DSA or ElGamal signatures are examples of this.

The New Method

The new method may be implemented in general non-abelian groups. A particularly attractive implementation in matrix groups will be discussed below.

Let $p(x)$ and $q(x)$ be two different irreducible polynomials of degree n over the field $F_2 = \{0,1\}$ consisting of the zero and unit element only. Let C and D be the corresponding companion matrices. To be specific, if, for example

$$p(x) = x^n + \sum_{i=0}^{n-1} c_i x^i$$

is the polynomial, then

$$
C = \begin{pmatrix}
0 & 0 & \cdots & \cdots & c_0 \\
1 & 0 & 0 & \ddots & c_1 \\
0 & 1 & \ddots & \ddots & \vdots \\
\vdots & \ddots & \ddots & 0 & c_{n-2} \\
0 & 0 & \cdots & 1 & c_{n-1}
\end{pmatrix}
$$

is the corresponding $n \times n$ companion matrix. Irreducibility implies that neither 0 nor 1 is a zero of the polynomials p and q. Moreover, no other divisors of p and q with smaller degrees exist (see, for example, Lidl & Pilz, 1997, p. 115).

Assume further that n as well as 2^n-1 are prime numbers. Such numbers 2^n-1 are called Mersenne primes, n is called Mersenne exponent (see Menezes et al., 1997, p. 142). Examples are exponents $n = 3, 7, 13, 17, 19, 31, 61, 89, 107, 127, 521, 607, \ldots$ It is important that if $p \neq q$, then $CD \neq DC$. This can be proved easily. It can be shown that C and D have order 2^n-1. This means that C^k or D^k is the identity matrix, if and only if k is a multiple of 2^n-1 or 0. It is also possible to prove that the set $\{D^i C^j \,|\, i, j \text{ natural numbers}\}$ contains $(2^n-1)^2$ different elements. For n large enough this is a set of large cardinality that may not be searched by successively looking at elements.

Let T_1 and T_2 be matrices such that

$$
T_1 C T_1^{-1} = diag(\lambda_1, \cdots, \lambda_n), \quad T_2 D T_2^{-1} = diag(\mu_1, \cdots, \mu_n)
$$

are diagonal matrices. Note that the components of T_1 and T_2 will not be elements of $F_2 = \{0,1\}$ but of a suitable field extension $G = F_{2^n}$. The elements of G may be represented as polynomials of degree less than n. Arithmetic in G is done by adding, subtracting, multiplying, and dividing polynomials modulo, an irreducible polynomial of degree n. Details may be found in Lidl and Niederreiter (2000, p. 83). Define $E = T_1 T_2^{-1}$.

To illustrate the potential use of the new method, we briefly sketch the key exchange corresponding to the Diffie-Hellman exchange method presented in the previous section.

- Alice chooses a polynomial $q(\alpha)$ where α is a zero of the characteristic polynomial of C or D. Note that α is an element of the extension field G. q is kept secret.

- Suppose Alice has published $C, D, E,$ and $q(\alpha)C^aED^b$ as her public key. a and b as well as C^a and D^b are kept secret as private keys.

- Bob chooses c and $d,$ which are kept secret; he also chooses a secret polynomial $r(\beta)$ with β being a zero of the characteristic polynomial of C or D, forms $r(\beta)C^cED^d$, as well as $r(\beta)q(\alpha)C^{a+c}ED^{b+d}$ and submits the latter matrix to Alice.

- Alice computes $(q(\alpha))^{-1}C^{-a}(r(\beta)q(\alpha)C^{a+c}ED^{b+d})D^{-b} = r(\beta)C^cED^d$. This is the secret key exchanged.

This illustrates the generalization of the Diffie-Hellman approach to a non-abelian group. However, none of the methods used to compute discrete logarithms in abelian groups generalize to the non-abelian case studied here (see, for example, Menezes et al., 1997, p. 103). This adds additional security to the new method presented here.

 The method presented may be implemented efficiently and quickly since powers of companion matrices may be computed rather quickly (more details may be found in Fiduccia [1985]). The remaining matrix multiplications are composed of field operations in G, which may be performed efficiently (see Lidl & Niederreiter, 2000, p. 83). Fast algorithms for multiplication of matrices are discussed, for example, in Aho and Ullman (1974, p. 242).

For the use of the new method, the existence and effective computation of irreducible polynomials is crucial. To generate irreducible polynomials, a randomized algorithm is suggested by Menezes et al. (1997, p. 156). Polynomials of degree n are generated by a random algorithm and tested. Note that there are $2(2^{n-1}-1)/n$ different irreducible polynomials of degree n. Then, the probability of generating an irreducible polynomial by means of the randomized algorithm is roughly $1/n$. This is sufficiently efficient, since these polynomials are needed only once to determine the public key used.

Powers of matrices may be expressed as sums of matrices of powers of lower order by the well-known Cayley-Hamilton theorem. Due to the construction of the matrix E, this approach does not allow the determination of C^a and D^b. Also, insertion of E prohibits the use of eigenvalues and eigenvectors of C and D to compute these matrix powers. Note that without the use of E, the Cayley-Hamilton theorem and/or the computation of eigenvalues and eigenvectors would allow to determine C^a and D^b. However, this would still require substantial computational and programming effort if n is large enough.

To summarize, the new method generalizes the approach of Diffie and Hellman to non-abelian groups. It may be implemented efficiently even on chip cards and offers high levels of security, for example, for $n = 31$.

A Watermarking Technique Based on the New Method

For the sake of briefness we will restrict ourselves to the case of watermarks for graphic images.

Basic Setup

Popular watermarking techniques are based on manipulating the least significant bit of an image (Wayner, 2002, p. 153). Such watermarks are not robust and can usually be easily removed or destroyed. In the case of our application domain, however, this is not an important issue.

Consider, for example, a financial institution that wishes to provide digital evidence in court. It has absolutely no interest in destroying or changing a watermark. Here, a watermark serves as some sort of digital signature that would guarantee the authenticity of the image (or video).

However, it is important in our case that there is no doubt about the authenticity of the image considered. This is achieved by embedding an encrypted watermark whenever an image is removed from the archiving device, for example, when it is printed. The private key should not be known outside the device. The correctness of the public key should be guaranteed by a third-party trusted server (trust center).

Authenticity can be checked by anyone knowing the public key. Figure 3 illustrates this process.

Figure 3. Embedding and verification of watermark

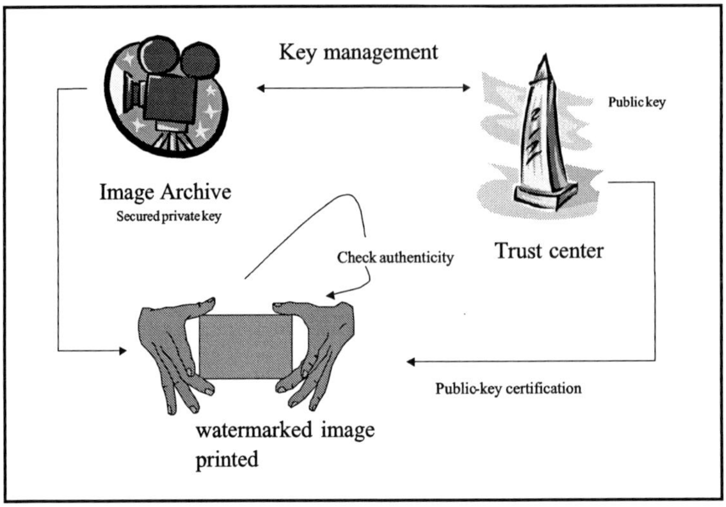

Technical Details

We now show how to apply the method initially presented earlier. Suppose that the archival device holds the private keys a, b, C^a, D^b, E and $q_1(\alpha)$, $q_2(\alpha)$ where a and b are natural numbers and C, D and E are $n \times n$ companion matrices with n being exponent of a Mersenne prime, e.g. $n = 31$. In that case there are $(2^{31}-1)^2$ different matrices $C^a E D^b$. q_1 and q_2 are polynomials as discussed in the last section. A trust center certifies the correctness of the public keys E, C, D and $P = q_1(\alpha)q_2(\alpha)C^a E D^b$.

The image is stored in the archival system in a file f. Let $H(f)$ be a hash value associated with this file by neglecting the least significant (or even some less significant bit). This can be done by setting them to 0. Here, H is a so-called Hash-function, that compresses the digital information in f to a bit string of length l. Refer to Menezes et al. (1997, p. 321) for details and potential hash-functions.

Suppose, e.g. that $l = 1922 = 2*31^2$. If l is smaller we may duplicate l a certain number of times and/or concatenate l with a certain number of zeros to get a length of 1922 bit. If l is larger we neglect the last bit. The first 961 components

Figure 4. Watermarking process

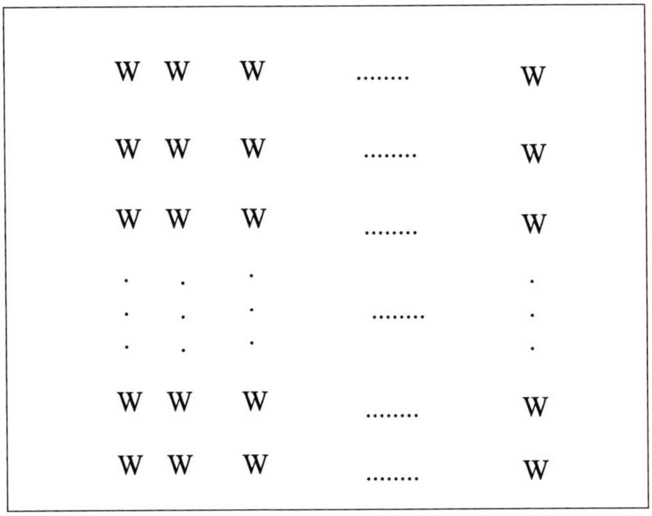

of l form components of a 31×31 matrix A, the last 961 components of l form components of a matrix B. A and B will now be interpreted as column vectors A^* and B^* of polynomials in G. Each row of A and B then represents coefficients of a polynomial and is regarded as a single component of a vector A^* or B^* in G.

If an output of the image is required, the archival device forms the matrix $W_1 = q_1(\alpha)q_2(\alpha)AC^aED^bB$. The device also forms $\alpha = q_1(\alpha)A^{*T}C^a$ and $\beta = q_2(\alpha)D^bB^*$. Finally the scalar product $\acute{a}\hat{a}$ is computed. Note that $\acute{a}$ is a row vector while β is a column vector of elements in G (thus representing two vectors of polynomials of degree less than 31). Then $\alpha\beta$ is an element of G. These results are combined into the matrix W as follows:

$$W = \begin{pmatrix} W_1 & \hat{a} \\ \acute{a} & \acute{a}\hat{a} \end{pmatrix}.$$

W_1 may be considered a 31×961 matrix of bit (31 rows and columns, each component is a polynomial of degree at most 30, giving $961 = 31^2$ columns in total). Hence, W is a 32×992 matrix. W may now be embedded into the least significant bit of the image by suitable tiling. Note that this may require a suitable number of repetitions depending on the number of pixels of the image (see Figure 4). Also, it may be necessary to suitably "cut" W at the borders.

Another possibility is to simply append the watermark at the end of the file. Since a pixel usually does not consist of a single bit but of a certain number of bits, even if resolution is small, the image size only moderately increases by this. This approach may be particularly useful if sophisticated compression techniques are used.

In order to prove the authenticity of an image, the watermark and its components are extracted. It may now be checked by computing the hash value of the image with removed watermark if some parts of the picture have been modified, for example, if W is not properly present everywhere or the hash value computed does not match A^* and B^*.

To check the correctness of W, the following steps will be executed:

(1) W_1, α and β are extracted from W. Also A^* and B^* are determined from the file without watermarking information.

(2)   Then, it is checked if $q_1(\alpha)q_2(\alpha)A^{*\mathrm{T}}\,C^a ED^b B^* = \acute{a}\hat{a}$ holds.

(3)   Next, two integers r and s and a polynomial r, as discussed in the last section, are chosen at random. The matrices $K = r(\beta)C^r PD^s$ and $L = r(\beta)C^r ED^s$ are formed. It is checked if $\alpha L\beta = A^{*\mathrm{T}}\,KB^*$.

(4)   In case all comparisons are true, the signature is accepted, otherwise the image is considered to be not authentic.

The third step ensures that the image has been signed by the archival device. Indeed, assume that a third party chooses two arbitrary matrices Q and R such that $QR = P$. Then a faked watermark, passing the test in step (2) may be implemented. The test in Step (3) assures that C^a and D^b are used in forming the watermark together with E and the polynomials q_1 and q_2. It can only be passed if a and b are guessed correctly modulo $(2^{30}-1)$ or modulo (2^n-1) in general. Higher security may be achieved by repeating Step (3) with new random integers r and s.

The trust center certifies the public key used. The signature scheme is a one-time signature scheme (cf. Menezes et al., 1997, p. 462). Hence, the public key should only be used for one verification procedure. The trust center may be used to distribute and administer different public keys for the archival device.

Conclusions

A new watermarking method for digital images has been presented. The method is especially useful in the context of surveillance of automated teller machines in financial institutions. Digital images of legal, as well as illegal, users are permanently taken. It should be possible to use these images in court as evidence, for example, in case of robbery or dispute.

Digital images may be manipulated rather easily. Hence, it is necessary to guarantee the authenticity of digital images. As soon as the image is retrieved from the archival device, an encrypted digital watermark assuring authenticity is added. The watermarking process is based on public-key cryptography in non-abelian groups. The public key is certified by a trusted third party (trust center). Authenticity may be verified by anyone who knows this certified public key.

The focus was on single digital images. The results, however, generalize to the case of digital videos. Digital videos merely are sequences of digital images. Therefore, a straightforward generalization would be to just apply the techniques presented on a single image basis. Other more efficient techniques may also be developed, of course. Digital videos are stored in files. Again, it is possible to compute hash values of such a file and to suitably embed a derived watermark in such a file. Details may depend on the compression technique used.

The method presented is a one-time digital signature scheme. This means that the public key may be used only once in watermarking an image. For this purpose, the trust center administers used and new public keys of the archival device. It is not clear if the method presented may be extended in such a way that the public key may be used more than once. This would reduce computational and administrative effort. Research in this direction continues.

The methods presented in this paper are protected under European patent EP 1 317 096 and German patent DE 101 59 690.

References

Aho, A.V., & Ullman, J.D. (1974). *The design and analysis of computer algorithms*. Reading, UK: Addison-Wesley.

Cox, I.J., Miller, M.L., & Bloom, J.A. (2002). *Digital watermarking.* Boston: Morgan Kaufmann.

Diffie, W., & Hellman, M.E. (1976). New directions in cryptography. *IEEE Transactions on Information Theory, 22,* 644–654.

Dugelay, J.-L., & Roche, S. (2000). A survey of current watermarking techniques. In S. Katzenbeisser & M. Petitcolas (Eds.), *Information hiding techniques for steganography and digital watermarking* (pp. 121–148). Boston: Artech House.

Fiduccia, C.M. (1985). An efficient formula for linear recurrences. *SIAM J. Computation, 14*(1), 106–112.

Johnson, N.F., Duric, Z., & Jajodia, S. (2001). *Information hiding, steganography and watermarking—Attacks and countermeasures.* Boston: Kluwer Academic.

Katzenbeisser, S.C. (2000). Principles of steganography. In S. Katzenbeisser & M. Petitcolas (Eds.), *Information hiding techniques for steganography and digital watermarking* (pp. 17–41). Boston: Artech House.

Koblitz, N. (1994). *A course in number theory and cryptography* (2nd ed.). New York: Springer.

Kutter, M., & Hartung, F. (2000). Introduction to watermarking techniques. In S. Katzenbeisser & M. Petitcolas (Eds.), *Information hiding techniques for steganography and digital watermarking* (pp. 97–120). Boston: Artech House.

Lee, E., & Park, J.H. (2003). Cryptanalysis of the public-key encryption based on braid groups. In E. Biham (Ed.), *Advances in cryptology— EUROCRYPT 2003. LNCS 2656* (pp. 477–490). New York: Springer.

Lidl, R., & Niederreiter, H. (1997). *Finite fields* (reprint 2nd ed.). Cambridge, UK: Cambridge University Press.

Lidl, R., & Pilz, G. (1997). *Applied abstract Algebra* (2nd ed.). New York: Springer.

Menezes, A.J., van Oorschot, P.C., & Vanstone, S.A. (1997). *Handbook of applied cryptography.* New York: CRC Press.

Rotman, J.J. (1994). *An introduction to the theory of groups* (4th ed.). New York: Springer.

Wayner, P. (2002). *Disappearing cryptography information hiding: Steganography and watermarking* (2nd ed.). Boston: Morgan Kaufmann.

Chapter V

Geometric Distortions Correction Using Image Moment in Image Watermarking

Zhang Li
Shenzen University, China

Sam Kwong
City University of Hong Kong, SAR China

Abstract

This chapter presents a method for detecting and recovering geometrical attacks in digital watermarking by making use of geometric moments of the original images. Digital image watermarking has become a popular technique for authentication and copyright protection. However, many proposed image watermarking techniques are sensitive to geometric distortions, such as rotation, scaling, and translation. In this chapter, we propose a new way of making this estimation by using the geometric moments of original image. The moment information can be used as a private key of extraction process. This method can be used as a preprocess of the extraction watermarking process. We have embedded different watermarks into original images in different domains including discrete wavelet transform (DWT), discrete cosine transfrom (DCT), fast Fourier transform, and spatial domain. The experimental results show that our method has a good robustness to wide geometric distortion parameters ranges and it is robust to Stirmark attacks.

Introduction

We are living in a digital world in that extensive information exchange can be performed quickly and easily in digital format over the Internet or different storing devices in a cost-effective way. Digital data, such as music, image, video, text, e-mail, and so forth, are easily copied and transferred without any degradation. Concerns over ownership protection, data protection, and other security issues have therefore arisen. Digital watermarking is a general solution that can be used to identify illegal copying and ownership, authentication, or other applications by inserting information into the digital data in an imperceptible way. However, the realization of valid copyright protection and information security has become an important problem (Dugelay & Petitcolas, 2000). Digital watermarking technique is an effective means to resolving these problems by embedding additional information (i.e., watermark information) into digital protected media. In order for a watermark to be useful, it must be perceptually invisible and have robustness against image processing and a variety of possible attacks by those who seek to pirate the material (Voloshynovskiy, Pereira, Herrigel, Baumgartner, & Pun, 2000; Voloshynovskiy, Pereira, Pun, Eggers, & Su, 2001). There has been much emphasis on the robustness of watermarking against common signal processing operations. However, recently it has become clear that even very small geometric distortions can prevent the detection of a watermark in many watermarking techniques. This problem is most pronounced for blind detection, that is, the original image is not available to the detector. Moreover, in many of these applications, attackers may attempt to defeat the watermark as a security feature by intentionally changing the scale and rotation of the media. Therefore, a robust watermarking system must be capable of re-synchronizing itself against scaling and rotation (Alattar & Meyer, 2003).

There are three advantages to using watermarking (Yiu, 2002). First, the watermark is embedded into the work in an imperceptible way, so that the information embedded is hidden and the effect on the appearance and function of the work is minimized or invisible. Second, the watermark is embedded within the data content and undergoes the same operations as the data experiences. It is supposed to survive even after encryption and decryption, digital-to-analog conversion, change of file format, compression, cropping, or resizing. Last, we deduce any changes made by checking the watermark since it is embedded in such a way as to locate the modified parts and even restore the original. Depending on different purposes, we can choose different watermark algorithms so that it can be used for broadcast data protection, copyright control, content authentication, identification, and proof of ownership. We can also apply broadcast monitoring, copy control, and convert communication. As a result, we can see that digital watermarking plays an important role in multimedia application and e-commerce.

During the last decade, digital technologies have grown dramatically. Digital audio, video, and software are widely used within home computers and open networks. Nevertheless, one particular drawback of digital content is its ability to be volatile and easily processed. Digital objects may be easily copied, manipulated, or converted without any control. The goal of watermarking is to embed unnoticeable information (called a mark) in the media content. Thus, the functionality of the medium is improved without altering the format.

One of the main obstacles in image watermarking systems is geometric manipulations of watermarked images. It is well known that a small amount of rotation and/or scaling can dramatically disable the receiver from detecting the watermark. Yet, how to design watermarking techniques with robustness against geometric transformations is still an unsolved issue. It is because geometric distortions will destroy the synchronization of the watermarking embedding and detection process. The detection of the watermark requires a synchronization step to locate the embedded watermark in the content. In audio, the watermark is commonly detected in real time. In practice, the position of the beginning of the sequence is not known and cannot be used as a reference. Consequently, the detector must preprocess the audio to know where the watermark is located. The case of digital watermarking for still images is similar because they can undergo geometrical transformations after analog-to-digital and digital-to-analog conversion such as printing and scanning the image. Resizing and rotating are also basic manipulations in image edition and require a synchronization step for detection of the watermark. In this paper, we assume that the detector is not informed of any parameters about geometric distortions. There are some watermarking techniques for embedding watermarks into digital images, including discrete cosine transform (DCT) (Hsu & Wu, 1999), discrete wavelet transform (DWT) (Inoue, Miyazaki, Yamamoto, & Katsura, 1998), discrete Fourier transform (DFT) (Lin, Wu, Bloom, Miller, Cox, & Lui, 2000, 2001), and spatial domain (Tirkel, Osborne, & Hall, 1998). They all perform well against compression, but lack robustness against geometric distortions. Some methods have been proposed in the Fourier domain (O'Ruanaidh & Pun, 1997; Pereira & Pun, 2000), which have proven to be robust against geometric distortions, but for DWT and DCT, such robustness is hard to achieve. Alghoniemy (Alghoniemy & Tewfik, 2000) presented a solution to estimate scaling factor and rotation angle based on computing-edges standard deviation ratio and average edges angle difference assuming that the detector has prior information regarding wavelet maxima of original images. Kutter (1998) proposed an approach in which the watermark itself is embedded several times at different horizontally and vertically shifted locations and it is used to estimate geometric distortions parameters. Alghoniemy further proposed another digital image watermarking technique based on its invariant moments (Alghoniemy & Tewfik, 2000). In Alattar and Meyer (2003), a log-polar mapping of the synchronization template is computed to convert the scaling factor and the rotation angle of the template into vertical and horizontal shifts. These shifts are then detected using a phase-only-matched (POM) filter, which concentrates the weak energy from all peaks into a single peak that is much easier to detect. The scaling factor and orientation angle are determined from the location of this peak. Simulation results of the method have shown that the method is very effective and produces accurate results. In Bas, Chassery, and Macq (2002), the authors proposed a watermarking technique to detect a geometrical transform that does not require the original image. In addition, they used a content-based technique to resynchronize both the local and global geometrical transformation. In Zhang, Kwong, and Wei (2002), we have presented the preliminary results on the use of geometric moments to detect and recover the geometric transformations of original images and we further to extend such a concept in this chapter.

An affine transformation is an important class of linear two-dimensional geometric transformations, which maps variables (e.g., pixel intensity values located at position (x_1, y_1) in an input image) into new variables (e.g., x_2, y_2) in an output image) by applying a linear combination of rotation, scaling, and translation. Before proceeding, it is important to define what we mean by geometric distortions of rotation, scaling, and flipping. The scaling operator performs a geometric transformation, which can be used to shrink or zoom the size of an image (or part of an image). Scaling is used to change the visual appearance of an image, to alter the quality of information stored in a scene representation, or as a low-level preprocessor in the multistage image processing chain, which operates on feature of a particular scale. The rotation operator performs a geometric transform, which maps the position (x_1, y_1) of a picture element in an input image onto a position (x_2, y_2) in an output image by rotating it through a user-specified angle θ about an original. Rotation is the most commonly used method to improve the visual appearance of an image, although it can be useful as a preprocessor in applications where directional operations are involved. The flipping operator performs a geometric transformation, which maps the position (x_1, y_1) of an input image to the position of $(-x_1, y_1)$ of an output image if the image was flipped in x direction. The translation operator performs a geometric transformation that maps the position (x_1, y_1) of an input image to the position of $(x_1 + a, y_1 + b)$ of an output image with the parameter of a and b in x and y directions, respectively. Scaling, rotation, translation, and flipping are considered as special cases of affine transformation and it will be discussed in later sections in detail. In fact, the use of affine transform has been proved to be very successful in the area of pattern recognition. We propose to apply this technique to detect the geometric transformation of an image.

The main contribution of this chapter lies in the development of a method to estimate geometric distortion parameters such as translation factor, the rotation angle, and scaling factor of a corrupted watermarked image using one or two geometric moments of the original image. We can then rotate the corrupted watermarked image back to its original orientation and/or rescale it back to its original size before the detection process, that is, we can recover the synchronization of watermarking embedding and detection processes. During the estimation process, only one or two geometric moments of an original image are used, which can be utilized as a private key to the watermarking. In the experiments, we estimate geometric distortion parameters using geometric moments of the original image with embedding different watermarks in DWT, DCT, FFT, and spatial domain to prove the robustness of our method. In order to test the robustness of the method we proposed in this chapter, we modify the Stirmark program with large ranges of rotation angle and scaling factor. The experiment results show a high precision is achieved even to large geometric distortion parameters ranges and it is very robust to Stirmark.

Background

Geometric attacks are very common techniques applied to images in that they do not actually remove the embedded watermark itself but distort the synchronization of the watermark detector. An affine transformation is a geometric transformation, which is equivalent to the composite effects of translation, rotation, scaling, and so on. In image watermarking, it is common to combine several different affine transformations to produce a resultant transformation. The transformation sequences applied to images are important since a translation followed by a rotation is not necessarily equivalent to the converse. Affine transformation can be written as follows:

$$\begin{vmatrix} x_2 \\ y_2 \end{vmatrix} = A \times \begin{vmatrix} x_1 \\ y_1 \end{vmatrix} + B \tag{1}$$

where (x_1, y_1) is the pixel of an input image, (x_2, y_2) is the pixel of the output image.

Here, we describe some properties that hold for an affine transformation.

Property 1: An affine transformation of the plane is defined uniquely by three pairs of points. That is, if a, b, and c are noncollinear points, and a', b', and c' are the corresponding points, then there exists a unique affine transformation mapping each of the three points to its corresponding point.

According to this property, given three pairs of corresponding points, we can compute the affine transformation parameters related by solving linear equations.

Property 2: Ratios of triangle areas are preserved. That is, given two sets of noncollinear points, $\{a, b, c\}$ and $\{d, e, f\}$ (not necessarily distinct from a, b, and c), if T is an affine transformation, then

$$\frac{\Delta_{abc}}{\Delta_{def}} = \frac{\Delta_{T(a)T(b)T(c)}}{\Delta_{T(d)T(e)T(f)}}$$

where Δ_x is the area of triangle.

These properties are important for our method to estimate the parameters of affine transformations. We will describe the affine transformation and its combined transformations such as flipping followed with rotation, rotation followed with flipping, flipping followed with scaling, and scaling followed with flipping in detail in the following section.

Scaling

The scale operator performs a geometric transformation, which can be used to shrink or zoom the size of an image (or part of an image). Image reduction, commonly known as *subsampling,* is performed by replacement (of a group of pixel values by one arbitrarily chosen pixel value from within this group) or by interpolating between pixel values in a local neighborhood. Image zooming is achieved by pixel *replication* or by interpolation. Scaling is used to change the visual appearance of an image, to alter the quantity of information stored in a scene representation, or as a low-level preprocessor in multistage image processing chain, which operates on features of a particular scale. Scaling is a special case of affine transformation.

Scaling compresses or expands an image along the coordinate directions. As different techniques can be used to subsample and zoom, each is discussed in turn. Scaling can be divided into two categories: one is symmetric scaling, which means that the scaling factor in the x direction is same as in the y direction; the other is nonsymmetric scaling, sometimes called shearing, which means that the scaling factors are different in two directions. Symmetric scaling can be considered as a special case of asymmetric scaling.

Figure 1 illustrates the two methods of subsampling. In the first method, one pixel value within a local neighborhood is chosen (perhaps randomly) to be representative of its surroundings. (This method is computationally simple but can lead to poor results if the sampling neighborhoods are too large.) The second method interpolates between pixel values within a neighborhood by taking a statistical sample (such as the mean) of the local intensity values.

An image (or regions of an image) can be zoomed either through pixel replication or interpolation. Figure 2 shows how pixel replication simply replaces each original image pixel by a group of pixels with the same value (where the group size is determined by the scaling factor). Alternatively, interpolation of the values of neighboring pixels in the original image can be performed in order to replace each pixel with an expanded group of pixels.

Figure 1. Methods of subsampling

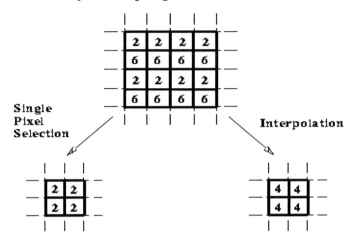

(a) Replacement with upper-left pixel   *(b) Interpolation using the mean value*

Figure 2. Methods of zooming

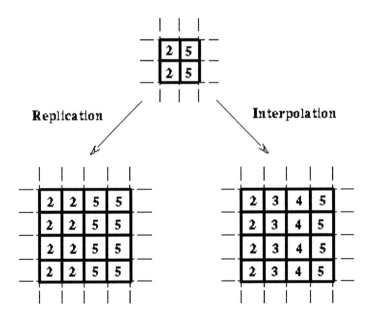

(a) Replication of a single pixel value   *(b) Interpolation*

Most implementations offer the option of increasing the actual dimensions of the original image, or retaining them and simply zooming a portion of the image within the old image boundaries.

Rotation

The rotation operator performs a geometric transform which maps the position (x_1, y_1) of a picture element in an input image onto a position (x_2, y_2) in the corresponding output image by rotating it through a user-specified angle θ about an original. Rotation is a special case of affine transformation. We assume that the watermarked image was rotated by the center normalized as $(0,0)$, which is showed in Figure 3.

We can obtain the following from Figure 3:

$$\begin{cases} x' = r\cos(\theta + \alpha) = r(\cos\theta\dfrac{x}{r} - \sin\theta\dfrac{y}{r}) = x\cos\theta - y\sin\theta \\ y' = r\sin(\theta + \alpha) = r(\sin\theta\dfrac{x}{r} + \cos\theta\dfrac{y}{r}) = x\sin\theta + y\cos\theta \end{cases} \quad (2)$$

The rotation operation produces output locations (x', y'), which do not fit within the boundaries of the image (as defined by the dimensions of the original input image). In such cases, destination elements, which have been mapped outside the image, are ignored by most implementations. Pixel locations out of which an image has been rotated are usually filled in with black pixels. The rotation algorithm, unlike that employed by translation, can produce coordi-

Figure 3. Sketch map of pixel rotation

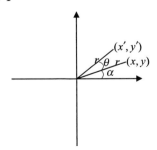

nates (x', y') which are not integers. In order to generate the intensity of the pixels at each integer position, different heuristics (or *resampling* techniques) may be employed. For example, two common methods include the following: (1) To allow the intensity level at each integer pixel position to assume the value of the nearest noninteger neighbor (x', y') and (2) To calculate the intensity level at each integer pixel position based on a weighted average of the n nearest noninteger values. The weighting is proportional to the distance or pixel overlap of the nearby projections. The second method produces better results but increases the computation time of the algorithm.

Translation

The translate operator performs a geometric transformation which maps the position of each picture element in an input image into a new position in an output image, where the dimensionality of the two images often is, but need not necessarily be, the same. Under the translation, an image element located at (x_1, y_1) in the original is shifted to a new position in the corresponding output image by displacing it through a user-specified translation (β_x, β_y). The treatment of elements near image edges varies with implementation. Translation is used to improve visualization of an image, but also has a role as a preprocessor in applications where registration of two or more images is required. Translation is a special case of affine transformation.

The translation operator performs a transformation of the form:

$$x_2 = x_1 + \beta_x \tag{3}$$

$$y_2 = y_1 + \beta_y \tag{4}$$

Since the dimensions of the input image are well defined, the output image is also a discrete space of finite dimension. If the new coordinates (x_2, y_2) are outside the image, the translate operator will normally ignore them, although, in some implementations, it may link the higher coordinate points with the lower ones so as to wrap the result around back onto the visible space of the image. Most implementations fill the image areas out of which an image has been shifted with black pixels.

Flipping, Flipping with Rotation, and Rotation with Flipping

The flipping operator maps the position (x_1, y_1) of an input image to the position of $(-x_1, y_1)$ of an output image if the image was flipped in x direction. For flipping followed with rotation, suppose (x_1, y_1) is the pixel of the original image, and (x', y') is the pixel of image flipped the original image in the x direction and (x_2, y_2) is the pixel of image rotated the flipped image with θ degree anticlockwise. Then we can obtain the following equations

$$\begin{cases} x' = -x_1 \\ y' = y_1 \end{cases} \tag{5}$$

$$\begin{cases} x_2 = x'\cos\theta - y'\sin\theta = -x_1\cos\theta - y_1\sin\theta \\ y_2 = x'\sin\theta + y'\cos\theta = -x_1\sin\theta + y_1\cos\theta \end{cases} \tag{6}$$

In this case, we can get that $A = \begin{vmatrix} -\cos\theta & -\sin\theta \\ -\sin\theta & \cos\theta \end{vmatrix}, B = \begin{vmatrix} 0 \\ 0 \end{vmatrix}$. For rotation followed with flipping, the result of rotating the flipped image with θ degree anticlockwise is same as flipping the rotated image with θ degree clockwise. We define the angle rotated anticlockwise as positive. So we can obtain that

$$\begin{cases} x' = x_1\cos(-\theta) - y_1\sin(-\theta) = x_1\cos\theta + y_1\sin\theta \\ y' = x_1\sin(-\theta) + y_1\cos(-\theta) = -x_1\sin\theta + y_1\cos\theta \end{cases} \tag{7}$$

$$\begin{cases} x_2 = -x' = -x_1\cos\theta - y_1\sin\theta \\ y_2 = y' = -x_1\sin\theta + y_1\cos\theta \end{cases} \tag{8}$$

We can see that the above two cases have the same results.

Flipping Followed with Scaling and Scaling Followed with Flipping

For flipping followed with scaling, suppose that (x_1, y_1) is the pixel of original image, (x', y') is the pixel of image flipped the original image in the x direction, and (x_2, y_2) is the pixel of image scaled the flipped image with a in x direction and b in y direction. So we can obtain the following equations

$$\begin{cases} x_2 = x'/a = -x_1/a \\ y_2 = y'/b = y_1/b \end{cases} \tag{9}$$

For this case, it is known that $A = \begin{vmatrix} -1/a & 0 \\ 0 & 1/b \end{vmatrix}$, $B = \begin{vmatrix} 0 \\ 0 \end{vmatrix}$. And for scaling followed with flipping, then the position of the pixel can be recomputed as follows

$$\begin{cases} x_2 = -x' = -x_1/a \\ y_2 = y' = y_1/b \end{cases} \tag{10}$$

We can see from above that even if the flipping and scaling were applied to the image with different sequences, the resultant effects are the same as shown in Equation (9).

Rotation Followed with Scaling and Scaling Followed with Rotation

For rotation followed with scaling, suppose that (x_1, y_1) is the pixel of an input image, (x', y') is the pixel of image rotated with θ degree anticlockwise, and (x_2, y_2) is the pixel of image scaled the rotated image with a in x direction and b in y direction. Their relationship can be shown as follows

$$\begin{cases} x' = x_1 \cos\theta - y_1 \sin\theta \\ y' = x_1 \sin\theta + y_1 \cos\theta \end{cases} \tag{11}$$

$$\begin{cases} x_2 = \dfrac{x'}{a} = \dfrac{x_1}{a}\cos\theta - \dfrac{y_1}{a}\sin\theta \\ y_2 = \dfrac{y'}{b} = \dfrac{x_1}{b}\sin\theta + \dfrac{y_1}{b}\cos\theta \end{cases} \tag{12}$$

For scaling followed with rotation, we can deduce that

$$\begin{cases} x_2 = x'\cos\theta - y'\sin\theta = \dfrac{x_1}{a}\cos\theta - \dfrac{y_1}{b}\sin\theta \\ y_2 = x'\sin\theta + y'\cos\theta = \dfrac{x_1}{a}\sin\theta + \dfrac{y_1}{b}\cos\theta \end{cases} \tag{13}$$

We can see for symmetric scaling, the above two cases have the same result and $A = \begin{vmatrix} \cos\theta/a & -\sin\theta/a \\ \sin\theta/a & \cos\theta/a \end{vmatrix}$, $B = \begin{vmatrix} 0 \\ 0 \end{vmatrix}$. However, it is different for asymmetric scaling.

Scaling Followed with Translation

Suppose (x_1, y_1), (x_2, y_2) are the pixel of original image, translated m and n in x and y direction, respectively, of watermarked image. Suppose scaling followed by translation is applied to the watermarked image, from the previous section, we can obtain that

$$\begin{cases} x_2 = x_1/a + m \\ y_2 = y_1/b + n \end{cases} \tag{14}$$

Suppose translation followed by scaling is applied to the watermarked image, we can obtain the following

$$\begin{cases} x_2 = (x_1 + m)/a \\ y_2 = (y_1 + m)/b \end{cases} \tag{15}$$

Summary on Existing Watermarking Resynchronization Solutions

Resynchronization is the essential topic for watermarking systems not to be sensitive to geometric distortions. There are several existing resynchronization solutions and we summarize them in this way. One solution is to exploit the theory of geometric invariants. This is to insert a watermark intrinsically to resist this sort of manipulations and to avoid the need of the synchronization pattern. After an image has undergone a geometric transformation, because spikes positions can assume only integer values, some uncertainties in determining if a point belongs or not to a line must be introduced, and this will result in an increasing number of false constellations. The second solution is in some way to resemble to the first solution and it is to embed the watermark with image normalization. Image normalization provides a convenient way to deal with geometric attack, the key idea is to geometrically transform the image into a standard form. The parameters of the normalized image are computed from the geometric moments of the image. The advantage of using geometric moments for normalization parameters computations is to let it to be more image dependent, which in turn makes the decoder able to estimate them without the need of the original image. The watermark is then embedded and detected in a transformed image. The disadvantage of image normalization is that before watermark embedding, the original image will be normalized, and after the watermark embedding, the inverted image normalization must be done to get the watermarked image. These transform will introduce the distortion and the computation is large. The third solution—the most used strategy for watermark detection after geometric distortions—is to try to identify what the distortions are and then invert them before applying the detector, for example, by introducing a template. Doing so requires the insertion and the detection of two watermarks, one of which is with no informative meaning. This approach requires in general exhaustive in a significant computational burden to estimating distortion parameters and applying the inverse attack to correct the geometric distortions.

In this chapter, we also present a way to estimate the geometric distortion parameters, but we use the moment to estimate them. And the experimental results show that this method requires small computation but high precision.

Methodology and Solutions

In this section, we will describe how to estimate the scaling factor and rotation angle of a previously scaled and/or rotated watermarked image in detail. In Bas et al. (2002), the authors claim that basically two levels of geometrical distortions can be found. They are the typical geometrical transformation commonly used in image edition and the one especially designed to desynchronized the mark without visual changes. Khun and Petitcolas (Petitcolas, Anderson, & Kuhn, 1998) developed the benchmark software called Stirmark. As we have mentioned in previous section, the objective of this work is to apply the affine transform technique to detect the geometrical transformation of the watermarked images. The proposed algorithm will try to test both categories of attacks, and the experimental results will be reported in the later section.

The Estimation of Single Affine Transformation Parameter

Scaling Factor Estimation

Suppose $f(\frac{x}{a}, \frac{y}{b})$ is the scaled watermarked image of the original image, $f(x,y)$, that is, scaling factor in the x direction is a and in the y direction is b. Define geometric moments, m_{pq}, of the original image, $f(x,y)$, as (Mukundan, Ong, & Lee, 2001)

$$m_{pq} = \iint x^p y^q f(x, y)\, dx\, dy \qquad (16)$$

where $p+q$ is the order of geometric moments. So geometric moments of scaled watermarked image can be defined as

$$m'_{pq} = \iint x^p y^q f(\frac{x}{a},\frac{y}{b})dxdy \tag{17}$$

Since the invariant moments results of Hu (1961) are also right here, we can deduce that

$$a(m'_{02} - \frac{m'^2_{01}}{m'_{00}}) = b(m'_{20} - \frac{m'^2_{10}}{m'_{00}}) \tag{18}$$

Since $m'_{10} = a^2 b m_{10}$, so the scaling factor a and b can be expressed as

$$a = \sqrt[3]{m'_{10}(m'_{20} - \frac{m'^2_{10}}{m'_{00}}) \Big/ ((m'_{02} - \frac{m'^2_{01}}{m'_{00}})m_{10})} \tag{19}$$

$$b = \sqrt[3]{m'_{10}(m'_{02} - \frac{m'^2_{01}}{m'_{00}})^2 \Big/ ((m'_{20} - \frac{m'^2_{10}}{m'_{00}})^2 m_{10})} \tag{20}$$

Where m'_{10}, m'_{01}, m'_{20}, and m'_{02} are the geometric moments of the scaled image. m_{10} is the geometric moment of the original image.

There has another way to estimate the scaling factor of the corrupted watermarked image. If we set the original image with size lx and ly, that is, lx is the length in x direction and ly is the length in y direction and the scaled watermarked image with size lx' and ly'. Suppose $r_0 = ly/lx$. We can deduce that $a/b = (lx'/lx)/(ly'/ly) = (lx'/ly')r_0$. The scaling factor can be estimated as

$$a = \sqrt[3]{m'_{10} lx' r_0 / (m_{10} ly')} \tag{21}$$

$$b = \sqrt[3]{m'_{10} ly'^2 / m_{10} lx'^2 r_0^2} \tag{22}$$

If we know r_0, we can estimate the scaling factor more easily from Equation (20) and (21), especially for the case where the original image has been normalized before watermark embedding.

Rotation Angle Estimation

We define $f(x', y')$ as rotated watermarked image rotated by θ degree, that is, the pixel (x', y') is obtained by rotating the pixel (x, y) by θ degree. Geometric moments of rotated watermarked image can be defined as

$$m'_{pq} = \iint x'^p \, y'^q \, f(x'y') dx' dy' = \iint (x\cos\theta - y\sin\theta)^p (x\sin\theta + y\cos\theta)^q \, f(x, y) dx dy \tag{23}$$

So we can obtain

$$m'_{10} = \iint (x\cos\theta - y\sin\theta) f(x, y) dx dy = m_{10} \cos\theta - m_{01} \sin\theta \tag{24}$$

$$m'_{01} = \iint (x\sin\theta + y\sin\theta) f(x, y) dx dy = m_{10} \sin\theta + m_{01} \cos\theta \tag{25}$$

$$m'_{10} \cos\theta + m'_{01} \sin\theta = m_{10} \tag{26}$$

Only m_{10} of the original image is used when we estimate the rotation angle θ. θ can be computed by numerical analysis. Supposed $\Delta = |m'_{10} \cos\theta + m'_{01} \sin\theta - m_{10}|$. Once θ is satisfied $\Delta < \varepsilon$, we will get the estimated result. Where ε is a positive value that is small enough and we set $\varepsilon = 10^{-5}$ in our experiments.

Translation Factor Estimation

Since the discrete wavelet transform coefficients of images are sensitive to the image position, it is important to have a robust watermarking algorithm against the translation distortion of digital image in DWT domain. Suppose that m_{10} and m_{01} are the geometric moments of original image and the translation parameters are p and q in the direction of x and y, respectively. So we can deduce that the geometric moments of translated watermarked image m'_{10} and m'_{01} are as follows:

$$m'_{10} = \iint x' f(x' y') dx' dy' = \iint (x + p) f(x, y) dx dy = m_{10} + p m_{00} \qquad (27)$$

$$m'_{01} = \iint y' f(x' y') dx' dy' = \iint (y + q) f(x, y) dx dy = m_{01} + q m_{00} \qquad (28)$$

Only the m_{10} and m_{01} of the original image are used for estimating the translation parameters in this case.

Flipping Estimation

Flipping is also a common operation often performed on watermarked images. It should be noted that the sign of m_{10} would always change with flipping in the x direction unless the image is symmetric around the y-axis, which is rare in real-world images. Supposed m'_{10} is the geometric moment of the corrupted watermarked image. If $m'_{10} \, m_{10} < 0$, we can judge that the image was flipped in the x direction.

The Estimation of Combined Affine Transformations Parameters

Flipping Followed with Scaling and Scaling Followed with Flipping

From previous section, we know that if $m_{10} \cdot m'_{10} < 0$, we can deduce that the image was flipped in the x direction. If the watermarked image has been flipped, the scaling factor is estimated after flipping back the watermarked image.

Flipping Followed with Rotation and Rotation Followed with Flipping

The rotation angle is estimated, as described above, after flipping back the watermarked image, if the watermarked image has been flipped.

Scaling Followed with Rotation

Suppose m_{10}, m_{01} and m'_{10}, m'_{01} and m''_{10}, m''_{01} are geometric moments of original image, corrupted watermarked image, and the scaled watermarked image, respectively. The corrupted watermarked image is obtained by scaling the watermarked image with a in x direction and b in the y direction, and then rotated the scaled image by θ degree anticlockwise. From previous sections, we can deduce that:

$$
\begin{cases}
m''_{10} = a^2 b m_{10} \\
m''_{01} = ab^2 m_{01} \\
m'_{10} = m''_{10} \cos\theta - m''_{01} \sin\theta \\
m'_{01} = m''_{10} \sin\theta + m''_{01} \cos\theta
\end{cases}
\tag{29}
$$

For asymmetric scaling, we can estimate the scaling factor and rotation angle as

$$\begin{cases} a = \sqrt{m_{00}'(m_{20}'m_{00}' - m_{10}'^2)/(m_{00}(m_{02}'m_{00}' - m_{01}'^2))} \\ b = \sqrt{m_{00}'(m_{02}'m_{00}' - m_{01}'^2)/(m_{00}(m_{20}'m_{00}' - m_{10}'^2))} \\ m_{10}' \cos\theta + m_{01}' \sin\theta - a^2 b m_{10} = 0 \end{cases} \tag{30}$$

For symmetric scaling, we can estimate the scaling factor and rotation angle as

$$\begin{cases} a = \sqrt{m_{00}'/m_{00}} \\ m_{10}' \cos\theta + m_{01}' \sin\theta - a^3 m_{10} = 0 \end{cases} \tag{31}$$

If r_0 of the original image is known, the scaling factor and rotation angle can be estimated as

$$\begin{cases} a = \sqrt{m_{00}' lx' r_0/(m_{00} ly')} \\ b = \sqrt{m_{00}' ly'/(m_{00} lx' r_0)} \\ m_{10}' \cos\theta + m_{01}' \sin\theta - a^2 b m_{10} = 0 \end{cases} \tag{32}$$

Rotation Followed with Scaling

Suppose (x, y), (x'', y''), and (x', y') are the pixel of original image, rotated by θ angle anticlockwise and the corrupted watermarked image, respectively, that is, the corrupted watermarked image is obtained by rotating the watermarked image by θ degree anticlockwise and then scaling it with a in the x direction and b in the y direction. From previous sections, we obtain

$$\begin{cases} x'' = x\cos\theta - y\sin\theta \\ y'' = x\sin\theta + y\cos\theta \\ x' = x''/a = (x\cos\theta - y\sin\theta)/a \\ y' = y''/b = (x\sin\theta + y\cos\theta)/b \end{cases} \qquad (33)$$

We can deduce that asymmetric scaling

$$\begin{cases} a = \sqrt{m'_{00}(m'_{20}m'_{00} - m'^2_{10})/(m_{00}(m'_{02}m'_{00} - m'^2_{01}))} \\ b = \sqrt{m'_{00}(m'_{02}m'_{00} - m'^2_{01})/(m_{00}(m'_{20}m'_{00} - m'^2_{10}))} \\ \dfrac{m'_{10}\cos\theta}{a^2 b} + \dfrac{m'_{01}\sin\theta}{ab^2} - m_{10} = 0 \end{cases} \qquad (34)$$

If we know r_0 of the original image, then we can obtain the following

$$\begin{cases} a = \sqrt{r_0 m'_{00} lx'/(ly' m_{00})} \\ b = \sqrt{m'_{00} ly'/(r_0 lx' m_{00})} \\ \dfrac{m'_{10}\cos\theta}{a^2 b} + \dfrac{m'_{01}\sin\theta}{ab^2} - m_{10} = 0 \end{cases} \qquad (35)$$

In these equations, m'_{10}, m'_{01} and m'_{00} are geometric moments of the corrupted watermarked image and m_{10}, m_{00} are geometric moments of the original image, which should be known to watermark detector before the detection process.

Image Enhancement

Image enhancement is another common manipulation of the image and there are many ways to enhance images. We assume that the contrast adjust will be used to enhance the image. Suppose the gray scope of original image, $f(x,y)$, is $[m,n]$ and the gray scope of enhanced image, $g(x,y)$, is $[M,N]$. In this case, M and N are known and we need to estimate m and n. m_{10} is not enough for estimating m and n, and we need the moment m_{00} of the original image. $g(x,y)$ can be expressed as follows

$$g(x,y) = \frac{N-M}{n-m}[f(x,y)-m]+M \qquad (36)$$

The moment m'_{10}, and m'_{00} of the enhanced image are

$$m'_{10} = \iint xg(x,y)dxdy = \frac{N-M}{n-m}m_{10} - \frac{Nm-Mn}{n-m}\iint xdxdy \qquad (37)$$

$$m'_{00} = \iint g(x,y)dxdy = \frac{N-M}{n-m}m_{00} - \frac{Nm-Mn}{n-m}\iint dxdy \qquad (38)$$

Then we can estimate the gray scope of the original image, m and n, which are only needed for two moments m_{00} and m_{10} of the original image

$$m = \frac{m'_{10}m_{10} - m_{10}m'_{00} + M(m_{10}\iint dxdy - m_{00}\iint xdxdy)}{m'_{10}\iint dxdy - m'_{00}\iint xdxdy} \qquad (39)$$

$$n = \frac{m'_{10}m_{10} - m_{10}m'_{00} + N(m_{10}\iint dxdy - m_{00}\iint xdxdy)}{m'_{10}\iint dxdy - m'_{00}\iint xdxdy} \qquad (40)$$

Experimental Results

In our experiments, we embed different watermarks, such as Gaussian noise, watermark predefined, and watermark adaptive to the original image into the original image in different domains including DWT, DCT, FFT, and spatial domain. We use many images as original images, such as Cameraman and Lena. In order to test the robustness of our estimation method, we embed watermarks large enough so that the embedded watermarks even degrade the image slightly. From the results, we can see that the estimation results are good enough, and during the estimation, we only use the geometric moments of the original image. Figure 4 shows Cameraman as the original image and Figure 5

Figure 4. Original image

Figure 5(a.) Watermarked image with Gaussian noise

Figure 5(b). Watermarked image adaptive to original

Figure 5(c). Watermarked image with image predefined

Figure 6(a). Watermark predefined

Figure 6(b). Watermark adaptive to original image

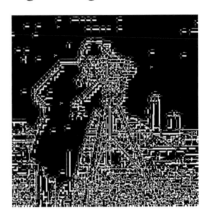

shows the watermarked images. Figure 6 shows watermarks including predefined image and the watermark adaptive to the original image. For the experiments, we used Stirmark to produce the affine transformation. In order to do more experiments, we modified the Stirmark program with larger ranges of scaling factor and rotation angle.

Results with Rotation Angle and Scale Factor Estimation

In order to compare to the results in Alghoniemy and Tewfik (2000), we use a cameraman image and a woman image to conduct the experiment and modify the rotation angles in the Stirmark program. The estimation results are listed in Table 1 with unit as degree. From the results, we can see that the rotation angle can be estimated with high precision even when the image is rotated with a large angle, such as 90 degrees or 180 degrees.

We use the cameraman image and Lena image to conduct the scaling factor estimation experiment and list the results in Table 2. We can see that our results are more efficient and the results change a little when the original image is changed. In the Stirmark benchmark, asymmetric scaling is also called aspect ration. From the results, we can see that the estimation results of scaling factor has a high precision.

Table 1.The experimental estimation results of rotation angle

The angle rotated factual (degree)	The estimated rotation angle with cameraman image (degree)	The estimated rotation angle with woman image (degree)	Results in (Alghoniemy & Tewfik, 2000) with cameraman image (degree)
3	3.000000000000682	3.000000000000372	Not reported
-3	-2.999999999986649	-3.000000000000838	Not reported
1	1.000000000000227	0.9999999999991640	Not reported
-1	-0.9999999999866477	-0.9999999999866477	-0.89
2	2.000000000000455	2.000000000000455	2.03
-2	-1.999999999986649	-1.999999999986649	-1.88
-0.5	-0.4999999999866478	-0.4999999999866478	-0.5068
-5	-5.000000000005951	-5.000000000005957	Not reported
5	4.999999999994047	4.999999999994051	Not reported
10	9.999999999994030	9.999999999994033	Not reported
15	14.99999999999401	14.99999999999403	Not reported
30	29.99999999999421	29.99999999999404	Not reported
45	44.99999999999441	44.99999999999402	Not reported
60	59.99999999999463	59.99999999999400	Not reported
90	89.99999999999832	90.00000000002046	Not reported
-90	-89.999999999858	-89.99999999998582	Not reported
-180	-179.99999999998	-179.9999999999807	Not reported

Table 2. Estimation results of scaling factor

	Scaling factor factual	Estimated scaling factor with cameraman	Estimated scaling factor with lena image	Results in (Alghoniemy & Tewfik, 2000) cameraman image
x direction	0.5	0.4996814661076497	0.4995280019526282	0.4715
y direction	0.5	0.4996814661076497	0.4995280019526282	0.4715
x direction	0.75	0.7500721392748826	0.7499987575603178	0.7445
y direction	0.75	0.7500721392748826	0.7499987575603178	0.7445
x direction	1.5	1.499047586910396	1.499460803117492	1.4831
y direction	1.5	1.499047586910396	1.499460803117492	1.4831
x direction	2.0	1.998086394443178	1.998926176430578	1.9482
y direction	2.0	1.998086394443178	1.998926176430578	1.9482
x direction	0.5	0.5001594335910921	0.5000007035944079	
y direction	0.75	0.7502391503866381	0.7500010553916119	Nil
x direction	1.5	1.499021494542371	1.499496930793576	
y direction	1.75	1.748858410299433	1.749413085925839	Nil
x direction	0.75	0.7493579365106440	0.7492803326037296	
y direction	0.5	0.4995719576737627	0.4995202217358197	Nil
x direction	1.75	1.748612060672134	1.749150670809605	
y direction	1.5	1.498810337718972	1.499272003551090	Nil
x direction	1.25	1.249495549938881	1.249777854073007	
y direction	1.5	1.499394659926657	1.499733424887608	Nil

Results for Estimating Flipping and Scaling Affine Transformations

We performed experiments by Stirmark with scaling and aspect ratio. Different watermarks embedded in different domains to test the method we proposed. For the experiments, we extended the parameters of scaling factor in the Stirmark program. Table 3 gives the estimation results of scaling attacked by Stirmark in DWT, DCT, FFT, and spatial domain.

Figure 7 shows the estimation results of flipping and symmetric scaling factors with watermarks embedded in DWT domain, which compared to the results in Alghoniemy and Tewfik (2000), where '△' are the results in Alghoniemy and Tewfik (2000) only with the geometric distortion of symmetric scaling and '*' are the results of our proposed method with geometric distortions of flipping and symmetric scaling. The data on the x-axis are the real scaling factor and the data on the y-axis are the estimated scaling factor. We can easily estimate flipping distortion in our method. From the figure comparison, we can see that our results perform better.

Table 3. Estimation results of scaling by Stirmark

Factual scaling factor	DWT domain estimation results	DCT domain estimation results	Comparison with (Mousand Alghoniemy & Ahmed H. Tewfik, 2000)
0.5	0.498289	0.498321	0.4715
0.75	0.749874	0.749808	0.7445
1.5	1.499924	1.499845	1.4831
2.0	1.999831	1.999861	1.9482
1.75	1.749519	1.749516	Not reported
2.5	2.499053	2.499034	Not reported
4.0	3.998064	3.998100	Not reported

Factual scaling factor	DFT domain estimation results	FFT domain estimation results
0.5	0.498746	0.498734
0.75	0.749364	0.749099
1.5	1.501256	1.501326
2.0	2.002506	2.002505
1.75	1.749906	1.748858
2.5	2.499112	2.498905
4.0	3.997864	3.998453

Figure 7. Results of estimating of scaling factor and comparison

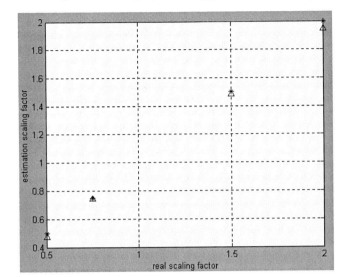

We can also estimate the flipping and asymmetric scaling factors, that is, aspect ratio, in DWT, DCT, FFT, and spatial domain by Stirmark and the results are shown in Table 4, where *Flipping* = 1 means flipping occurred and *Flipping* = 0 means no flipping occurred.

Experimental Results for Translation Affine Transformations

We estimated the translation parameters of different watermarks embedded in different images, and the results are shown in Table 5.

Experimental Results for Flipping and Rotation Affine Transformations

For rotation experiments, different watermarks were embedded in different domains to test the method we proposed. For the experiments, we extended the parameters of rotation angle range in the Stirmark program. Table 6 shows the estimation results of rotation by Stirmark.

Table 4. Results of estimation flipping and aspect ratio

Flipping	Factual Factor in x	Factual factor in y	DWT domain		DCT domain	
			Estimated x	Estimated y	Estimated x	Estimated y
1	0.5	0.75	0.4988	0.7482	0.4991	0.7487
0	0.5	0.75	0.5002	0.7502	0.4990	0.7485
1	1.5	1.75	1.4999	1.7499	1.4999	1.7497
0	1.5	1.75	1.4990	1.7489	1.4996	1.7496
1	1.25	1.5	1.24999	1.49999	1.2499	1.4998
0	1.25	1.5	1.2495	1.4994	1.2498	1.4997

Flipping	Factual Factor x	Factual factor y	FFT domain		Spatial domain	
			Estimated x	Estimated y	Estimated x	Estimated y
1	0.5	0.75	0.4991	0.7486	0.4991	0.7485
0	0.5	0.75	0.4990	0.7486	0.4990	0.7486
1	1.5	1.75	1.4997	1.7496	1.4997	1.7495
0	1.5	1.75	1.4996	1.7495	1.4996	1.7498
1	1.25	1.5	1.2498	1.4998	1.2498	1.4999
0	1.25	1.5	1.2498	1.4997	1.2497	1.4997

Table 5. Results of estimation translation

X factor	Y factor	Cameraman x factor	Cameraman y factor	Woman x factor	Woman y factor
1.0	1.0	0.99999999999991	1.00000000000067	1.0000000000003	1.0000000000002
1.0	2.0	1.00000000000067	1.9999999999998	1.0000000000002	2.0000000000001
2.0	2.0	1.9999999999998	1.99999999999999	2.0000000000005	2.0000000000001
3.0	3.0	2.9999999999996	2.9999999999991	3.0000000000005	3.0000000000004
3.0	30.0	2.9999999999996	29.999999999994	3.0000000000005	30.000000000003
5.0	5.0	4.9999999999995	4.9999999999993	5.0000000000002	5.0000000000008
10.0	5.0	9.9999999999996	4.9999999999993	10.000000000002	5.0000000000008
10.0	20.0	9.9999999999996	19.999999999997	10.000000000001	20.000000000002

Figure 8 shows the estimation results of flipping and rotation with watermarks embedded in the DWT domain and compares the results to those of Alghoniemy and Tewfik (2000), where '*' are the results of our method with geometric distortions of flipping and rotation and 'Δ' are the results in Alghoniemy and Tewfik (2000) only with the geometric distortion of rotation. The data on the x-axis are the real rotation angle and the data on the y-axis are the estimated rotation angle. It is clear that our estimation results are closer to the real rotation angle.

Table 6. Estimation results of rotation angle by Stirmark

Original angle	Estimation results	Original angle	Geometric moment estimation
1	0.9999999999940481	2	1.999999999994049
-1	-1.000000000005952	-2	-2.000000000005953
3	2.999999999994050	5	4.999999999994047
-3	-3.000000000005954	-5	-5.000000000005951
6	5.999999999994044	7	6.999999999994040
8	7.999999999994037	9	8.999999999994033
10	9.999999999994030	11	10.99999999999403
-10	-10.00000000000593	12	11.99999999999402
13	12.99999999999402	14	13.99999999999402
15	14.99999999999401	-15	-15.00000000000592
16	15.99999999999401	17	16.99999999999402
18	17.99999999999404	30	29.99999999999421
60	59.99999999999463	90	89.99999999999321
-90	-90.00000000000512		

Figure 8. Results of estimation rotation angle

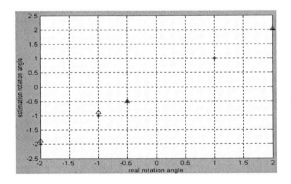

Experimental Results for Rotation and Scaling Affine Transformations

No matter what order of geometric distortions of rotation and scaling was done to the watermarked images, we used the same estimation method as mentioned above. Table 7 shows the estimation results of rotation and scaling in DWT, DCT, FFT, and spatial domain. We also performed the experiments of

Table 7. Estimation results of rotation and scaling in different domains

Real angle	x real scale	y real scale	DWT domain			DCT domain		
			Estimated angle	Estimat-ed x	Estimat-ed y	Estimation angle	Estimat-ed x	Estimat-ed y
2	0.5	0.5	2.0000000000004	0.49874	0.49874	1.999999999994	0.49873	0.49873
2	0.75	0.75	2.0000000000004	0.74940	0.74940	1.999999999994	0.74910	0.74910
2	1.5	1.5	2.0000000000004	1.50126	1.50126	1.999999999994	1.50132	1.50132
2	2.0	2.0	2.0000000000004	2.00251	2.00251	1.999999999994	2.00250	2.00250
2	1.25	1.5	2.0000000000004	1.25083	1.50099	1.999999999994	1.25088	1.50101
-1	0.5	0.5	-0.99999999998	0.49874	0.49875	-1.000000000005	0.49873	0.49873
-1	0.75	0.75	-0.99999999998	0.74940	0.74940	-1.000000000005	0.74909	0.74909
-1	1.5	1.5	-0.99999999998	1.50126	1.50126	-1.000000000005	1.50133	1.50133
-1	2.0	2.0	-0.99999999998	2.00251	2.00251	-1.000000000005	2.00250	2.00250
-1	1.25	1.5	-0.99999999998	1.25084	1.50101	-1.000000000005	1.25088	1.50106

Real angle	x real scale	y real scale	FFT domain			Spatial domain		
			Estimated angle	Estimat-ed x	Estimat-ed y	Estimation angle	Estimat-ed x	Estimat-ed y
2	0.5	0.5	1.999999999999	0.49875	0.49875	1.999999999994	0.49876	0.49876
2	0.75	0.75	1.999999999999	0.74941	0.74941	1.999999999994	0.74907	0.74907
2	1.5	1.5	1.999999999999	1.50125	1.50125	1.999999999994	1.50215	1.50215
2	2.0	2.0	1.999999999999	2.00256	2.00256	1.999999999994	2.00251	2.00251
2	1.25	1.5	1.999999999999	1.25081	1.50100	1.999999999994	1.25083	1.50099
-1	0.5	0.5	-0.999999999999	0.49876	0.49876	-1.000000000009	0.49879	0.49879
-1	0.75	0.75	-0.999999999999	0.74939	0.74939	-1.000000000009	0.74925	0.74925
-1	1.5	1.5	-0.999999999999	1.50120	1.50120	-1.000000000009	1.50125	1.50125
-1	2.0	2.0	-0.999999999999	2.00253	2.00253	-1.000000000009	2.00259	2.00259
-1	1.25	1.5	-0.999999999999	1.25083	1.50107	-1.000000000009	1.25084	1.50100

geometric distortions as rotation followed by asymmetric scaling and asymmetric scaling followed by rotation by Stirmark. For our experiments, we found that even with different watermarks embedded in different domains, the results are nearly the same and the estimation results have a high precision.

From the experimental results, we can see that even when several affine transformations are combined in the watermarked image, estimation results of the proposed method perform well.

Figure 9. Image enhancement. (a) Enhanced with [0.2,0.9] (b) Enhanced with [0.4,0.8]

(a)   (b)

Table 8. Results on image enhancement

	Gray scope of enhanced image	Estimated gray scope of the image	Gray scope of the original image	Correlation between original image and the restored image
Min	0.2	0.02745098039191914	0.02745098039215686	
Max	0.9	0.9921568627454210	0.9921568627450981	1
Min	0.4	0.02745098039434069	0.02745098039215686	
Max	0.8	0.9921568627418390	0.9921568627450981	1
Min	0.3	0.02745098039295670	0.02745098039215686	
Max	0.7	0.9921568627438852	0.9921568627450981	1
Min	0.5	0.02745098040473985	0.02745098039215686	
Max	0.6	0.9921568627263803	0.9921568627450981	0.9999999999999992

Experiment Results on Image Enhancement

We used the cameraman image to perform image enhancement experiment, and the results are listed in Table 8. The effect after the image enhancement is shown in Figure 9. The results show that the estimated gray scope is very near the gray scope of the original image and the correlation between the restored image and the original image is close to one.

Conclusions and Future Work

In this chapter, we presented a novel approach to estimate the scaling factor and rotation angle for a previously geometrically distorted watermarked image using geometric moments of the original image, which can be used as a private key in the watermark extraction process. It is useful in watermarking and data-hiding applications since by scaling and/or rotating the image, the hidden information will be out of synchronization. This may cause the decoder to be unable to detect the watermark correctly. If we can estimate the scaling factor and rotation with high precision, we can restore the corrupted watermarked image back to its original size and original orientation, that is, we can recover the synchronization and detect the watermark. This method can be imple-mented without any prior information regarding the original image. In our approach, we described how to estimate the geometric distortion parameters of geometric distortions when several affine transformations are combined with the watermarked image by the Stirmark benchmark. We performed experi-ments to embed different watermarks into the original image in different domains including DWT, DCT, FFT, and spatial domain. Experimental results of our proposed estimation method show that it has a good robustness even to large s geometric distortion ranges and it is very robust to Stirmark attacks. There are still many issues that need to be further investigated in this work. Currently, we still need one or two moments for detecting the geometrical transformation of the images. Although this information can be stored in the database of some types of cryptographic systems, it would be ideal if the information could be embedded in the image and retrieved later on. This can be done by using the algorithm proposed by Huang and Shi (2002). One of the drawbacks of their work is that the algorithm works only in the DCT domain.

Acknowledgments

This work is supported by City University strategic grant number 7001488.

References

Alattar, A.M., & Meyer, J. (2003). Watermark re-synchronization using log-polar mapping of image autocorrelation. Paper presented at the *Proceed-ings of the 2003 International Symposium of Circuits and Systems*, Bangkok, Thailand.

Alghoniemy, M., & Tewfik, A.H. (n.d.). Geometric distortions correction in image watermarking. Paper presented at the *SPIE on Security and Watermarking of Multimedia Content II*, San Jose, CA.

Alghoniemy, M., & Tewfik, A.H. (2000b). Image watermarking by moment invariants. Paper presented at the *Proceedings of the 2000 International Conference on Image Processing*.

Bas, P., Chassery, J.-M., & Macq, B. (2002). Geometrically invariant watermarking using feature points. *IEEE Transactions on Image Processing, 11*(9), 1014–1028.

Dugelay, J.L., & Petitcolas, F. (2000). Possible counter attacks against random geometric distortions. Paper presented at the *Proceedings of SPIE, Security and Watermarking of Multimedia Contents II*, San Jose, CA.

Hsu, C.-T., & Wu, J.-L. (1999). Hidden digital watermarks in images. *IEEE Transactions on Image Processing, 8*(1), 58–68.

Hu, M.-K. (1961). Pattern recognition by moment invariants. Paper presented at the *Proceedings of IRE*.

Huang, J., & Shi, Y.Q. (2002). Reliable information bit hiding. *IEEE Transactions on Circuits and Systems for Video Technology, 12*(10), 916–920.

Inoue, H., Miyazaki, A., Yamamoto, A., & Katsura, T. (1998). A digital watermark based on the wavelet transform and its robustness on image compression. Paper presented at the *ICIP 98*.

Kutter, M. (1998). Watermarking resisting to translation, rotation, and scaling. Paper presented at the *Proceedings of SPIE: Multimedia Systems and Applications*, Boston, MA.

Lin, C.-Y., Wu, M., Bloom, J.A., Miller, M.L., Cox, I., & Lui, Y.M. (2000). Rotation, scale and translation resilient public watermarking for images. Paper presented at the *ISPIE Security and Watermarking of Multimedia Contents II*, San Jose, CA.

Lin, C.-Y., Wu, M., Bloom, J.A., Miller, M.L., Cox, I., & Lui, Y.M. (2001). Rotation, scale, and translation resilient public watermarking for images. *IEEE Transactions on Image Processing, 10*(5), 767–782.

Mukundan, R., Ong, S.H., & Lee, P.A. (2001). Image analysis by Tchebichef moments. *IEEE Transactions on Image Processing, 10*(9), 1357–1364.

O'Ruanaidh, J. J. K., & Pun, T. (1997). Rotation, scale and translation invariant digital image watermarking. Paper presented at the *International Conference on Image Processing*.

O'Ruanaidh, J.J.K., & Pun, T. (1998). Rotation, scale and translation invariant spread spectrum digital image watermarking. *Signal Processing, 66*(3), 303–317.

Pereira, S., & Pun, T. (2000). Robust template matching for affine resistant image watermarks. *IEEE Transactions on Image Processing, 9*(6), 1123–1129.

Petitcolas, F.A.P., Anderson, R.J., & Kuhn, M.G. (1998). Attacks on copyright marking systems. Paper presented at the Second *Workshop on Information Hiding*.

Tirkel, A.Z., Osborne, C.F., & Hall, T.E. (1998). Image and watermark registration. *Signal Process, 66,* 373–383.

Voloshynovskiy, S., Pereira, S., Herrigel, A., Baumgartner, N., & Pun, T. (2000). Generalized watermarking attack based on watermark estimation and perceptual remodulation. Paper presented at the *Proceedings of SPIE 3971, Security and Watermarking of Multimedia Content II*, San Jose, CA.

Voloshynovskiy, S., Pereira, S., Pun, T., Eggers, J.J., & Su, J. K. (2001). Attacks on digital watermarks: classification, estimation based attacks, and benchmarks. *IEEE Communications Magazine, 39*(8), 118–126.

Yiu, C.N. (2002). *Watermarking for image authentication and protection.* Unpublished MSc Thesis, City University of Hong Kong, Hong Kong.

Zhang, L., Kwong, S., & Wei, G., (2003, May). Geometric moment in image watermarking. *Proceedings of the 2003 International Symposium of Circuits and Systems,* Bangkok, Thailand.

Chapter VI

Audio Watermarking:
Requirements, Algorithms, and Benchmarking

Nedeljko Cvejic
University of Oulu, Finland

Tapio Seppänen
University of Oulu, Finland

Abstract

This chapter provides an overview of digital audio watermarking systems, including a description of recently developed watermarking algorithms and insights into effective attack strategies against audio watermarking methods. Audio watermarking algorithms are characterized by a number of defining properties, ranging from robustness requirements to computational complexity and cost of implementation. This chapter provides a comprehensive list of signal modifications that are usually used by adversaries in order to distort the embedded watermark and prevent detection of the hidden data. At the end, application areas that have recently been developed and possible future applications areas are listed.

Introduction

The focus of this chapter is the watermarking of digital audio (i.e., audio watermarking), including a description of developed watermarking algorithms and insights into effective strategies against attacks on audio watermarking. Even though the number of published papers on watermarking and information hiding increased sharply since 1992, algorithms were primarily developed for digital images and video sequences (Bender, Gruhl, Morimoto, & Lu, 1996; Cox & Miller, 2001); interest and research in audio watermarking started slightly later (Hartung & Kutter, 1999; Swanson, Zhu, & Tewfik, 1999). In the past few years, several algorithms for embedding and extraction of watermarks in audio sequences have been presented. It is clear that audio watermarking initially started as a subdiscipline of digital signal processing, focusing mainly on convenient signal processing techniques to embed additional information to audio sequences. This included the investigation of a suitable transform domain for watermark embedding and schemes for imperceptible modification of the host audio. Only recently has watermarking been based on a stronger theoretical foundation, becoming a more mature discipline with a proper basis in both communication modeling and information theory.

Watermarking algorithms can be characterized by a number of defining properties (Cox, Miller, & Bloom, 2001). In Section 2, six requirements are highlighted that are important for audio watermarking algorithms (Arnold, Wolthusen, & Schmucker, 2003). For example, the amount of data that can be embedded transparently into an audio sequence is considerably lower than the amount that can be hidden in images, as audio signal has a dimension less than two-dimensional image files.

All of the developed algorithms take advantage of the perceptual properties of the human auditory system (HAS) in order to add a watermark into a host signal in a perceptually transparent manner. Embedding additional information into audio sequences is a more tedious task than in the case of images, due to the dynamic supremacy of the HAS over the human visual system (Bender et al., 1996). In Section 3, psychoacoustic models of the HAS that are exploited in order to preserve the subjective quality of the watermarked audio during the watermarking process will be reviewed.

A literature survey of audio watermarking algorithms that form the mainstream research is presented in Section 4. The algorithms are categorized by the statistical method used for detection and extraction of watermark bits, with references to specific algorithms using different signal domains for watermark embedding.

When the perceptual transparency requirement has been fulfilled, the design objective is to increase robustness and achieve a practical watermark bit rate. Section 5 gives a general framework of the audio watermark systems' performance in the presence of attacks. Many attacks that are malicious against image watermarking algorithms (e.g., geometrical distortions, spatial scaling, etc.) cannot be implemented against audio watermarking schemes, while some of the signal modifications are specific for audio watermarking. Section 6 presents application areas for the audio watermarking algorithms, while Section 7 gives an overview of the chapter.

Requirements for Audio Watermarking Algorithms

Watermarking algorithms can be characterized by a number of defining properties (Cox et al., 2001). In this section, six of them that are important for audio watermarking algorithms will be highlighted. The relative importance of a particular property is application dependent, and in many cases, even the interpretation of a watermark property varies with the application.

Perceptual Transparency

In most of the applications, the watermark embedding algorithm has to insert additional data without affecting the perceptual quality of the audio host signal (Zwicker & Fastl, 1999). Fidelity of the watermarking algorithm is usually defined as perceptual similarity between the original and the watermarked audio sequence. However, the quality of the watermarked audio is usually degraded, either intentionally by an adversary or unintentionally in the transmission process before a person perceives it. In that case, it is more adequate to define the fidelity of a watermarking algorithm as perceptual similarity between watermarked audio and host audio at the point at which they are presented to a consumer (Cox et al., 2001).

In perceptual audio coding, the quality of codecs is often evaluated by comparing an original signal, called reference, with its coded version. This general principle is applied to the quality evaluation of the watermarking systems as well. Instead of evaluating the coded version (as is the case in codec quality assessment), the watermarked version is analyzed. There are three objective measurement methods usually utilized for quality evaluation of the watermarked audio tracks. Those quality measurement systems are perceptual audio quality measure (PAQM) (Beerends & Stemerdink, 1992), perceptual evaluation of audio quality (PEAQ) (ITU-R, 1998), and selected parameters of the noise-to-mask ratio (NMR) (Brandenburg & Sporer, 1992) measurement system.

1. PAQM derives an estimate of the signals on the cochlea and compares the representation of the reference signal with that of the signal being tested. The weighted difference of these representations is mapped to the five-grade impairment scale as used in the testing of speech and audio coders. Table 1 shows this subjective grades (SG) scale (Sporer, 1996).

2. The PEAQ system has been developed in order to obtain a perceptual measurement scheme that estimates the results of real-world listening tests as faithfully as possible. In listening tests for very high quality signals, the test subjects sometimes confuse the coded signal and the original one and grade the original signal below an SG of 5.0. Therefore, the difference between the grades for the original signal and the signal under test is used as a normalized output value for the result of the listening test. Table 2 lists the corresponding subjective diff-grades (SDG), which are the output values of the PEAQ system.

3. Overall NMR_{total} value expressed in dB indicates the averaged energy ratio of the difference signal with respect to a signal that is just masked (masking threshold). Usually, at NMR_{total} values below -10 dB, there is no audible difference between the processed and the original signal.

Table 1. Subjective grades (SG) scale

SG	Description
5.0	Imperceptible
4.0	Perceptible, but not annoying
3.0	Slightly annoying
2.0	Annoying
1.0	Very annoying

Table 2. Subjective diff-grades (SDG)

SDG	Description
0.0	Imperceptible
-1.0	Perceptible, but not annoying
-2.0	Slightly annoying
-3.0	Annoying
-4.0	Very annoying

In addition to objective measurements, listening tests are usually performed as well. A number of audio sequences that represent a broad range of music genres are used as test signals; the usual duration of test clips is 10–20s. In the first part of the test, participants listen to the original and the watermarked audio sequences and are asked to report dissimilarities between the two signals, using a five-point impairment scale: (5 = imperceptible; 4 = perceptible, but not annoying; 3 = slightly annoying; 2 = annoying; 1 = very annoying). Results of the test should show the lowest and the highest value from the impairment scale and average MOS for the given audio excerpt. In the second part, test participants are randomly presented with unwatermarked and watermarked audio clips and asked to determine which one the watermarked one is. Values near 50% show that the two audio clips (original audio sequence and watermarked audio signal) cannot be discriminated.

Watermark Bit Rate

One of the most important properties of an audio watermarking system is watermark bit rate, usually determined by specific demands of the application that the system is designed for. The bit rate of the embedded watermark is the number of embedded bits within a unit of time and is usually given in bits per second (bps).

In some applications, for example, hiding speech in audio or compressed audio stream in audio, algorithms have to be able to embed watermarks with a bit rate that is a significant fraction of the host audio bit rate, up to 150 kbps. It is a well-known fact in the audio compression community that only a few bits per sample are needed to represent music with a quality near compact disc-quality music (Johnston, 1988). This implies that, for uncompressed music, a significant level of noise can be injected into the signal without it being perceptible to the end user. Contrary to compression methods where this fact is utilized to decrease the file size of the audio clip, it is used in information hiding to maximize the bit rate of the inserted watermark inside the perceptual requirements of the HAS. High-capacity hiding algorithms are usually not robust to signal processing modifications of the watermarked audio. However, Chou, Ramchandran, and Ortega (2001) describe a system with a watermark bit rate of 100 kbps, which does not cause distortion of the host audio sequence and is able to perfectly extract the hidden bits at a signal-to-noise ratio of 15 dB.

Some audio watermarking applications, such as copy control, require insertion of a serial number or author ID, with average bit rate of up to 0.5 bps (Cox et al., 2001). On the other hand, such applications demand a very high level of robustness and usually have to survive all the modifications listed in Section 5. For broadcast monitoring, the watermark bit rate is higher, caused by the necessity of embedding an ID signature of a commercial within the first second at the start of the broadcast clip, with the average bit rate up to 15 bps (Cox et al., 2001).

Robustness

Robustness of the algorithm is defined as the ability of the watermark detector to extract the embedded watermark after common signal processing manipulations. A detailed overview of robustness tests is given in Section 5. Applications usually require robustness in the presence of a predefined set of signal processing modifications, so that the watermark can be reliably extracted at the detection side. For example, in radio broadcast monitoring, the embedded watermark needs only to survive distortions caused by the transmission process, including dynamic compression and low-pass filtering, as watermark detection is done directly from the broadcast signal. On the other hand, in some algorithms robustness is completely undesirable and those algorithms are labeled as fragile audio watermarking algorithms.

The ultimate goal of any watermarking system is reliable watermark extraction. In general, extraction reliability for a specific watermarking scheme relies on features of the original data, on the embedding distortion, and on the attack distortion. Watermark extraction reliability is usually analyzed for different levels of attack distortion and fixed data features as well as embedding distortion. Different reliability measures are used for watermark decoding and watermark detection.

In the performance evaluation of watermark decoding, digital watermarking is considered as a communication problem. A watermark message is embedded into the host signal and must be reliably decodable from the received signal. The decoding reliability is usually described by word error probability (WER) or bit-error probability (BER).

Watermark detection is defined as the decision of whether the received data is watermarked (hypothesis H_1) or unwatermarked (hypothesis H_0). In general, both hypotheses cannot be separated perfectly. Thus, we define the probability p_{fp} (false positive) as the case of accepting H_1 when H_0 is true and the probability p_{fn} of accepting H_0 when H_1 is true (false negative). In many applications, the hypothesis test must be designed to ensure a limited false positive probability, for example, $p_{fp} < 10^{-12}$ was proposed for watermark detection in the context of DVD copy protection (Cox et al., 2001). Another option for the evaluation of watermark detection is the investigation of the total detection error probability p_e, which measures both of the possible error types.

Blind and Informed Watermark Extraction

The complete process of embedding and extraction of the watermark is modeled as communications channel where the watermark is distorted due to the presence of strong interference and channel effects. Strong interference is caused by the presence of the host audio, and channel effects correspond to signal processing operations.

In some applications, the detection algorithm may use the original host audio to extract the watermark from the watermarked audio sequence (informed extraction). It often significantly improves detector performance in that the original audio can be subtracted from the watermarked copy, resulting in the watermark sequence alone. However, if the detection algorithm does not have access to the original audio (blind extraction), this inability substantially decreases the amount of data that can be hidden in the host signal.

In most blind watermarking schemes, such as blind spread spectrum watermarking, the host signal is considered as interfering noise during the watermark extraction. Nevertheless, recently it has been realized that blind watermarking can be modeled as communication with side information at the encoder. This has been published in Chen and Wornell (1999) and Cox, Miller, and McKellips (1999) independently. The main idea is that, although the blind receiver does not have access to the host signal, the encoder can exploit his/

her knowledge of the host signal to reduce the influence of the host signal on the watermark detection and decoding.

Security

Security measures the impact on the detection capability of intentional process-ing dedicated to a certain class of watermarking techniques. They are some-times called malicious attacks in the sense that the pirates are perfectly familiar with the watermark embedding and detection algorithms, and they look for flaws in this targeted technique.

The watermark algorithm must be secure in the sense that an adversary must not be able to detect the presence of embedded data, let alone remove the embedded data. The security of the watermark process is interpreted in the same way as the security of encryption techniques, using the Kerckhoffs principle. Hence, the security of the cryptosystem must only stem from storing the secret key in a safe place, the rest of the system being public. The system cannot be broken unless the authorized user has access to a secret key that controls watermark embedding. An unauthorized user should be unable to extract the data in a reasonable amount of time even if he/she knows that the host signal contains a watermark and is familiar with the exact watermark embedding algorithm. Security requirements vary with application and the most stringent of them are found in cover communications applications, and in some cases, data are encrypted prior to embedding them into host audio.

Computational Complexity and Cost

Implementation of an audio watermarking system is a tedious task and it depends on the business application involved. The principal issue from the technical point of view is computational complexity of embedding and detection algorithms and the number of embedders and detectors used in the system. For example, in broadcast monitoring, embedding and detection must be done in real time, while in copyright protection applications, time is not a crucial factor for practical implementation. One of the economic issues involved in the design of embedders and detectors, which can be implemented as hardware or software plug-ins, is the difference in processing power of different devices (laptop, PDA, mobile phone, etc.).

Summary

In Section 2, six of the properties by which audio watermarking algorithms can be characterized are highlighted. These properties include perceptual transparency, watermark bit rate, robustness in the presence of attacks, type of watermark detection (blind/informed), security, and computational complexity. The relative importance of a particular property is application dependent, and in many cases, even the interpretation of a watermark property varies with the application.

HAS-Based Perceptual Transparency

Watermarking of audio signals is more challenging compared to watermarking of images or video sequences, due to the wider dynamic range of the HAS in comparison with the human visual system (HVS). The HAS perceives sounds over a range of power greater than one billion to one and a range of frequencies greater than one thousand to one. Sensitivity of the HAS to additive white Gaussian noise (AWGN) is high as well; this noise in a sound file can be detected as low as 70 dB below the ambient level. On the other hand, opposite to its large dynamic range, the HAS contains a fairly small differential range. As a result, loud sounds generally tend to mask weaker sounds. Additionally, it is insensitive to a constant relative phase change in a static waveform, and some specific spectral distortions are interpreted as natural.

It is important to take into account the interaction of different frequencies and the subsequent processing of the HAS to have a profound understanding of the relation between acoustic stimuli and hearing sensation. Auditory perception is based on critical band analysis in the inner ear where a frequency-to-place transformation takes place along the basilar membrane. The power spectra of the received sounds are not represented on a linear frequency scale but on limited frequency bands called critical bands (Zwicker & Fastl, 1999). The auditory system is usually modeled as a band pass filterbank, consisting of band pass filters with bandwidths around 100 Hz for bands with central frequency below 500 Hz and up to 5,000 Hz for bands placed at high frequencies. If we limit the highest frequency to 24,000 Hz, 26 critical bands have to be taken into account. Table 3 gives an overview of the first 24 critical bands and corresponding frequencies inside the HAS frequency range.

Table 3. Critical bands and corresponding frequencies

z/Bark	f_{low} [Hz]	f_{up} [Hz]	Δf [Hz]	z/Bark	f_{low} [Hz]	f_{up} [Hz]	Δf [Hz]
0	0	100	100	13	2,000	2,320	320
1	100	200	100	14	2,320	2,700	380
2	200	300	100	15	2,700	3,150	450
3	300	400	100	16	3,150	3,700	550
4	400	510	110	17	3,700	4,400	700
5	510	630	120	18	4,400	5,300	900
6	630	770	140	19	5,300	6,400	1,100
7	770	920	150	20	6,400	7,700	1,300
8	920	1,080	160	21	7,700	9,500	1,800
9	1,080	1,270	190	22	9,500	12,000	2,500
10	1,270	1,480	210	23	12,000	15,500	3,500
11	1,480	1,720	240	24	15,500		
12	1,720	2,000	280				

Critical bands are an essential model for description of the auditory sensation as they show the nonlinear behavior of the HAS. Two analytical expressions are used to describe the relation of critical band rate and critical bandwidth over the HAS frequency range

$$z = 13\arctan\left(0.76\frac{f}{kHz}\right) + 3.5\arctan\left(\frac{f}{7.5kHz}\right)^2 \quad [Bark] \quad (1)$$

$$\Delta f_G = 25 + 75\left[1 + 1.4\left(\frac{f}{kHz}\right)^2\right]^{0.69} \quad [Hz] \quad (2)$$

Two properties of the HAS dominantly used in watermarking algorithms are frequency (simultaneous) masking and temporal masking. The concept of using perceptual "holes" of the HAS is taken from wideband audio coding (MPEG 1 compression, layer 3, usually called MP3). In the compression algorithms, the "holes" are used to decrease the amount of bits needed to encode audio signal, without causing perceptual distortion to the audio. On the other hand, in an information-hiding scenario, masking properties are used to embed additional bits into existing bit stream, again, without generating audible noise in the host audio sequence.

Frequency Masking

Frequency masking is a frequency domain phenomenon where a low-level signal (the maskee) can be made inaudible (masked) by a simultaneously appearing stronger signal (the masker), if masker and maskee are close enough to each other in frequency (Zwicker & Fastl, 1999). A masking threshold can be derived below which any signal will not be audible. Without a masker, a signal is inaudible if its sound pressure level (SPL) is below the threshold in quiet, which depends on frequency and covers a dynamic range of more than 70 dB as depicted in the lower curve of Figure 1. The masking threshold depends on the masker and on the characteristics of the masker and maskee (narrowband noise or pure tone). For example, with the masking threshold for the SPL equal to 60 dB, masker in Figure 1 at around 1 kHz, the SPL of the maskee can be surprisingly high—it will be masked as long as its SPL is below the masking threshold. The slope of the masking threshold is steeper toward lower frequencies; in other words, higher frequencies tend to be more easily masked than lower frequencies. It should be pointed out that the distance between maskee SPL and masking threshold is smaller in noise-masks-tone case than in tone-masks-noise case, due to the sensitivity of the HAS toward additive noise. Noise and low-level signal components are masked inside and outside the particular critical band if their SPL is below the masking threshold (Zwicker & Fastl, 1999). Noise can arise from coding, inserted watermark sequence, aliasing distortions, and so forth.

The qualitative sketch of Figure 2 gives more details about the masking threshold. The distance between the SPL of the masker (masking tone SPL in Figure 2) and the minimum masking threshold is called signal-to-mask ratio (SMR). Its maximum value is at the left end of the critical band. Let SNR(m) be the signal-to-noise ratio resulting from watermark insertion in the subband m; the perceivable distortion in a given subband is then measured by the noise-to-mask ratio (NMR):

$$NMR\ (m) = SMR\text{-}SNR\ (m) \qquad (3)$$

Figure 1. Frequency masking in the human auditory system (HAS)

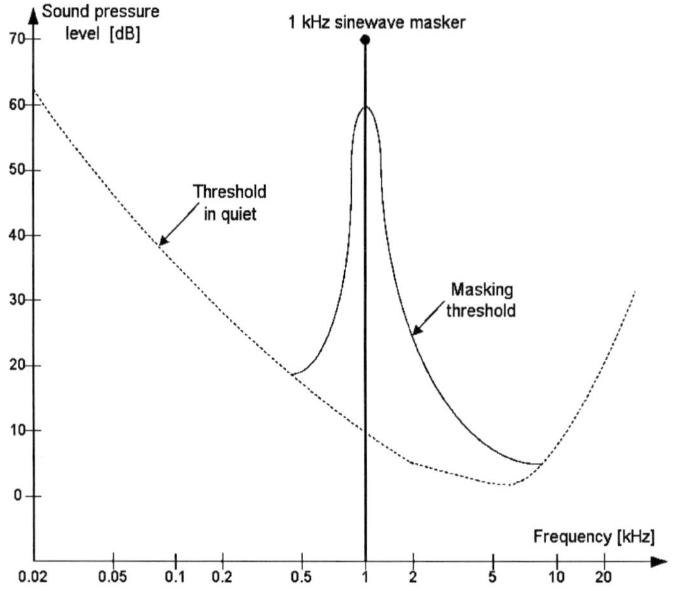

The noise-to-mask ratio NMR(m) expresses the difference between the watermark noise in a given subband and the level where a distortion may just become audible. If a watermarking system needs to embed inaudible watermarks, NMR(m) value in dB must be kept negative during watermark embedding. Thus, within a critical band, noise caused by watermark embedding (given as quantization noise in Figure 2) will be inaudible as long as the SNR of the band is higher than its SMR. It is clear that the embedding of a watermark with a higher amplitude will cause a decrease in the SNR value and increase the SPL of the noise above the minimum threshold level.

This description is the case of masking by only one masker. If the source signal consists of many simultaneous maskers, a global masking threshold can be computed. It describes the threshold of just noticeable distortion (JND) as a function of frequency. The calculation of the global masking threshold is based on the high-resolution short-term amplitude spectrum of the audio signal, sufficient for critical band-based analysis. In the first step, all the individual masking thresholds are determined, depending on signal level, type of masker (tone or noise) and frequency range. After that, the global masking threshold is determined by adding all individual masking thresholds and the threshold in quiet. The effects of frequency masking reaching over critical band bounds must be included in the calculation as well. Finally, the global signal-to-noise ratio is

Figure 2. Definition of signal-to-noise (SNR) ratio and signal-to-mask ratio (SMR)

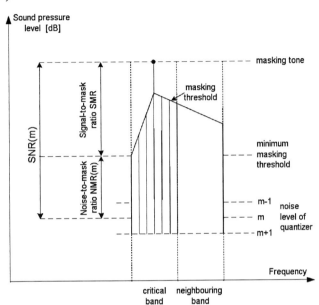

determined as the ratio of the maximum of the signal power and the global masking threshold.

Temporal Masking

In addition to frequency masking, two phenomena of the HAS in time domain have an important role in human auditory perception. Those are pre-masking and post-masking in time. The temporal masking effects appear before and after a masking signal has been switched on and off, respectively (Figure 3). Temporal masking is the characteristic of the HAS where a maskee is inaudible due to a masker, which has just disappeared, or even after a masker which is about to appear. Therefore, if the SPL of the maskee is below the curve drawn in Figure 3, it will not be perceived by the HAS because of the temporal masking. The temporal masking threshold increases as the appearance of the masker is approaching, and decreases as the appearance of the masker has passed. The duration of the pre-masking phenomenon is significantly less than one tenth of the post-masking, which is in the interval of 50 to 200 milliseconds. Both pre- and post-masking have been exploited in MPEG audio compression algorithm and in the most significant audio watermarking methods.

Figure 3. Frequency masking phenomena

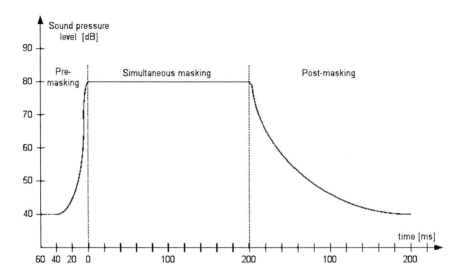

Summary

Section 3 reviewed the psychoacoustic models of the HAS that are exploited in order to preserve the subjective quality of the watermarked audio during the watermarking process. Phenomena of frequency and temporal masking are presented as well as the concept of critical bands and definitions for NMR, SMR, JND, and masking thresholds.

Audio Watermarking Algorithms

Watermarking algorithms were primarily developed for digital images and video sequences; interest and research in audio watermarking started slightly later. In the past few years, several concepts for embedding and extraction of watermarks in audio sequences have been presented. A large majority of the developed algorithms take advantage of the perceptual properties of the HAS in order to add a watermark into a host signal in a perceptually transparent manner. A broad scale of embedding techniques ranges from simple least significant bit (LSB) scheme to the various spread spectrum methods.

Watermark embedder design consists of adjusting the watermark signal to satisfy the perceptual transparency and simultaneously maximize the power of the watermark signal to provide high robustness. It usually contains a psychoacoustic analysis block that provides the embedding algorithm with a frequency masking threshold, maximum allowable phase difference, a temporal masking threshold, or similar parameters necessary for optimal watermark embedding. Selection of the particular psychoacoustic analysis block depends on the domain used for watermark embedding in a specific algorithm.

After the watermarked signal is generated, it is subjected to common audio signal distortions, including dynamic compression, filtering, and perceptual coding. The effect of those distortions on the embedded watermark is usually considered to be in the form of stationary additive Gaussian noise, although many watermark attacks are more appropriately modeled as fading-like (Kundur & Hatzinakos, 2001). A well-defined model for the distortion introduced by a certain attack is a necessary precondition for the design of an optimal watermark detector.

The ultimate goal of any watermarking system is reliable watermark extraction. It is important to make a term separation between watermark decoding and watermark detection during the watermark extraction. Communicating a watermark message is the essence of embedding and decoding of a digital watermark, while verifying whether the received audio sequence is watermarked or not is watermark detection.

Least Significant Bit Coding

One of the earliest techniques studied in the information-hiding and watermarking area of digital audio (as well as other media types [Fridrich, Goljan, & Du, 2001; Fridrich, Goljan, & Du, 2002; Lee & Chen, 2000] is LSB coding (Yeh & Kuo, 1999). A simple approach in watermarking audio sequences is to embed watermark data by alternation of certain bits of the digital audio stream, having the amplitude resolution of 16 bits per sample. It usually does not use any psychoacoustics model to perceptually weight the noise introduced by LSB replacement. However, there are some advanced methods of LSB coding (Cvejic & Seppänen, 2002; Lee & Chen, 2000) that introduce a certain level of perceptual shaping.

The watermark encoder usually selects a subset of all available host audio samples chosen by a secret key. The substitution operation on the LSBs is performed on this subset. The extraction process simply retrieves the watermark by reading the value of these bits. Therefore, the decoder needs all the samples of the watermarked audio that were used during the embedding process. The random selection of the samples used for embedding introduces low-power additive white Gaussian noise. As noted in Section 3, HAS is very sensitive to the AWGN and this fact limits the number of LSBs that can be imperceptibly modified.

The main advantage of the method is a very high watermark channel capacity; use of only one LSB of the host audio sample gives the capacity of 44.1 kbps (all samples used). The obvious disadvantage is extremely low robustness, due to the fact that random changes of the LSBs destroy the coded watermark (Mobasseri, 1998). In addition, it is very unlikely that the embedded watermark would survive digital-to-analog and subsequent analog-to-digital conversion. As no calculation-demanding transformation of the host signal in the basic version of this method needs to be done, this algorithm has a very small computational complexity. This allows the use of this LSB in real-time applications. This algorithm is a good basis for steganographic applications for audio signals and a basis for steganalysis of digital media (Chandramouli & Memon, 2001; Dumitrescu, Wu, & Wang, 2003).

Watermarking the Phase of the Host Signal

Algorithms that embed a watermark into the phase of the host audio do not use the masking properties of the HAS, but the fact that the HAS has a low sensitivity to relative phase change (Bender et al., 1996). There are two main approaches used in watermarking the host signal's phase: phase coding (Bender et al., 1996; Ruiz & Deller, 2000) and phase modulation (Ciloglu & Karaaslan, 2000; Lancini, Mapelli, & Tubaro, 2002; Tilki & Beex, 1997).

Phase Coding

The basic phase coding method was presented in Bender, Gruhl, Morimoto, and Lu (1996). The basic idea is to split the original audio stream into blocks and embed the whole watermark data sequence into the phase spectrum of the first block. One drawback of the phase coding method is considerably low payload as only the first block is used for watermark embedding. In addition, the watermark is not dispersed over the entire data set available, but is implicitly localized and can thus be removed easily by the cropping attack. It is a nonblind watermarking method, which limits the number of applications that it is suitable for.

Phase Modulation

Watermark insertion in this method is performed using independent multiband phase modulation (Gang, Akansu, & Ramkumar, 2001; Kuo, Johnston, Turin, & Quackenbush, 2002). The original signal is segmented into M blocks containing N samples using overlapping windows

$$win(n) = \sin\left(\frac{\pi(n + 0.5)}{N}\right) \quad 0 \leq n \leq N-1 \tag{4}$$

To ensure perceptual transparency by introducing only small changes in the envelope, the performed phase modulation has to satisfy the following constraint

$$\left|\frac{\Delta\phi(z)}{\Delta z}\right| < 30^0 \tag{5}$$

where $\Phi(z)$ denotes the signal phase and z is the Bark scale. Each Bark constitutes one critical bandwidth; conversion of frequency between Bark and Hz is given in Table 3. Using a long block size N (e.g., $N=2^{14}$) algorithm attains a slow phase change over time. The watermark is converted into phase modulation by having one integer Bark scale carry one message bit of the watermark. Each message bit is first represented by a phase window function, which centers at the end of the corresponding Bark band and spans two adjacent Barks. The phase window function is defined as follows

$$\phi(z) = \sin^2\left(\frac{\pi(z+1)}{2}\right), \quad -1 \leq z \leq 1 \tag{6}$$

Denote $a_1, a_2, \ldots, a_l$ the sequence of weights used for watermark embedding the kth block of host audio. The sign $a_k \in \{-1, 1\}$ of the phase window function is determined by the kth watermark bit $m_k \in \{-1,1\}$. The total phase modulation is obtained as linear combination of the overlapped phase window functions

$$\Phi_k(z) = \sum_{j=1}^{J} a_k[j]\phi(z-j), \; 0 \le z \le J \qquad (7)$$

Using the $F_k(z)$, the bits are embedded into the phases in the kth audio block by multiplying the Fourier coefficients with the phase modulation function

$$\mathbf{A}_{wk}[f] = \mathbf{A}_{ok}[f] \times e^{i\Phi_k[f]} \qquad (8)$$

with the frequency in Hz.

The watermarked signal is computed by inverse Fourier transformation of the modified Fourier coefficients $\mathbf{A}_{wk}$. All the blocks are windowed and overlap added to create watermarked signal. The robustness of the modulated phase can be increased by using n_z Bark values carrying one watermark bit.

Watermark extraction requires a perfect synchronization procedure to perform a block alignment for each watermarked block, using the original signal as a reference. The watermark bits from the kth block are extracted from the phase modulation $\hat{\Phi}_k$ for that block. A matching of the particular segments of the modulated phase to the encoded watermark bits is possible if no significant distortions of the watermarked signal took place. Here is the extraction algorithm in detail (Arnold et al., 2003)

1. Calculate phase modulation function $\hat{\Phi}_k$ by applying the window function from above and performing the Fourier transformation $\mathbf{C}_{wk} = F\{\mathbf{c}_{wk}\}$ of the kth block.

2. Formulate the $\hat{\Phi}_k$ as an observation sequence $\mathbf{o}[f] = \{\mathbf{o}_t[f]\}_{t=1}^{T}$ where f covers the frequency range for the t-th bit.

3. Calculate the weight factor sequence $\beta[f]$, where $\beta[f] = \{\beta_t[f]\}_{t=1}^{T}$, using:

$$\beta_t[f] = \min\left(\left|\mathbf{A}_{wt}[f]\right|^2, \left|\mathbf{A}_{ot}[f]\right|^2\right),$$

$$for \ f = 0, \ldots, K-1 \ and \ \sum_f \beta_t[f] = 1 \tag{9}$$

The particular weight factor of the observation sequence is determined by the smaller value of two values: energy of the original and energy of the watermarked signal. This weighting is based on the hypothesis that smaller spectrum components and their corresponding phase are more likely to be distorted by watermark attacks.

1.   Calculate the cost function

$$c_t^{ij} = \frac{1}{K}\sum_{f=0}^{K-1}\left|p_t^{ij}[f] - o_t[f]\beta_t[f]\right| \quad for \ 0 \pounds i, \ j \pounds 1, \ 1 \pounds t \pounds T \tag{10}$$

2.   Perform the Viterbi search algorithm (Stein, 2000) with the calculated cost function to find the best sequence of possible state transitions, which in turn yields the kth sequence of bits.

The data rate of the phase modulation algorithm depends on three factors: the amount of redundancy added, the frequency range used for watermark embedding and the energy distribution of the host audio. For signals sampled at 44.1 kHz, 0–15 kHz (0–24 in Bark scale) proved to be a sensible range for watermark embedding. If, for example, two Barks carry one watermark bit, the watermark data rate is $(24/2)(2^{14}/44100)=32$ bps.

Echo Hiding

A number of developed audio watermarking algorithms (Foo, Yeo, & Huang, 2001; Huang & Yeo, 2002; Ko, Nishimura, & Suzuki, 2002) are based on the echo-hiding method, described for the first time in Bender et al. (1996). Echo-hiding schemes embed watermarks into a host signal by adding echoes to produce a watermarked signal. An echo hiding audio watermarking algorithm

Figure 4. Parameters of echo-embedding watermarking method

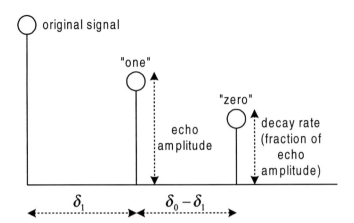

is a blind watermarking algorithm, designed especially for audio signals (it is not used in image or video watermarking). It is highly robust against standard watermarking attacks and the watermark bit rate of several tens of bps.

The nature of the echo is to add resonance to the host audio, therefore, the acute problem of sensitivity of the HAS toward the additive noise is circumvented in this method. After the echo has been added, the watermarked signal retains the same statistical and perceptual characteristics. The offset (or delay) between the original and watermarked signal is small enough so that the echo is perceived by the HAS as an added resonance. The four major parameters, initial amplitude, decay rate, "one" offset, and "zero" offset, are given in Figure 4.

The watermark embedding process can be represented as a system that has one of two possible system functions. In the time domain, the system functions are discrete time exponential differing only in the delay between impulses. Processing a host signal through any kernel in Figure 4 will result in an encoded signal. The delay between the original signal and the echo is dependent on the kernel being used, δ_1 if the "one" kernel is used and δ_0 if the "zero" kernel is used.

The host signal is divided into smaller portions for encoding more than one bit. Each individual portion can then be considered as an independent signal and echoed with the desired bit. The final watermarked signal (containing several bits) is composite of all independently encoded signal portions. A smooth transition between portions encoded with different bits should be adjusted using different methods to prevent abrupt changes in the resonance in the watermarked signal. Information is embedded into a signal by echoing the original signal with one of two delay kernels. Therefore, extraction of the embedded information is to detect the spacing between the echoes. The magnitude of the autocorrelation of the encoded signal's cepstrum

$$F^{-1}\left\{\log\left(\left|F(x)\right|^2\right)\right\}$$

(11)

where F represents the Fourier transform and F^{-1} the inverse Fourier transform can be examined at two locations, corresponding to the delays of the "one" and "zero" kernels, respectively. If the autocepstrum is greater at δ_1 than it is at δ_0, the embedded bit is decoded as "one." For multiple echo hiding, all peaks present in the autocepstrum are detected. The number of peaks corresponding to the delay locations of the "one" and "zero" kernels are then counted and compared. If there are more peaks at the delay locations for the "one" echo kernel, the watermark bit is decoded as "one."

Increased robustness of the watermark algorithm requires high-energy echoes to be embedded, which increases audible distortion. There are several modifications to the basic echo-hiding algorithm. Xu, Wu, Sun, and Xin (1999) proposed a multi-echo embedding technique to reduce the possibility of echo detection by third parties. The technique has clear constraints regarding the increase of the robustness, as the audio timbre is noticeably changed with the sum of pulse amplitude (Oh, Seok, Hong, & Youn, 2001). Oh, Seok, Hong, and Youn (2001) propose an echo kernel comprising multiple echoes by both positive and negative pulses with different offsets (closely located) in the kernel, of which the frequency response is plain in lower bands and large ripples in high frequency.

Spread Spectrum

In a number of the developed algorithms (Bassia, Pitas, & Nikolaidis, 2001; Cox, Kilian, Leighton, & Shamoon, 1997; Kirovski & Malvar, 2003; Neubauer, Herre, & Brandenburg, 1998; Swanson, Zhu, Tewfik, & Boney, 1998), watermark embedding and extraction are carried out using spread-spectrum (SS) technique. An SS sequence can be added to the host audio samples in time domain (Bassia et al., 2001; Cvejic, Keskinarkaus, & Seppänen, 2001), to

Figure 5. General model for SS-based watermarking

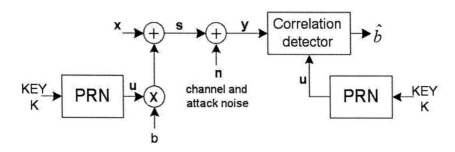

FFT coefficients (Ikeda, Takeda, & Itakura, 1999; Seok & Hong, 2001; Swanson et al., 1998), in subband domain (Kirovski & Malvar, 2001; Li & Yu, 2000; Tachibana, Shimizu, Kobayashi, & Nakamura, 2002), to cepstral coefficients (Lee & Ho, 2000; Li & Yu, 2000), and in compressed domain (Neubauer & Herre, 2000; Cheng, Yu, & Xiong, 2002). If embedding takes place in a transform domain, it should be located in the coefficients invariant to common watermark attacks as amplitude compression, resampling, low-pass filtering, and other common signal processing techniques. The idea is that, after the transform, any significant change in the signal would significantly decrease the subjective quality of the watermarked audio. Thus, spread spectrum watermarking is an extremely robust, blind watermarking algorithm, with the watermark bit rate from a few bps to several dozen bps.

The watermark is spread over a large number of coefficients and distortion is kept below the just-noticeable-difference level by using the occurrence of masking effects of the human auditory system. Change in each coefficient can be small enough to be imperceptible, because correlator detector output still has a high signal-to-noise ratio, as it despreads the energy present in a large number of coefficients.

A general system for SS-based watermarking is shown in Figure 5. Vector $\mathbf{x}$ is considered to be the original host signal already in an appropriate transform domain. The vector $\mathbf{y}$ is the received vector, in the transform domain, after channel distortions. A secret key $\mathbf{K}$ is used by a pseudo-random number generator (Furon & Duhamel, 2003; Tefas, Nikolaidis, Nikolaidis, Solachidis, Tsekridou, & Pitas, 2003) to produce a **spreading sequence u** with zero mean and elements equal to $+\sigma_u$ or $-\sigma_u$. The sequence $\mathbf{u}$ is then added to or subtracted from signal $\mathbf{x}$ according to variable b, where b assumes the values of $+1$ or -1 according to the bit (or bits) to be transmitted by the watermarking process (in multiplicative algorithms, multiplication operation is performed instead addition (Barni, Bartolini, De Rosa, & Piva, 2003). The signal **s** is the watermarked audio signal. A simple analysis of SS-based watermarking leads to a simple formula for the probability of error. Thus, if we consider the definitions of inner product and norm

$$\langle \mathbf{x}, \mathbf{u} \rangle = \sum_{i=0}^{N-1} x_i u_i \ and \ \|\mathbf{x}\| = \sqrt{\langle \mathbf{x}, \mathbf{x} \rangle} \qquad (12)$$

where **N** is the length of the vectors **x, s, u, n**, and **y** in Figure 5.

Without loss of generality, we assume that we are embedding one bit of information in a vector **s** of N transform coefficients. That bit is represented by the variable b, whose value is either +1 or "1. Embedding is performed by

$$\mathbf{s} = \mathbf{x} + b\mathbf{u} \qquad (13)$$

The distortion in the embedded signal is defined by $\|\mathbf{s} - \mathbf{x}\|$. It is easy to see that for the embedding equation (13), we have

$$D = \|b\mathbf{u}\| = \|\mathbf{u}\| = \sigma_u \qquad (14)$$

The channel is modeled as additive noise **y=s+n,** and watermark extraction is usually performed by calculation of the normalized sufficient statistic (Box, 1978) r

$$r = \frac{\langle \mathbf{y}, \mathbf{u} \rangle}{\langle \mathbf{u}, \mathbf{u} \rangle} = \frac{\langle b\mathbf{u} + \mathbf{x} + \mathbf{n}, \mathbf{u} \rangle}{\sigma_u^2} = b + x + n \qquad (15)$$

and estimating the embedded bit as $\hat{b} = sign(r)$, where $x = \langle \mathbf{x}, \mathbf{u} \rangle / \|\mathbf{u}\|$ and $n = \langle \mathbf{n}, \mathbf{u} \rangle / \|\mathbf{u}\|$.

Simple statistical models for the host audio $\mathbf{x}$ and the attack noise $\mathbf{n}$ are assumed. Both vectors are modelled as uncorrelated white Gaussian random processes (Box, 1978)

$$x_i \approx N\left(0, \sigma_x^2\right) and \ n_i \approx N\left(0, \sigma_n^2\right) \tag{16}$$

Then, it is easy to show (Box, 1978) that the sufficient statistic r is also a Gaussian variable, that is

$$r \approx N\left(m_r, \sigma_r^2\right), \ m_r = E[r] = b\sigma_r^2 = \frac{\sigma_x^2 + \sigma_n^2}{N\sigma_u^2} \tag{17}$$

Specifically, let us elaborate the case when b is equal to 1. In that case, an error occurs when r<0, and therefore, the error probability p is given by

$$p = \Pr\{\hat{b} < 0 \mid b = 1\} = \frac{1}{2} erfc\left(\frac{m_r}{\sigma_r \sqrt{2}}\right) = \frac{1}{2} erfc\left(\sqrt{\frac{\sigma_u^2 N}{2\left(\sigma_x^2 + \sigma_n^2\right)}}\right) \tag{18}$$

where erfc(*) is complementary error function. The equal error probability is obtained under the assumption that b=-1. A plot of that probability as a function of the SNR m_r/σ_r is given in Figure 6.

For example, from Figure 6, it is clear that if an error probability lower than 10^{-3} is needed, then we get

$$\frac{m_r}{\sigma_r} > 3 \Rightarrow N\sigma_u^2 > 9\left(\sigma_x^2 + \sigma_n^2\right) \tag{19}$$

Figure 6. Error probability as a function of the SNR

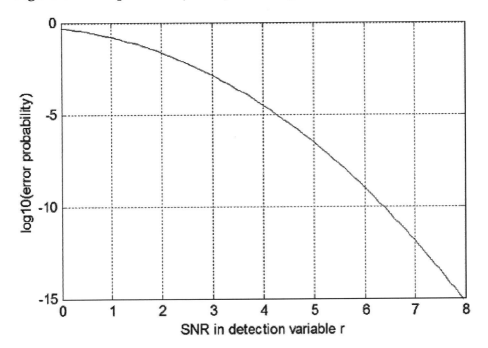

or more generally, to achieve an error probability p, we need

$$N\sigma_u^2 > 2\left(erfc^{-1}(p)\right)^2 \left(\sigma_x^2 + \sigma_n^2\right) \tag{20}$$

The equation above shows that we can make a trade-off between the length of the spreading sequence N and the energy of the spreading sequence σ_u^2. It allows us to simply compute either N or σ_u^2, given the other variables involved.

Improved Spread Spectrum

Development of the improved spread spectrum (ISS) method was gradual and consisted of several phases. In Cox, Miller, and McKellips (1999), the authors described the importance of decreasing the influence of the host signal on the watermark extraction process, analyzing a spread spectrum system with the fixed cross-correlation value. Using the framework from Cox et al. (1999), the authors have derived three different watermarking approaches corresponding to the cases of "maximized robustness," "maximized correlation coefficient," and "constant robustness." Still, the problem of minimizing the bit error rate, at a fixed average distortion level during watermark embedding process, is not addressed. The final ISS method has been proposed in Malvar and Florencio (2003). It removes the host signal as a source of interference, gaining significantly on robustness, compared with the standard SS algorithm, with the same watermark bit rate.

The main idea behind the ISS is that by using the encoder knowledge about the signal (or more precisely, x, the projection of **x** on the watermark), we can enhance performance by modulating the energy of the inserted watermark to compensate for the signal interference. The new embedding approach is defined by a slight modification to the SS embedding, that is, the amplitude of the inserted spreading sequence is varied by a function μ(x,b):

$$\mathbf{s} = \mathbf{x} + \mu(x, b)\mathbf{u} \tag{21}$$

where, as in the standard SS method $x = \langle \mathbf{x}, \mathbf{u} \rangle / \|\mathbf{u}\|$. It is obvious that the traditional SS is a particular case of ISS. In this notation, SS is a case of the ISS in which the function μ is made independent of x. The simplest version of the ISS is to restrict μ to be a linear function. Not only is this much simpler to analyze, but it also provides a significant part of the gains in relation to traditional SS. In this case and due to the symmetry of the problem in relation to x and b, we have

$$\mathbf{s} = \mathbf{x} + (\alpha b - \lambda x)\mathbf{u} \tag{22}$$

The parameters α and λ control the distortion level and the removal of the carrier distortion on the detection statistic. Traditional SS is obtained by setting α=1 and λ=0. If white Gaussian channel noise model is used as we did for SS method, the receiver sufficient statistic is

$$r = \frac{\langle \mathbf{y}, \mathbf{u} \rangle}{\|\mathbf{u}\|} = \alpha b + (1 - \lambda)x + n \tag{23}$$

Therefore, as λ tends to 1, the more the influence of x is removed from r. The detector is the same as in SS, that is, the detected bit is sign(r). The expected distortion of the ISS system is given by

$$E[D] = E[\|s - x\|] = E[\|\alpha b - \lambda x\|^2 \sigma_u^2] = \left(\alpha^2 + \frac{\lambda^2 \sigma_x^2}{N\sigma_u^2}\right)\sigma_u \qquad (24)$$

To force the average distortion of the ISS system to be equal to that of the traditional SS system, we force $E[D] = \sigma_u$ and therefore

$$\alpha = \sqrt{\frac{N\sigma_u^2 - \lambda^2 \sigma_x^2}{N\sigma_u^2}} \qquad (25)$$

In order to compute the error probability, the mean and the variance of the sufficient statistic r are needed. They are given by

$$m_r = \alpha b \ and \ \sigma_r^2 = \frac{\sigma_n^2 + (1-\lambda)^2 \sigma_x^2}{N\sigma_u^2} \qquad (26)$$

Thus, the error probability of the ISS system can be computed as

$$p = \Pr\{r < 0 \,|\, b = 1\} = \frac{1}{2}\,erfc\left(\frac{m_r}{\sigma_r \sqrt{2}}\right) = \frac{1}{2}\,erfc\left(\sqrt{\frac{N\sigma_u^2 - \lambda^2 \sigma_x^2}{2(\sigma_n^2 + (1-\lambda)^2 \sigma_x^2)}}\right) \qquad (27)$$

Error probability function p can be rewritten as a function of the relative power of the SS sequence $N\sigma_u^2 / \sigma_x^2$ and the SNR σ_x^2 / σ_u^2

$$p = \frac{1}{2} erfc\left(\frac{1}{\sqrt{2}}\sqrt{\dfrac{\dfrac{N\sigma_u^2}{\sigma_x^2} - \lambda^2}{\dfrac{\sigma_n^2}{\sigma_x^2} + (1-\lambda)^2}}\right) \qquad (28)$$

In Figure 7, error probability is drawn as a function of various values of SNR and $N\sigma_u^2 / \sigma_x^2$. Note that by proper selection of the parameter λ, the error probability in the proposed method can be made several orders of magnitude better than the traditional SS.

For example, with a signal-to-interference ratio of 10 (i.e., 10 dB), we get a reduction in the error rate from $p_0 = 10^{-5}$ for traditional SS to $p = 1.55 \times 10^{-43}$ for the ISS method, which is a reduction of over 37 orders of magnitude in the error probability. Higher SNR values, which can happen in practical applications, lead to even higher gains. As it can be inferred from Figure 7, the error probability varies with λ, with the optimum value usually close to one. The expression for the optimum value for can be computed from the error probability by setting $\partial p / \partial \lambda = 0$ and is given by

Figure 7. Error probability as a function of the SNR

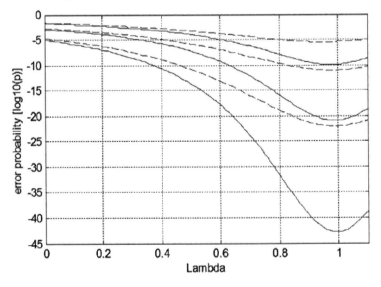

$$\lambda_{OPT} = \frac{1}{2}\left(\left(1 + \frac{\sigma_n^2}{\sigma_x^2} + \frac{N\sigma_u^2}{\sigma_x^2}\right) - \sqrt{\left(1 + \frac{\sigma_n^2}{\sigma_x^2} + \frac{N\sigma_u^2}{\sigma_x^2}\right)^2 - 4\frac{N\sigma_u^2}{\sigma_x^2}}\right) \tag{29}$$

In addition, it is clear from that for N large enough, $\lambda_{OPT} \rightarrow 1$ as SNR $\rightarrow \infty$.

Patchwork Method

The patchwork technique was first presented in Bender et al. (1996) for embedding watermarks in images. It is a statistical method based on hypothesis testing and relying on large data sets. As one second of CD quality stereo audio contains 88,200 samples, the patchwork approach is applicable for watermarking of audio sequences as well. The watermark embedding process uses a pseudo-random process to insert a certain statistic into the host audio data set, which is extracted with the help of numerical indices (like the mean value) describing the specific distribution. The method is usually applied in a transform domain (Fourier, DCT, wavelet, etc.) in order to spread the watermark in time domain and to increase robustness against signal processing modifications (Arnold, 2000; Sugihara, 2001; Yeo & Kim, 2003). The patchwork algorithm does not require the original host signal in the process of watermark detection (blind watermarking detection). Watermark bit rate is 1–10 bps, if a high robustness in the presence of attacks is required. Watermark embedding steps are summarized as follows:

1. Map the secret key and the watermark to the seed of a random number generator. After that, generate an index set $I = \{I_1, ..., I_{2n}\}$ whose elements are pseudo-randomly selected integer values from $[K_1, K_2]$, where $1 \leq K_1 \leq K_2 \leq N$. Note that two index sets, I^0 and I^1, are needed to denote watermark bits 0 and 1, respectively. The choice of K_1 and K_2 is a crucial step in embedding the watermark because these values control the trade-off between the robustness and the inaudibility of the watermark.

2. Let $F = \{F_1, ..., F_N\}$ be the coefficients whose subscript denote frequency range from the lowest to the highest frequencies. Define $A = \{a_1, ..., a_n\}$ as the subset of F whose subscript corresponds to the first n elements of the index set I^0 or I^1 according to the embedded code with similar definition

for B={$b_1,...,b_n$} with the last n elements, that is a_i=F_I and b_i=F_{In+I}, for i=1,...,n.

3   Calculate the sample means $\bar{a} = \frac{1}{n}\sum_{i=1}^{n} a_i$ and $\bar{b} = \frac{1}{n}\sum_{i=1}^{n} b_i$, respectively, and the pooled sample standard error

$$S = \sqrt{\frac{\sum_{i=1}^{n}(a_i - \bar{a})^2 + \sum_{i=1}^{n}(b_i - \bar{b})^2}{n(n-1)}} \qquad (30)$$

4.   The embedding function presented below introduces a location-shift change

$$a_i^* = a_i + sign(\bar{a} - \bar{b})\sqrt{C}\frac{S}{2} \text{ and } b_i^* = b_i - sign(\bar{a} - \bar{b})\sqrt{C}\frac{S}{2} \qquad (31)$$

where C is a constant and sign is the sign function. This function makes the large value set larger and the small value set smaller, so that the distance between the two sample means is always larger than $d = \sqrt{C}S$.

Finally, replace the selected elements a_i and b_i by a_i* and b_i*, respectively, and then apply the inverse DCT.

Since the proposed embedding method introduces relative changes of two sets in location, a natural test statistic which is used to decide whether or not the watermark is embedded should concern the distance between the means of A and B. Thus, the watermark extracting process is done as follows

1.   Map the secret key and watermark to the seed of random number generator and then generate the index sets I^0 and I^1, which was applied to the encoding process.

2.   Obtain the subsets A_1 and B_1 from F={$F_1,...,F_N$} and compute the sample means and the pooled sample standard errors. Obtain the subsets

$A_0=\{a_{01},...,a_{0n}\}$ and $B_0=\{b_{01},...,b_{0n}\}$ from the index set I^0, $A_1=\{a_{11},...,a_{1n}\}$ and $B_1=\{b_{11},...,a_{1n}\}$ from the index set I^1, all from $F=\{F_1,...,F_N\}$ and compute the sample means $\bar{a}_0, \bar{b}_0, \bar{a}_1$ and $\bar{b}_1$ and the pooled standard errors S_0 and S_1.

3. Calculate the test statistics

$$T_0^2 = \frac{\left(\bar{a}_0 - \bar{b}_0\right)^2}{S_0^2} \text{ and } T_1^2 = \frac{\left(\bar{a}_1 - \bar{b}_1\right)^2}{S_1^2} \tag{32}$$

and define T^2 as the larger value obtained from two statistics.

4. Compare T^2 with the threshold M and decide that watermark is embedded if $T^2>M$. Only when $T^2>M$ is bit 0 assigned if $T_0^2 > T_1^2$, and bit 1 otherwise.

Methods Using Various Characteristics of the Host Audio

Several audio watermarking algorithms developed in recent years use different statistical properties of the host audio and modify them in order to embed watermark data. Those properties are pitch values, number of salient points, difference in energy of two adjacent blocks, and so forth. However, modifications of the host signal statistical properties do influence the subjective quality of the audio signal and have to be performed in a way that does not produce distortions above the audible threshold. Usually, these methods are robust to signal processing modifications, but offer low watermark capacity.

The paper by Xu, Wu, and Sun (1999) introduce content-adaptive segmentation of the host audio according to its characteristics in time domain. Since the embedding parameters are dependent of the host audio, it is in the right direction to increase tamper resistance. The basic idea is to classify the host audio into a predetermined number of segments according to its properties in time domain, and encode each segment with an embedding scheme, which is designed to best suit this segment of audio signal, according to its features in frequency domain.

In the paper by Lemma, Aprea, Oomen, and Van de Kerkhof (2003), the temporal envelope of the audio signal is modified according to the watermark.

A number of signal processing operations are needed for embedding a multibit payload watermark. First, the filter extracts the part of the audio signal that is suitable to carry the watermark information. The watermarked audio signal is then obtained by adding an appropriately scaled version of the product of watermark and filtered host audio to the host signal. The watermark detector consists of two stages: the symbol extraction stage and the correlation and decision stage.

An algorithm presented in Kaabneh and Youssef (2001) embeds the watermark by deciding for each mute period in the host audio whether to extend it by a predefined value. In order to detect the watermark, the detector must have access to the original length of all mute periods in the host audio.

A method described in Hiujuan, Patra, and Chan (2002) uses pitch scaling of the host audio, realized using short-time Fourier transform, to embed the watermark. The correlation ratio, computed during embedding procedure, is quantized with different quantization steps in order to embed bit 0 and 1 of the watermark stream.

In Hsieh and Sou (2002) and Mansour and Tewfik (2001), salient points are used as bases for watermark embedding resistant to desynchronization attacks. A salient point is defined as the energy fast-climbing part of the host audio signal; it defines the synchronization point for the watermarking process without embedding additional synchronization tags. Embedding of the watermark bits in Hsieh and Sou (2002) is performed using statistical mean manipulation of the cepstral coefficients and in Mansour and Tewfik (2001) by changing the distance between two salient points.

Algorithms presented in Hiujuan, Patra, and Chan (2002) and Xu and Feng (2002) use feature extraction of the host audio signal in order to tailor a specific embedding algorithm for the given segment of the host audio. In Hiujuan et al. (2002), the authors use neural networks for feature extraction and classification, while in Xu and Feng (2002), feature extraction is done using a nonlinear frequency scale technique.

The algorithm proposed in Lie and Chang (2001) embeds watermarks using relative energy relations between consecutive sample sections of the host audio in time domain. Discontinuities between boundaries of adjacent sections that would cause significant audible distortions are "blurred" using progressive weighting near section boundaries.

Summary

Section 4 provides an overview of state-of-the-art audio watermarking algorithms. Generally, the developed algorithms use the masking properties of the HAS in order to inaudibly embed a watermark into a host signal. The broad range of algorithms extends from the simple LSB scheme to various spread spectrum methods.

Attacks Against Audio Watermarking Algorithms

Subjective quality of the watermarked signal and robustness of the embedded watermark to various modifications are general requirements for all watermarking systems. Since the requirements of robustness, inaudibility, and high capacity ("magic triangle") cannot be fulfilled simultaneously, various variations and design criteria are significant for certain applications of audio watermarking. The most important requirement addresses the inaudibility of the inserted watermark; if the quality of audio signal cannot be preserved, the method will not be accepted by industry or users. When the perceptual transparency requirement has been fulfilled, the design objective is to maximize robustness inside the limits imposed by perceptual requirements, obtaining at the same time a practical watermark bit rate.

Common signal processing manipulations are frequently applied to the watermarked audio. They significantly modify frequency content and dynamics of the host signal and therefore distort the embedded watermark. Furthermore, third parties may attempt to modify the watermarked signal in order to prevent detection of the embedded data.

An example of a signal manipulation is preparation of audio material to be transmitted at a radio station. The audio sequence is first normalized and compressed to fit the loudness level of the broadcast transmission. Equalization is used as well to optimize the quality of received audio. A denoiser (dehisser) reduces unwanted parts of the audio information and filters are used to cut off any frequency that cannot be transmitted. If a watermark is used for tracking of broadcasted commercials, it has to be robust against all the attacks described above, or the extraction will be impossible. Another case is Internet distribution, for example, when a company wants to embed watermarks as copyright protection. Thus, the watermark has to be robust against all operations usually applied to the material. In this case, the most common attack will be lossy MPEG or AAC compression, usually at high compression rates.

To evaluate robustness of audio watermarking algorithms, attacks can be grouped by the manner in which signal manipulations distort the embedded watermark. Based on the attack models, the following groups of attacks are usually identified (Steinebach, Petitcolas, Raynal, Dittmann, Fontaine, Seibel, et al., 2001):

Dynamics—These modifications change the loudness profile of the watermarked audio, amplification, and decreasing being the most basic attacks. Limiting, expansion, and compression are more complicated, as they consist of nonlinear changes depending on the input audio signal. There are even several frequency-dependent compression algorithms, which only affect a part of the frequency range.

Examples:

1. Amplitude compression with compression rates dependent on the amplitude A: (8.91:1 for A>-29dB, 1.73:1 for –46dB<A<-29dB and 1:1.61 for A<-46dB).

2. Denoising, usually utilized to remove noise from audio. A parameter is used to set the loudness of signals interpreted as noise, similar to a gate (usually set at –60 or –80 dB).

Filtering—Filters cut off or increase a selected part of the spectrum. The basic filters are high-pass and low-pass filters, but equalizers can also be seen as filters. They are used to increase or decrease certain subbands of audio spectrum.

Examples:

1. High-pass filter removes all frequencies lower than a threshold, for example, 100 Hz.

2. Low-pass filter removes all spectral components higher than a threshold, for example, 6 kHz.

3.   8-band equalizer, signal randomly suppressed or amplified by 6 dB in each band.

Ambience—Audio effects simulating the presence of a room. The most common effects are reverb and delay that offer various parameters to set the quality of effect.

Examples:

1.   Delay—A delayed replica of the original signal is added to it in order to simulate wide spaces. For example, delay time 100 ms, amplitude decay 50%.

Conversion—Watermarked audio is often subject to format changes. Mono data can be mixed up in order for it to be used in stereo environments and stereo signal can be down mixed to mono. Sampling frequencies range fro 32 kHz to 96 kHz, while sample resolution goes from 8 to 24 bits per sample.

Examples:

1.   Resampling, for example, from 44.1 KHz to 11.025 kHz and back to 44.1 kHz.
2.   Sample resolution modification, from 16 bps to 8 bps and back to 16 bps.

Lossy compression—Audio compression algorithms based on psychoacoustic effects used to reduce the size of audio files by factor 10 or more.

Examples:

1.   Watermarked audio clips compressed to MPEG-1 files, at a rate of 128 kb/s.
2.   Audio sequences were encoded with Advanced Audio Coder at the rate of 96 kb/s.

Noise—Noise can be the result of most attacks described in this section, and most of the hardware components introduce noise into the signal. Adversaries usually attack the watermarked audio by adding AWGN of certain amplitude.

Examples:

1.   Random number addition to the values of audio samples, constrained by a parameter giving the relative amount of the number compared with the watermarked signal. Up to 0.91% of the original sample value could be added as noise without decreasing the subjective quality of the watermarked signal.

Modulation—Modulation effects such as vibrato, chorus, amplitude modulation, or flanging are usually not implemented in the broadcasting, but as most audio processing software includes such effects, they can be used as attacks to remove watermarks.

Examples:

1.   Chorus—A modulated echo is added to the signal with various delay time, modulation strength, and number of voices. For example, four voices, maximum delay 20 ms, delay rate 1.5 Hz, feedback 10%, voice spread 50 ms, vibrato depth 6 dB, vibrato rate 2 Hz, dry out (unmodified signal) 100%, and wet out (effect signal) 5%.
2.   Flanger—Flanging is usually created by mixing a signal with a lightly delayed copy of itself, where the delay length is continuously changing.
3.   Enhancer—Used to increase the power of signal in higher frequencies, thereby increasing the subjective brilliance. Effect is also known as "exciter."

Time stretch and pitch shift—These attacks either change the length of an audio sequence without changing its pitch or change the pitch of audio content without changing its length. They are used for fine-tuning or fitting audio sequences into predefined time windows.

Examples:

1.   Pitch shifter—Used to change the base frequency without changing the speed of audio signal. This is one of the most sophisticated algorithms used in audio editing, with many different algorithms providing different output quality, depending on the characteristics of the original signal. For example, pitch increased by 5 cents (a 480th of an octave).

2.   Time stretch—Effect similar to the pitch shift, used to increase the length of watermarked audio signal without changing its pitch. For example, attacked watermarked audio sequence is 2% longer the original watermarked sequence.

Sample permutations—This group consists of the algorithms not used for audio manipulation in common environments. These attacks represent a specialized way to attack embedded watermarks in time domain.

Examples:

1.   Zero-cross-inserts—Attack consists of search with the value 0 and addition of, for example, 20 zeros at this position, creating a short pause in the signal.

2.   Copy samples—Samples are randomly chosen and repeated in the signal, increasing its total duration. For example, 20 sample repetitions in half a second.

3.   Flip samples—The positions of randomly chosen samples are permuted. For example, 40 sample permutations in half a second.

4.   Cut samples—A sequence of randomly chosen samples is deleted from the signal: to make the modification inaudible, a maximum length of the deleted sequence should be lower than 50.

Although a complete benchmark for the audio watermarking has not yet been implemented, there were some attempts to introduce unified testing environment for audio watermarking algorithms. Multiple advantages of unified third-party benchmark are obvious. First, researchers and software programmers would just provide a table of test results that would show summary of performances of the proposed algorithm. Researchers could compare different algorithms and improve methods by adding some new features to it. Second, end users would get information whether their basic application requirements are fulfilled. Third, industry can properly estimate the risks associated with the use of a particular solution by having information about level of reliability of the proposed solution.

Applications of
Digital Audio Watermarking

The basic goal is that embedded watermark information follows the watermarked multimedia and endures unintentional modifications and intentional removal attempts. The relative importance of the described properties significantly depends on the application for which the algorithm is designed. For copy protection applications, the watermark must be recoverable even when the watermarked signal undergoes a considerable level of distortion, while for tamper assessment applications, the watermark must effectively characterize the modification that took place. In this section, several application areas for digital watermarking will be presented and advantages of digital watermarking over standard technologies examined.

Ownership Protection

In the ownership protection applications, a watermark containing ownership information is embedded to the multimedia host signal. The watermark, known only to the copyright holder, is expected to be very robust and secure (i.e., to survive common signal processing modifications and intentional attacks) so the owner can demonstrate the presence of this watermark in case of dispute to demonstrate his ownership. Watermark detection must have a very small false alarm probability. On the other hand, ownership protection applications require small embedding capacity of the system, because the number of bits that can be embedded and extracted with small probability of error does not have to be large.

Proof of Ownership

It is even more demanding to use watermarks not only in the identification of the copyright ownership, but as an actual proof of ownership. The problem arises when adversary uses editing software to replace the original copyright notice with his/her own one and then claims to own the copyright him-/herself. Can the owner protect his/her rights and avoid the cost of copyright registration by applying a watermark to his/her multimedia file? In the case of early watermark systems, the problem was that the watermark detector was readily available to adversaries. As elaborated in Cox et al. (2001), anybody who can detect a watermark can probably remove it as well. Therefore, because the adversary can easily obtain a detector, he/she can remove the owner's watermark and replace it with his/her own. To achieve the level of security necessary for proof of ownership, it is indispensable to restrict the availability of the detector. When an adversary does not have the detector, the removal of a watermark can be extremely difficult. However, even if the owner's watermark cannot be removed, an adversary might try to undermine the owner. As described in Cox et al. (2001), an adversary, using his/her own watermarking system, might be able to make it appear as if his/her watermark data was present in the owner's original host signal.

This problem can be solved using a slight alteration of the problem statement. Instead of a direct proof of ownership by embedding, for example, a Dave owns this image watermark signature in the host image; algorithm will instead try to prove that the adversary's image is derived from the original watermarked image. Such an algorithm provides indirect evidence that it is more probable the real owner owns the disputed image, because he is the one who has the version from which the other two were created.

Authentication and Tampering Detection

In the content authentication applications, a set of secondary data is embedded in the host multimedia signal and is later used to determine whether the host signal was tampered. The robustness against removing the watermark or making it undetectable is not a concern as there is no such motivation from the attacker's point of view. However, forging a valid authentication watermark in an unauthorized or tampered host signal must be prevented. In practical applications, it is also desirable to locate (in time or spatial dimension) and to discriminate the unintentional modifications (e.g., distortions incurred due to moderate MPEG compression) from content tampering itself. In general, the watermark embedding capacity has to be high to satisfy the need for more additional data than in ownership protection applications. The detection must be performed without the original host signal because either the original is unavailable or its integrity has yet to be established. This kind of watermark detection is usually called a noncoherent detection.

Fingerprinting

Additional data embedded by watermark in this application is used to trace the originator or recipients of a particular copy of multimedia file. For example, watermarks carrying different serial or ID numbers are embedded in different copies of music CDs or DVDs before distributing them to a large number of recipients. The algorithms implemented in fingerprinting applications must show high robustness against intentional attacks and signal processing modifications such as lossy compression or filtering. Fingerprinting also requires good anti-collusion properties of the algorithms, that is, it is not possible to embed more than one ID number to the host multimedia file, otherwise the detector is not able to distinguish which copy is present. The embedding capacity required by fingerprinting applications is in the range of the capacity needed in copyright protection applications, with a few bits per second.

Broadcast Monitoring

A variety of applications for audio watermarking are in the field of broadcasting. Watermarking is an obvious alternative method of coding identification information for an active broadcast monitoring. It has the advantage of being embedded within the multimedia host signal itself, rather than exploiting a particular segment of the broadcast signal. Thus, it is compatible with the already-installed base of broadcast equipment, including digital and analog communication channels. The primary drawback is that the embedding process is more complex than a simple placing of data into file headers. There is also a concern, especially on the part of content creators, that the watermark would introduce distortions and degrade visual or audio quality of multimedia. A number of broadcast monitoring watermark-based applications are already available on commercial basis. These include program-type identification; advertising research, broadcast coverage research, and so forth. Users are able to receive a detailed proof of the performance information that allows them to

1. Verify that the correct program and its associated promos aired as contracted;
2. Track advertising within programming; and

3.   Automatically track multimedia within programs using automated software online.

Summary

This chapter provides an overview of digital audio watermarking systems, including a description of developed watermarking algorithms and insights into effective attack strategies against audio watermarking methods. Audio watermarking algorithms are characterized by a number of defining properties, ranging from robustness requirements to computational complexity and cost of implementation. The relative importance of a particular property is application dependent, and in many cases, even the interpretation of a watermark property varies with the application. Psychoacoustic models of the HAS that are exploited in order to preserve the subjective quality of the watermarked audio during the watermarking process are briefly reviewed. In the past few years, several concepts for embedding and extraction of watermarks in audio sequences have been presented. A large majority of the developed algorithms uses the properties of the HAS in order to inaudibly embed a watermark into a host signal. A broad range of embedding techniques goes from simple LSB scheme to various spread spectrum methods. The most important requirement for audio watermarking schemes is the inaudibility of the inserted watermark. When this requirement has been fulfilled, the design objective is to maximize robustness inside the limits imposed by inaudibility, obtaining at the same time a practical watermark bit rate. The chapter provides a comprehensive list of signal modifications that are usually used by adversaries in order to distort the embedded watermark and prevent detection of the hidden data. To conclude, application areas that have recently been developed as well as future applications areas are given.

References

Arnold, M. (2000). Audio watermarking: Features, applications and algorithms. *Proceeding of the IEEE International Conference on Multimedia and Expo*, 1013–1016.

Arnold, M., & Huang, Z. (2001). Blind detection of multiple audio watermarks. *Proceedings of the International Conference on Web Delivering of Music*, 12–19.

Arnold, M., Wolthusen, S., & Schmucker, M. (2003). *Techniques and applications of digital watermarking and content protection.* Artech House.

Barni, M., Bartolini, F., De Rosa, A., & Piva, A. (2003). Optimum decoding and detection of multiplicative watermarks. *IEEE Transactions on Signal Processing, 51*(4), 1118–1123.

Bassia, P., Pitas, I., & Nikolaidis, N. (2001). Robust audio watermarking in the time domain. *IEEE Transactions on Multimedia, 3*(2), 232–241.

Beerends, J., & Stemerdink, J. (1992). A perceptual audio quality measurement based on a psychoacoustic sound representation. *Journal of the Audio Engineering Society, 40*(12), 963–972.

Bender, W., Gruhl, D., Morimoto, N., & Lu, A. (1996). Techniques for data hiding. *IBM Systems Journal, 35*(3), 313–336.

Box, G.E.P. (1978). *Statistics for experimenters: An introduction to design, data analysis, and model building.* John Wiley & Sons.

Brandenburg, K., & Sporer, T. (1992). NMR and masking flag: Evaluation of quality using perceptual criteria. *Proceedings of the International Audio Engineering Society Conference on Audio Test and Measurement*, 169–179.

Chandramouli, R., & Memon, N. (2001). Analysis of LSB based image steganography techniques. *Proceedings of IEEE International Conference on Image Processing*, 1019–1022.

Chen, B., & Wornell, B. (1999). Dither modulation: A new approach to digital watermarking and information embedding. *Proceedings of SPIE: Security and Watermarking of Multimedia Contents*, 342–353.

Cheng, S., Yu, H., & Xiong, Z. (2002). Enhanced spread spectrum watermarking of MPEG-2 AAC. *Proceedings of the IEEE International Conference on Acoustics, Speech, and Signal Processing*, 3728–3731.

Chou, J., Ramchandran, K., & Ortega, A. (2001). High capacity audio data hiding for noisy channels. *Proceedings of the International Conference on Information Technology: Coding and Computing*, 108–111.

Ciloglu, T., & Karaaslan, S. (2000). An improved all-pass watermarking scheme for speech and audio. *Proceedings of the IEEE International Conference on Multimedia and Expo*, 1017–1020.

Cox, I., & Miller, M. (2001). Electronic watermarking: The first 50 years. *Proceedings of the IEEE Workshop on Multimedia Signal Processing*, 225–230.

Cox, I., Kilian, J., Leighton, F., & Shamoon, T. (1997). Secure spread spectrum watermarking for multimedia. *IEEE Transactions on Image Processing, 6*(12), 1673–1687.

Cox, I., Miller, M., & Bloom, J. (2001). *Digital watermarking*. Morgan Kaufmann.

Cox, I., Miller, M., & McKellips, A. (1999). Watermarking as communications with side information. *Proceedings of the IEEE, 87*(7), 1127–1141.

Cvejic, N., & Seppänen, T. (2002). Increasing the capacity of LSB-based audio steganography. *Proceedings of the IEEE International Workshop on Multimedia Signal Processing*, 336–338.

Cvejic, N., Keskinarkaus, A., & Seppänen, T. (2001). Audio watermarking using m-sequences and temporal masking. *Proceedings of the IEEE Workshop on Applications of Signal Processing to Audio and Acoustics*, 227–230.

Dumitrescu, S., Wu, W., & Wang, Z. (2003). Detection of LSB steganography via sample pair analysis. *IEEE Transactions on Signal Processing, 51*(7), 1995–2007.

Fridrich, J., Goljan, M., & Du, R. (2001). Distortion-free data embedding. *Lecture Notes in Computer Science, 2137*, 27–41.

Fridrich, J., Goljan, M., & Du, R. (2002). Lossless data embedding—New paradigm in digital watermarking. *Applied Signal Processing, 2002*(2), 185–196.

Foo, S.W., Yeo, T.H., & Huang, D.Y. (2001). An adaptive audio watermarking system. *Proceedings of the IEEE Region 10 International Conference on Electrical and Electronic Technology*, 509–513.

Furon, T., & Duhamel, P. (2003). An asymmetric watermarking method. *IEEE Transactions on Signal Processing, 51*(4), 981–995.

Gng, L., Akansu, A., & Ramkumar, M. (2001). MP3 resistant oblivious steganography. *Proceedings of the IEEE International Conference on Acoustics, Speech and Signal Processing*, 1365–1368.

Hartung, F., & Kutter, M. (1999). Multimedia watermarking techniques. *Proceedings of the IEEE, 87*(7), 1709–1107.

Hiujuan, Y., Patra, J.C., & Chan, C.W. (2002). An artificial neural network-based scheme for robust watermarking of audio signals. *Proceedings of the IEEE International Conference on Acoustics, Speech, and Signal Processing*, 1029–1032.

Hsieh, C.T., & Sou, P.Y. (2002). Blind cepstrum domain audio watermarking based on time energy features. *Proceedings of the International Conference on Digital Signal Processing*, 705–708.

Huang, D.Y., & Yeo, Y.H. (2002). Robust and inaudible multi-echo audio watermarking. *Proceedings of the IEEE Pacific-Rim Conference on Multimedia*, 615–622.

Ikeda, M., Takeda, K., & Itakura, F. (1999). Audio data hiding use of band-limited random sequences. *Proceedings of the IEEE International Conference on Acoustics, Speech, and Signal Processing*, 2315–2318.

ITU-R draft new recommendation ITU-R BS. (1998). Method for objective measurements of perceived audio quality.

Johnston, J. (1988). Estimation of perceptual entropy using noise masking criteria. *Proceedings of the IEEE International Conference on Acoustics, Speech, and Signal Processing*, 2524–2527.

Kaabneh, K.A., & Youssef, A. (2001). Muteness-based audio watermarking technique. *Proceedings of the International Conference on Distributed Computing Systems*, 379–383.

Kirovski, D., & Malvar, H. (2001). Robust covert communication over a public audio channel using spread spectrum. *Proceedings of the Information Hiding Workshop*, 256–269.

Kirovski, D., & Malvar, H. (2003). Spread-spectrum watermarking of audio signals. *IEEE Transactions on Signal Processing, 51*(4), 1020–1033.

Ko, B.S., Nishimura, R., & Suzuki, Y. (2002). Time-spread echo method for digital audio watermarking using PN sequences. *Proceedings of the IEEE International Conference on Acoustics, Speech, and Signal Processing*, 2001–2004.

Kundur, D., & Hatzinakos, D. (2001). Diversity and attack characterization for improved robust watermarking. *IEEE Transactions on Signal Processing, 29*(10), 2383–2396.

Kuo, S.S., Johnston, J., Turin, W., & Quackenbush, S. (2002). Covert audio watermarking using perceptually tuned signal independent multiband phase modulation. *Proceedings of the IEEE International Conference on Acoustics, Speech, and Signal Processing*, 1753–1756.

Lancini, R., Mapelli, F., & Tubaro, S. (2002). Embedding indexing information in audio signal using watermarking technique. *Proceedings of EURASIP-IEEE Region 8 International Symposium on Video/Image Processing and Multimedia Communications*, 257–261.

Lee, S.K., & Ho, Y.S. (2000). Digital audio watermarking in the cepstrum domain. IEEE *Transactions on Consumer Electronics, 46*(3), 744–750.

Lee, Y.K., & Chen, L.H. (2000). High capacity image steganographic model. *IEEE Proceedings on Vision, Image and Signal Processing, 147*(3), 288–294.

Lemma, A.N., Aprea, J., Oomen, W., & Van de Kerkhof, L. (2003). A temporal domain audio watermarking technique. *IEEE Transactions on Signal Processing, 51*(4), 1088–1097.

Li, X., & Yu, H. (2000a). Transparent and robust audio data hiding in cepstrum domain. *Proceedings of the IEEE International Conference on Multimedia and Expo*, 397–400.

Li, X., & Yu, H. (2000b). Transparent and robust audio data hiding in subband domain. *Proceedings of the International Conference on Information Technology: Coding and Computing*, 74–79.

Lie, W.N., & Chang, L.C. (2001). Robust and high-quality time-domain audio watermarking subject to psychoacoustic masking. *Proceedings of the IEEE International Symposium on Circuits and Systems*, 45–48.

Malvar, H., & Florencio, D. (2003). Improved spread spectrum: A new modulation technique for robust watermarking. *IEEE Transactions on Signal Processing, 51*(4), 898–905.

Mansour, M., & Tewfik, A. (2001). Audio watermarking by time-scale modification. *Proceedings of the IEEE International Conference on Acoustics, Speech and Signal Processing*, 1353–1356.

Mobasseri, B. (1998). Direct sequence watermarking of digital video using m-frames. *Proceedings of the International Conference on Image Processing*, 399–403.

Neubauer, C., & Herre, J. (2000). Audio watermarking of MPEG-2 AAC bit streams. *Proceedings of the Audio Engineering Society Convention.*

Neubauer, C., Herre, J., & Brandenburg, K. (1998). Continuous steganographic data transmission using uncompressed audio. *Proceedings of the Information Hiding Workshop*, 208–217.

Oh, H.O., Seok, J.W., Hong, J.W., & Youn, D.H. (2001). New echo embedding technique for robust and imperceptible audio watermarking. *Proceedings of the IEEE International Conference on Acoustic, Speech and Signal Processing*, 1341–1344.

Ruiz, F., & Deller, J. (2000). Digital watermarking of speech signals for the national gallery of the spoken word. *Proceedings of the IEEE International Conference on Acoustics, Speech, and Signal Processing*, 1499–1502.

Seok, J.W., & Hong, J.W. (2001). Audio watermarking for copyright protection of digital audio data. *Electronics Letters, 37*(1), 60–61.

Sporer, T. (1996). Evaluating small impairments with mean opinion scale— reliable or just a guess? *Proceedings of the Audio Engineering Society Convention.*

Stein, J. (2000). *Digital signal Processing: A computer science perspective.* Wiley-Interscience.

Steinebach, M., Petitcolas, F., Raynal, F., Dittmann, J., Fontaine, C., Seibel, S., et al. (2001). Stirmark benchmark: Audio watermarking attacks. *Proceedings of the International Conference on Information Technology: Coding and Computing*, 49–54.

Sugihara, R. (2001). Practical capacity of digital watermark as constrained by reliability. *Proceedings of the International Conference on Information Technology: Coding and Computing*, 85–89.

Swanson, M., Zhu, B., & Tewfik, A. (1999). Current state-of-the-art, challenges and future directions for audio watermarking. *Proceedings of the IEEE International Conference on Multimedia Computing and Systems*, 19–24.

Swanson, M., Zhu, B., Tewfik, A., & Boney, L. (1998). Robust audio watermarking using perceptual masking. *Signal Processing, 66*(3), 337–355.

Tachibana, R., Shimizu, S., Kobayashi, S., & Nakamura, T. (2002). An audio watermarking method using a two-dimensional pseudo-random array. *Signal Processing, 82*(10), 1455–1469.

Tefas, A., Nikolaidis, A., Nikolaidis, N., Solachidis, V., Tsekeridou, S., & Pitas, I. (2003). Performance analysis of correlation-based watermarking schemes employing Markov chaotic sequences. *IEEE Transactions on Signal Processing, 51*(7), 1979–1994.

Tilki, J., & Beex, A. (1997). Encoding a hidden auxiliary channel onto a digital audio signal using psychoacoustic masking. *Proceedings of the IEEE South East Conference*, 331–333.

Xu, C., & Feng, D. (2002). Robust and efficient content-based digital audio watermarking. *Multimedia Systems, 8*(5), 353–368.

Xu, C., Wu, J., & Sun, Q. (1999). Robust digital audio watermarking technique. *Proceedings of the International Symposium on Signal Processing and Its Applications*, 95–98.

Xu, C., Wu, J., Sun, Q., & Xin, K. (1999). Applications of watermarking technology in audio signals. *Journal of the Audio Engineering Society, 47*(10).

Yeh, C.H., & Kuo, C.J. (1999). Digital watermarking through quasi m-arrays. *Proceedings of the IEEE Workshop on Signal Processing Systems*, 456–461.

Yeo, I.K., & Kim, H.J. (2003). Modified patchwork algorithm: A novel audio watermarking scheme. *IEEE Transactions on Speech and Audio Processing, 11*(4), 381–386.

Yu, H., Kundur, D., & Lin, C.Y. (2001). Spies, thieves, and lies: The battle for multimedia in the digital era. *IEEE Multimedia, 8*(3), 8–12.

Zwicker, E., & Fastl, H. (1999). *Psychoacoustics: Facts and models.* Springer-Verlag.

Chapter VII

MPEG Standards and Watermarking Technologies

Jong-Nam Kim
Pukyong University, Republic of Korea

Byung-Ha Ahn
Gwangju Institute of Science and Technology, Republic of Korea

Abstract

This chapter introduces the watermarking technologies of the MPEG standards and gives information about a framework of watermarking technology for intellectual property protection (MPEG IPMP technology). An overview of MPEG-2/4, IPMP standard of MPEG-2/4, and watermarking technologies of MPEG-2/4 IPMP is described, and the concept of IPMP system and required normative technical items is summarized. MPEG-21 and its Part 11, PATs (Persistent Association Technologies) methodologies, PATs requirements, and evaluation methods of PATs are described and future trends of the MPEG-related watermarking technologies are discussed, including technical requirements.

Introduction

This chapter discusses some recent developments in watermarking technologies related to MPEG international standards and suggests technical requirements and evaluation methods of video watermarking technologies for broadcasting applications. Many watermarking technologies have been developed for intellectual property protection, metadata descriptions, and other purposes. Initial intellectual property protection systems employing watermarking technologies could not assure compatibility between different protection tools. Lack of fair evaluation tools for comparing various watermarking technologies led to several international standards.

MPEG-2/4/21, CPTWG, SDMI, STEP, and CIDF have been developed for interoperability and reliable evaluation of watermarking technologies. Of these international standards, MPEG-2/4/21 watermarking technologies are being developed and would seem to have the potential to affect the industrial world by protecting intellectual property by making persistent associations between content and metadata. The other watermarking standards are in active state or have stopped development. MPEG-2/4 watermarking technology is mainly used for IPMP (intellectual property management and protection), and specific technology parameters for audio and video watermarking are specified. MPEG-21 Part 11, on the other hand, deals with evaluation methods for audio watermarking. Current MPEG-21 Part 11 defines the evaluation methods of audio PATs leaving video, still image, and text watermarking to version 2 of MPEG-21 Part 11. Technical requirements and evaluation methods have been proposed for video watermarking required in broadcasting and other video applications. The proposed requirements and evaluation methods for video watermarking technologies will be useful in developing the second version of MPEG-21 Part 11, designing video watermarking system, and evaluating various video watermarking technologies.

This chapter explains the watermarking technologies of the MPEG standards and gives information about a framework of watermarking technology for intellectual property protection (MPEG IPMP technology). Additionally, the details of audio/video watermarking technology in MPEG-2/4 IPMP, and technical requirements as well as evaluation methods of audio/video watermarking technologies in MPEG-21 are discussed.

Background

Recent reports on watermarking technologies cover extensive applications of authentication, traitor tracking, copyright protection, and copy protection. The problem of interoperability was raised due to concern over these various methodologies of watermarking, for instance, the many watermarking methods from various companies for copy protection (Katzenbeisser & Petitcolas, 2000; Johnson, Duric, & Jajodia, 2001; Cox, Miller, & Bloom, 2002). However, these watermarking methods from different companies are not interoperable. That is, one watermark detector from one company cannot be used on a watermark embedded by another different company.

This interoperability problem gives rise to the need of international standards. From another viewpoint, reliable evaluation methods for benchmarking tests are needed. With objective and reliable evaluation methods, users can select a desired watermarking technology and compare the candidate technologies clearly. MPEG-2/4/21, CPTWG, SDMI, and CIDF promote international standards of watermarking. Standards besides MPEG-2/4/21 have become inactive or obsolete. MPEG-2/4/21 watermarking technologies are the only continuing standard for investigation.

After great success of audio/video coding in MPEG-2/4 (Wang, Ostermann, & Zhang, 2002; Puri & Chen, 2000), standards of other functions were strongly promoted. Of these standards, IPMP-related standards in MPEG-2/4, employing watermarking technologies as a protection tool, is important to intellectual property (Koenen, 2002; Lacy, Rump, & Kudumakis, 1998; Koenen, 2001; Ming, Chiariglione, Alberti, Kudumakis, Kaneko, & Schultz, 2003; Schultz, 2002; ISO/IEC FDIS 13818-11, 2003). IPMP-using watermarking technologies in MPEG-2/4 specify technical parameters of watermarking, syntax, and corresponding semantics.

MPEG-21 Part 11 Evaluation Tools for Persistent Association Tools have developed as a technical report with objective evaluation methods of watermarking technologies and provides a yardstick for benchmarking tests. Current MPEG-21 Part 11 deals only with audio watermarking evaluation methods. Video, still image, and text watermarking will be specified in version 2 of MPEG-21 Part 11. Video watermarking is particularly important and necessary in various broadcasting and communication applications. However, a reliable evaluation method has not been found to fairly compare video watermarking technologies.

An overview of MPEG-2/4, IPMP standard of MPEG-2/4, and watermarking technologies of MPEG-2/4 IPMP is given in Section 3 of this chapter. Because watermarking technology in IPMP standard of MPEG-2/4 is used only in IPMP framework and not by itself, an introduction to MPEG-2/4 and IPMP technology is needed. Because MPEG-2/4 IPMP standard is extensive, we will briefly summarize the concept of IPMP system and the required normative technical items. Then, audio/video watermarking technologies as one of MPEG-2/4 IPMP tools will be described. The many message parameters necessary for detecting the embedded watermark in audio/video data and the detection results of watermarks are also described.

In Section 4, we overview MPEG-21 and its Part 11, PAT methodologies, PAT requirements, and PAT evaluation methods. The description of MPEG-21 Part 11 and definition of PAT include watermarking technology associating the user's metadata to original contents. Additionally, four PATs and their characteristics are described, and their technical requirement and evaluation methods are explained.

In Section 5, future trends of MPEG-related watermarking technologies are discussed, including technical requirements and evaluation methods of video watermarking, and requirements and evaluation methods are suggested. Finally, the conclusion follows in Section 6.

Watermarking Technologies for IPMP and MPEG-2 and MPEG-4

This section discusses watermarking technologies in MPEG-2 and MPEG-4, which are used for IPMP. MPEG-2/MPEG-4 IPMP systems are described as well as their architecture, overall walk-through of the systems, watermarking technology as an IPMP tool, and specific normative syntax and semantics of audio and video watermarking technologies.

Overview of MPEG-2 and MPEG-4

MPEG-2 is a successful international standard and strongly affects real-world industries in the fields of broadcasting, communication, and storage. The original target for the MPEG-2 standard was TV-resolution video and up-to-five-channel audio of very good quality at about 4 to 15 Mbit/sec for applications such as digital broadcast TV and digital versatile disk. The standard either has been deployed or is likely to be deployed for a number of other applications including digital cable or satellite TV, video on asynchronous transfer mode (ATM), networks, and high-definition TV (HDTV). Based on the target applications, a number of primary requirements were derived, which include interlaced video coding, random access, scalable coding, and so on. The MPEG standard is formally referred to as ISO/13818 and consists of the Part 1 System to Part 11 IPMP on MPEG-2 system (Puri & Chen, 2000).

Since the MPEG-2 has been successfully developed, the MPEG-4 standard was designed to address the requirements of a new generation of highly interactive multimedia applications, while simultaneously supporting traditional applications. Such multimedia applications also require additional advanced functionalities such as interactivity with individual objects, scalability of contents, and a high degree of error resilience. The MPEG-4 standard provides a set of technologies to satisfy the needs of authors, service providers, and end users alike.

Additionally, MPEG-4 enables the production of content that has far greater reusability, has greater flexibility than is possible today with individual technologies such as digital television, animated graphics, and Web pages and their extensions. Also, it is now possible to better manage and protect content owner rights. For network service providers, MPEG-4 offers transparent information, which can be interpreted and translated into the appropriate native signaling messages of each network with the help of relevant standards bodies. MPEG-4 brings higher levels of interaction with content for end users within the limits set by the author. It also brings multimedia to new networks, including those employing relatively low bit rate and mobile ones (Wang et al., 2002).

IPMP Technology of MPEG-2 and MPEG-4

With the successful development of the MPEG-2 and MPEG-4, almost all contents were moved to the digital domain, where there is no distinction between original and pirated versions. The idea for protection of intellectual property rises from the concern of the holder of the rights of the content. In April 1997, MPEG issued a call for proposals (CfP) for the identification and protection of content in MPEG-4. The CfP covered the following:

- Identification of content
- Automated monitoring and tracking of creations
- Prevention of illegal copying
- Tracking object manipulation and modification history
- Supporting transactions between users, media distributors, and rights holders

In response to the CfP, a number of different proposals were received, ranging from watermarking technologies to complete DRM system. The call brought together a good number of DRM experts, who defined two different pieces of technology: one for the identification of copyright and the other to enable its protection. The identification part of intellectual property identifies the following:

- Whether the content is protected by an IPMP system
- The type of the content (audiovisual, audio, visual, still picture)
- The registration authority that hands out unique numbers for the type of content: ISAN, ISBN, ISRC, and so forth.
- The number that identifies the content according to such a system
- Variable-length fields for titles and supplementary information
- References to separate data streams with such information

MPEG views protection as an integral part of the management of content, which can be called DRM (digital rights management). The conclusion of the CfP is as follows

- It was not desirable to enforce IPMP tools upon all MPEG-4 content and MPEG-4 players
- It was neither feasible nor desirable, at that point in time, to standardize a complete DRM system (Koenen, 2001)

Hence, MPEG employed the hooks approach as shown in Figure 1, and MPEG-4 integrates the hooks tightly with the MPEG-4 system layer (Lacy et al., 1998).

Figure 1. High-level view of the IPMP architecture with hooks approach

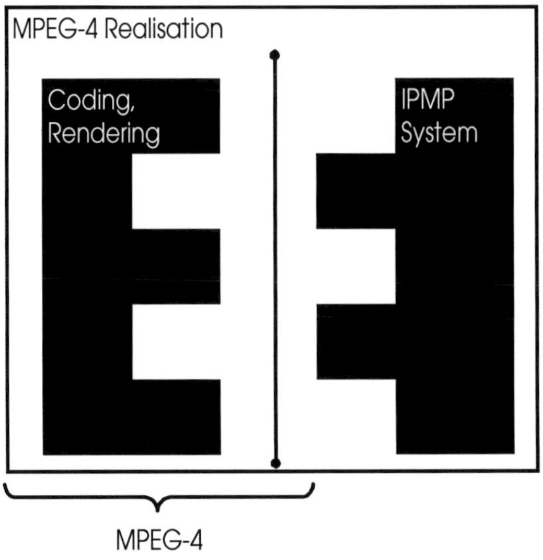

In basic MPEG-4 object descriptors, there are two simple extensions, which are IPMP–Descriptors (IPMP-Ds) and IPMP–Elementary Streams (IPMP-ES). The former is part of the MPEG-4 objects descriptor that describes how an object can be accessed and decoded. These IPMP-Ds are used to denote the IPM system that was used to encrypt the object. An independent registration authority (RA) is used so that any party can register its own IPMP system and identify this without collisions. Meanwhile, all MPEG objects are represented by elementary streams that can reference each other. These special elementary streams can be used to convey IPMP-specific data. Their syntax and semantics are not specified in the hook approach.

After development of IPMP hooks, concerns were voiced within MPEG that many similar devices might be built by different manufactures without their being able to interwork. They would incorporate different, non-interworking protection schemes, thus interworking is not guaranteed. In July 2000, MPEG issued a new CfP for IPMP extension to overcome these problems and began an extension to the MPEG-4 systems standard in the form of an amendment (Schultz, 2002). As a result of the extension works, extended IPMP system architecture was produced, as shown in Figure 2.

This walk-through identifies the technologies required for interoperability and renewability of IPMP Tools. The diagram works as follows

Figure 2. Architecture diagram of IPMPX for walk-through concepts

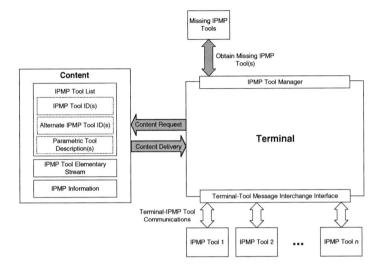

1) Users request specific content.

    The manner in which content is requested is out of scope of the IPMPX. However, the following recommendations are made for the order in which different parts of the content are received and used:

    •   IPMP requirements on the terminal should be placed with or before media requirements on the terminal.

    •   Access information and/or restrictions should precede media stream delivery information.

2) Terminal accesses IPMP tools description.

    •   Using the IPMP tool list, the terminal determines the IPMP tools required for consuming the content.

3) Terminal retrieves IPMP tools.

    •   IPMP tools retrieved out of band are outside the scope of IPMP extensions spec. Missing IPMP tools may be retrieved through an IPMP tool stream if available.

4) Terminal instantiates of IPMP tools.

    •   The terminal instantiates the IPMP tool(s) locally or remotely.

    •   The instantiated tools are provided with initial IPMP information from the content.

5) Terminal IPMP initializes and updates IPMP tools in parallel with content consumption.

- The message router routes IPMP information to the IPMP tools.
- The terminal consumes the content if allowed by the requisite IPMP tools.
- During content consumption, the complete walk-through can be requested again. Requests for content consumption are implicit within the process, or are requested by the user.

The following normative elements from the above walk-through are identified as areas of standardization. Therefore, these elements must be satisfied and provided in the user's terminal.

1) IPMP Tool List

The IPMP tool list supports indication of independent or alternative tools. For each tool in the IPMP tool list, the following information is provided; IPMP tool identifier, possible alternatives to a given tool, and optional tool list signature.

2) Parametric Infrastructure

The exact values of parameters controlling a parametrically described tool are carried in parametric configuration. Such information shall be carried in the content or generated by other IPMP tools during content consumption.

3) Tools in the Content

Specific IPMP tool implementations may be carried within the bitstream. In such case, the representation format shall be carried in the information describing such a stream. The representation indicates the interface implementation, binary representation, packaging mechanism, instantiation, and initialization for the specific tool implementation, and is provided by a registration authority. Registration of tool implementation-specific information not only applies to tools in the content but elsewhere.

4) Instantiation of IPMP Tools

Instantiation creates an instance of protection for a specific context, and results in a mechanism of communication from the message router to the IPMP tool. The actual instantiation mechanism is implement dependent and is not described in this specification although supported via the use of a registration authority.

5)   Mutual Authentication

Tools that must communicate with one another or with the terminal must do so in a way that meets the security requirements of the tools and the terminal. Tools may establish trust with the terminal and possibly with one another to enable secure communication. Support for the establishment of a communication channel that reflects the nature of inter-tool trust can be accomplished via the use of secure, trusted authenticated channels. Mutual authentication is the first part of protocols designed for such communication.

6)   IPMP Information

IPMP information is of two types. The first type is based on a fixed syntax that is meant for use both by the terminal and the IPMP tool to initialize or configure the tool to protect specific media streams in the content. The second type is fully opaque and is meant for use only by the IPMP tool. Note that one or both types of information may be contained in a single IPMP message or IPMP tool message. IPMP information may come from four sources which contain the content, the terminal resources, remote resources, and another IPMP tool.

7)   IPMP Information Routing

IPMP information routing mechanisms depend on the following parameters: a unique identification of the sender of the IPMP information and a unique identification of the intended recipient of the IPMP information. Routing considerations are manifested by encapsulating the IPMP information in an IPMP tool message or IPMP message, or are implicit by the location of the IPMP information in a bitstream.

8)   Consumption Permission

The course of processing content involves a number of different types of application-specific content use. Although communications required to query rights processing and governance tools is out of the scope of these specifications, the specifications provide a message, IPMP_CanProcess, to allow tools to notify the terminal of the ability to proceed with and/or continue processing the given content.

Figure 3. MPEG-2 IPMPX system architecture

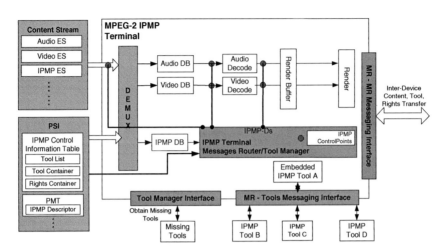

MPEG made MPEG-2 and MPEG-4 IPMPX system architecture satisfy the abovementioned normative elements, as shown in Figure 3 and Figure 4 (Schultz, 2002; ISO/IEC FDIS 13818-11, 2003). Because of the different system syntax and architecture between MPEG-2 and MPEG-4, IPMP information is located at different positions in the stream. IPMP information in MPEG-2 IPMPX is contained in the PSI section, and IPMP information in MPEG-4 IPMPX is contained in an object descriptor.

Figure 4. MPEG-4 IPMPX system architecture

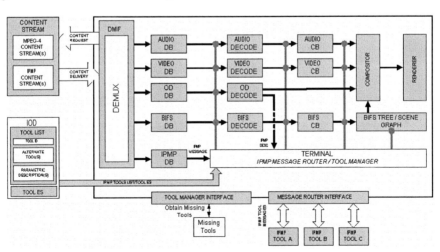

Watermarking Technology of MPEG-2 and MPEG-4 IPMPX

Audio Watermarking Syntax and Semantics

Watermarking is used as an IPMP tool in MPEG-2 and MPEG-4 IPMP-X (Intellectual Property Management and Protection Extension). There are two types of IPMP data for audio watermarking, which are IPMP_AudioWatermarkingInit data and IPMP_SendAudioWatermark data. The former could be carried in either IPMP descriptor or IPMP stream, and sent to a watermarking tool in order to initialize the process of insertion or extraction of the watermarking payload into or from an audio stream. The watermarking tool receives the audio stream and in case of watermarking extraction, constructs an IPMP_SendAudioWatermark data, either sending it upstream or informing the terminal with an IPMP_MessageFromTool message carrying the IPMP_SendAudioWatermark data.

- Audio watermarking parameters in IPMP_AudioWatermarkingInit data

   The IPMP_AudioWatermarkingInit data delivers to an audio watermarking tool all information about the characteristics of the audio content, the type of action to be performed on it, and possibly other related proprietary data required by the watermarking tool. The syntax of the IPMP_AudioWatermarkingInit data is shown in Table 1 (Schultz, 2002; ISO/IEC FDIS 13818-11, 2003).

There are four types of required operations RequiredOp as shown in Table 2.

In Table 3, the compression detection is used considering the audio material that has been distributed only in a noncompressed legacy (CD) format. Thus, if compression is detected, it will be considered unauthorized content. This implies that the watermarking tool will be able to discriminate compression from other common signal processing manipulations which may have also taken place in the signal but are not considered prohibited (as expressed by the rights attached to the particular audio stream), such as sample rate conversion, tremble/bass, spatialization, echo, and so forth. It should be clear that this is only an example of the possible uses of this flag. Its goal in general is to facilitate means and technologies for distinguishing legal from illegal audio content.

Table 1. The syntax of IPMP_AudioWatermarkingInit data

```
class IPMP_AudioWatermarkingInit extends IPMP_Data_BaseClass :
    bit(8) tag = IPMP_AudioWatermarkingInit_tag
{
    bit(8) inputFormat;
    bit(4) requiredOp;
    bit(1) hasOpaqueData;
    const bit(3) reserved = 0b000;
    if (inputFormat == PCM)
    {
        bit(8) nChannels;
        bit(8) bitPerSample;
        bit(32) frequency;
    }
    if ((requiredOp == INSERT_WM)||(requiredOp == REMARK_WM))
    {
        bit(16) wmPayloadLen;
        bit(8) wmPayload[wmPayloadLen];
    }
    if ((requiredOp == EXTRACT_WM)||(requiredOp ==
DETECT_COMPRESSION))
    {
        bit(32) wmRecipientId;
    }
    if (hasOpaqueData)
    {
        bit(16) opaqueDataSize;
        bit(8) opaqueData[opaqueDataSize];
    }
}
```

Table 2. Four types of required operations

insertion	the watermarking payload to be inserted
extraction	the ID of the recipient of the watermarking payload is provided
remarking	the watermarking payload to be inserted
compression	the ID of the recipient of the decision (that compression has taken place or not) is provided

- Audio watermarking parameters in IPMP_SendAudioWatermarking data

  An audio watermarking tool, which has been required to perform payload extraction, will construct this IPMP data and either send it upstream or wrap this IPMP data in IPMP_MessageFromTool message and send this message to wmRecipientId each time a new watermarking payload is extracted from the audio content. An audio watermarking tool, which

Table 3. Semantics of IPMP_AudioWatermarkingInit data

InputFormat	The format of the audio input stream to be maintained by a registration authority. It shall contain at least the PCM format, signaled by the value "0x01" and all audio formats indicated in "ObjectTypeIndication values" of [W3C recommendation, Extensible Markup Language (XML) 1.0 (2nd Edition)]
RequiredOp	The operation that the watermarking tool is required to perform on the audio stream. The following values are allowed: INSERT_WM = 0 EXTRACT_WM=1 REMARK_WM =2 DETECT_COMPRESSION =3 ISO reserved = 4..10 User defined = 11..15
NChannels	The number of audio channels (1 = mono, 2 = stereo…) of the input stream
Frequency	The number of samples per second (in Hz, e.g., 44,100) of the input audio stream
BitPerSample	The number of bits per sample (e.g., 8, 16) of the input audio stream
WmPayloadLen	The length of the watermarking payload in bytes to be inserted in the audio content
WmPayload	The watermarking payload to be inserted in the audio content
WmRecipientId	The destination tool identified by the IPMP_Descriptor_ID to which the watermarking payload and compression information must be delivered. A value of 0 indicates the terminal
HasOpaqueData	A flag that indicates if the message also carries opaque data information for the watermarking tool
OpaqueDataSize	The length of the opaque data field in bytes
OpaqueData	The opaque data field carrying proprietary information to the watermarking tool (e.g., initialization parameters, such as specific algorithm ID, keys, etc.)

detects if compression has taken place on a raw (PCM) audio stream, will construct this IPMP data and either send it upstream or wrap this IPMP data in an IPMP_MessageFromTool message and send this message to wmRecipientId each time it detects that the raw audio stream has either been compressed (and as such perhaps has been illegally distributed) or not. Table 4 to Table 7 shows the syntax and semantics of IPMP_SendAudioWatermark data (Schultz, 2002; ISO/IEC FDIS 13818-11, 2003).

Table 4. The syntax of IPMP_SendAudioWatermark data

```
class IPMP_SendAudioWatermark extends IPMP_Data_BaseClass :
    bit(8) tag = IPMP_SendAudioWatermark_tag
{
    bit(2) wm_status;
    bit(2) compression_status;
    bit(1) hasOpaqueData;
    bit(3) reserved = 0b000;
    if (wm_status == WM_PAYLOAD)
    {
        ByteArray payload;
    }
    if  (hasOpaqueData)
    {
        ByteArray opaqueData;
    }
}
```

Table 5. Important information in IPMP_SendAudioWatermark data

wm_status	The result of the check if watermarking was present. If watermark was detected, then this value also says if the payload extracted is carried inside the message or not
compression_status	The result of the check if the audio stream was compressed. Possible values are listed in Table D-2 below
hasOpaqueData	A flag indicating whether this message carries opaque data
payload	The watermarking payload extracted from the audio content
opaqueData	Opaque data from the watermarking tool

Table 6. The semantics of wm_status

00	WM_PAYLOAD	Watermarking was present in the audio stream; payload is carried in the message
01	WM_NOPAYLOAD	Watermarking was present in the audio stream; no payload is carried in the message
10	NO_WM	Watermarking was not present in the audio stream
11	WM_UNKNOWN	Watermarking tool was unable to detect whether watermarking was present in the audio stream

Table 7. The semantics of compression_status

00	COMPRESSION	The audio stream was compressed
01	NO_COMPRESSION	The audio stream was not compressed
10	COMP_UNKNOWN	The watermarking tool was unable to detect if the audio stream was compressed
11	ISO Reserved	Reserved

Video Watermarking Syntax and Semantics

The two types of IPMP data for video watermarking are IPMP_VideoWatermarkingInit and IPMP_SendVideoWatermark data. It could also be carried in either IPMP descriptor or IPMP stream and sent to a video watermarking tool in order to initialize the process of insertion/extraction of the watermarking payload into/from an video stream. The watermarking tool receives the video stream and in case of watermarking extraction, constructs an IPMP_SendVideoWatermark data and either sends it upstream or informs the terminal with an IPMP_MessageFromTool message carrying the IPMP_SendAudioWatermark data. The IPMP_videoWatermarkingInit data delivers information to a watermarking tool about the characteristics of the video content, the type of action to be performed on it, and possibly other proprietary related data required by the watermarking tool. The syntax of the IPMP_videoWatermarkingInit data is the same as the IPMP_audioWatermarkingInit data except for the inputFormat. The syntax and semantics of the inputFormat are represented in Table 8 and Table 9. IPMP_SendVideoWatermark data also play the same role as

Table 8. The syntax of the inputFormat in IPMP_videoWatermarkingInit data

```
if (inputFormat == YUV)
    {
        bit(16) frame_horizontal_size;
        bit(16) frame_vertical_size;
        bit(8) chroma_format;
    }
```

Table 9. The semantics of the inputFormat in IPMP_videoWatermarkingInit data

inputFormat	The format of the video input stream to be maintained by a registration authority. It shall contain at least all video formats indicated in "ObjectTypeIndication values" of [W3C recommendation, Extensible Markup Language (XML) 1.0 (2nd Edition)].
frame_horizontal_size	Horizontal size of the yuv frame
frame_vertical_size	Vertical size of the yuv frame
chroma_format	chroma_format: 0x01=4:2:0, 0x02=4:2:2, 0x03=4:4:4 ISO reserved =0x04..0xA0 User defined = 0xA1..0xFE Forbidden: 0x00, 0xFF

IPMP_SendAudioWatermark with video stream instead of audio stream (ISO/ IEC FDIS 13818-11, 2003).

Evaluation Methods of Watermarking Technologies in MPEG-21

This section presents an overview of MPEG-21 and PATs of MPEG-21, which include watermarking technology, their requirements, and evaluation methodologies.

Overview of MPEG-21 and PATs

MPEG has developed international standards in terms of data compression and multimedia data description, which include MPEG-2, MPEG-4, and MPEG-7. MPEG-2 and MPEG-4 mainly deal with audio/video compression and MPEG-7 deals with multimedia data description. However, these standards are far from building an infrastructure for the production, delivery, and consumption of multimedia content. That is, there is no "big picture" to describe these environments from the production to consumption of multimedia content. MPEG-21 aims at describing how these various elements fit together and provides a unified environment to augment use of contents.

MPEG started to develop new standards to answer the above problem and contain other relevant standards if necessary. MPEG-21 defines a multimedia framework to enable transparent and augmented use of multimedia resources across a wide range of networks and devices used by different communities. Additionally, MPEG-21 uses a new term "digital item" instead of contents or media, which contains resources and metadata. MPEG-21 has developed from Part 1 to Part 13 (Bormans & Hill, 2002; Rump, 2002). The 11th part of MPEG-21 (ISO/IEC TR 21000-11) specifies the evaluation methods of PATs, which link additional information to the original contents to identify and describe the contents. PATs can be used for description, identification, and IPMP of contents. The purpose of MPEG-21 Part 11 is to prove objective evaluation methods of various PATs and fair measurements. MPEG-21 Part 11 is composed of the methodologies, use case scenarios, requirements, characteristics, and evaluation methods of PATs. Four kinds of PATs methodologies are classified: head insertion, digital signature, fingerprinting, and watermarking. The first two methods require additional storage to link the information to the original content, but the last two methods do not require it. MPEG-21 Part 11 specifies the requirements and evaluation methods of fingerprinting and watermarking (Rump & Jessop, 2003).

PAT Methodologies

PATs-associated content with user information is called metadata. Figure 5 shows the concept of PATs and the environment of PATs in which there are association tools and detection tools. Four kinds of technologies for PATs include headers, digital signatures, fingerprinting, and watermarking (Rump & Jessop, 2003).

PAT-Using headers

Insertion of a header into a file is a simple methodology for associating information with the contents. Within the context of the multimedia framework as specified by various parts of ISOIEC 21000, there can be similar methods of this approach. Figure 6 shows PAT reference model using headers, in which user information—Data 1 and Data 2—are associated with DID (digital item declaration) and resource by association tools (Bormans & Hill, 2002). Users can extract the information with the proper detection tool. In MPEG-21, DID is used for modeling the description of additional information about the resources. Here, user information Data 1 is added into a statement of DID. The other information, Data 2, can be added to the beginning or end of a resource

Figure 5. Generic PATs concept and usage environment

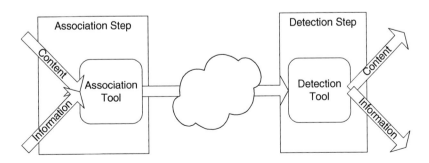

Figure 6. PAT reference model using headers

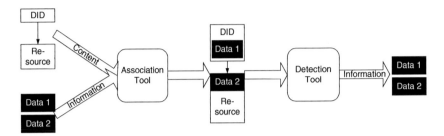

referenced from the DID. Of course, the information can be added to one or several data blocks that are interspersed throughout a resource referenced from the DID.

Digital Signatures

Digital signatures can be used to authenticate information that has been associated using other technologies, including but not limited to information provided via headers. Also, information provided via watermarking and fingerprints can be authenticated using digital signatures. Figure 7 illustrates the concept of a PAT reference model using digital signatures. The user wanting to use digital signatures acquires a certificate from a certification agency and then uses this certificate and a signature algorithm to sign the DID with the ID included in the following steps

- Calculate a hash sum over the DID with the ID
- Use the signature algorithm and the certificate to create a signature
- Add the signature into the DID

Upon receipt of a digitally signed DID the detection tool will

- Calculate a hash sum over the DID—without the signature
- Use the signature algorithm and the association tool's certificate to calculate a "reverse" signature
- Compare this reverse signature with the hash sum

Figure 7. PAT reference model using digital signatures

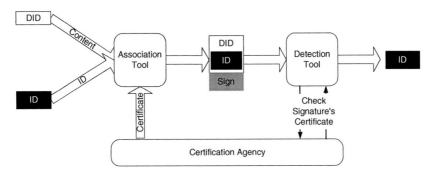

Fingerprinting

Fingerprinting technologies work by extracting characteristics of a piece of content and storing them in a database. Unlike fingerprinting as a watermarking technology, the fingerprinting in the section does not add any information to original contents. It uses the inherent characteristics of the contents as shown in Figure 8. When the technology is presented with an unidentified piece of content, characteristics of that piece are calculated and matched against those stored in the database. In populating the database stage, as shown in Figure 8, fingerprints are generated from the Resource 1 via fingerprint generator, and then corresponding Metadata 1 and the fingerprints are stored in the database.

Figure 8. PAT reference model using fingerprinting

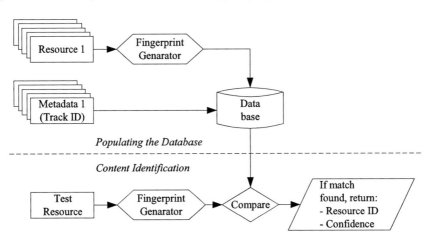

Figure 9. PAT reference model using watermarking

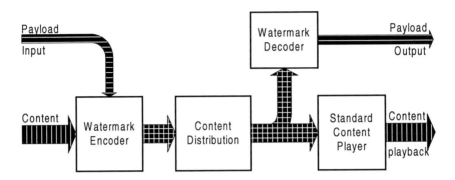

For the content identification, a user wanting resource generates fingerprints via the fingerprint generator. Two kinds of fingerprints are then compared: one from the population stage and ones from the database.

Watermarking

While fingerprints do not affect the signal quality of the content with information persistently associated with it, watermarks do have an effect on the signal quality of the content because they add additional watermarking signals to the original one. The additional watermarking signals degrade the signal quality. As with fingerprinting, watermarking is usually used with nontext-based resources only. As illustrated in Figure 9, the user's information is embedded into the original contents via the watermark encoder. The watermark decoder, though, separates the original contents and the user's information and extracts the user's information.

PAT Requirements

MPEG-21 requirement group specified the PAT requirements as design principles, capability, reliability, resilience, and obtrusiveness. Users can select the most appropriate watermarking technology according to their requirements (Bormans, 2003).

Design Principles

- Good cryptographic practice

  A PAT shall declare explicitly its cryptographic approach. In particular, it shall declare whether it relies on the secrecy of an algorithm or of a global secret.

- Recover from compromise

  A PAT should be able to recover from compromise.

- Complexity

  It shall be possible to implement a PAT on an appropriate terminal without placing undue computational demands on the terminal. The benchmark for this requirement is that computational requirements of the PAT should normally be considerably lower than those of the tool rendering the resource. Some resource types may justify a higher computational demand, for instance, because of their value.

- Multiple technologies

  Where more than one technology is used in different PATs, it shall be possible to determine which technology is in use. This requirement could be fulfilled by the use of a single meta-PAT to indicate which PAT is in use, or by exhaustively checking for the existence of all relevant PATs.

Capability

- Capacity

  A PAT shall declare its information capacity, that is, the maximum amount of information that may be associated with a digital item or resource, measured where appropriate over a standard quantity of the resource (time, bytes, etc.). This capacity shall be sufficient to allow the operation of expected use cases.

- Association of identifiers

  A PAT shall be able to associate an identifier for a digital item or resource with that digital item or resource. Such an identifier shall be compliant with the MPEG-21 digital item identification standard.

- Association of transaction information

A PAT shall be able to associate an identifier for a transaction with a digital item or resource.

- Association of users

  A PAT shall be able to associate an identifier for a user with a digital item or resource.

- Association of temporal information

  A PAT shall be able to associate temporal information, such as a time stamp, with a digital item or resource.

- Multiple associations

  A PAT shall be capable of associating multiple sets of information with a digital item or a resource. The information shall be independently retrievable. The different sets of information may be associated in different ways with different characteristics.

- Validation

  A PAT shall provide a capability to verify the authenticity of an association and to resolve conflicts in associated information.

- Removal

  A PAT shall allow a user creating an association to change or remove it. This does not imply that a watermark must be reversible—a user creating an association by using a watermark can always revert to the unwatermarked version. However, it may be important to be able to change or delete the associated information when this is not embedded in a resource.

- Streaming application

  A PAT shall be usable in a streaming environment.

- Off-line use

  A PAT shall declare whether it is usable in systems that are never connected to networks. Also, a PAT shall declare whether it is usable in systems that are only intermittently connected to networks.

Reliability

- Repeatability

  A PAT shall declare its performance with respect to repeatability, that is, the probability that under given circumstances a terminal using the tool on the same digital item or resource multiple times will recover the same associated information (whether this was the originally associated information or not).

- Accuracy

  A PAT shall declare its performance with respect to accuracy, that is, the probability that under given circumstances a terminal using the tool on a digital item or resource will recover the same associated information as that was originally associated. This requirement refers to degradation after adaptation rather than attack.

Resilience

- Adaptation

  The association created by a PAT shall be able to survive the types of adaptation typically encountered in the life of a digital item and its resources. These adaptations include conversions to and from the analog domain.

- Malicious Attack

  It is intended that the association created by a PAT shall persist under adaptations performed with the deliberate intent of preventing the recovery of the information from a digital item or resource. In the event that such damage occurs, the perceived quality of a digital item or resource shall no longer be fit for the purpose for which it was intended. For example, removing a watermark from audio or visual material should degrade its quality so that the listening or viewing experience is no longer satisfactory.

- Forensic Survival

  When the association is removed deliberately and without the authorization of the user creating it, sufficient evidence of the former existence of an association shall remain to allow a forensic examination to identify that an association formerly existed.

Obtrusiveness

- Audibility, Visibility, and So Forth

  A PAT shall not create impairments in rendered resources that exceed certain well-defined limits.

Evaluation Methods for PATs

This section contains, for each characteristic listed above, a "procedure" on how to conduct an evaluation. The evaluation procedure is for the characteristics that must be tested. Inherent characteristics must also be evaluated and weighted in importance for a given application. The six types of dimensions of evaluation criteria for PATs are reliability, perceptibility, size/payload, robustness, granularity, and computational complexity. Until now, these evaluation methods have not been completed and are under construction. This section only treats the evaluation methods of audio and video watermarking in MPEG-21 Part 11 (Rump & Jessop, 2003).

Evaluation of Reliability

This evaluation is to measure the reliability of the watermarking detection with several statistical indexes, which are as follows:

- False negative and false positive
- Correct recognition rate
- Rate of unidentified
- Bit error rate

Evaluation of Perceptibility

Perceptibility describes how perceptible changes of audiovisual content are due to using a persistent association process. Therefore, this yardstick deals with subjective and objective testing methods that estimate the degradation of persistently associated content in comparison to the respective original content. Subjective testing means that human beings are involved in the test, whereas objective measurements try to simulate the outcome of subjective tests by means of a machine.

- Audio watermarking

  Without being exhaustive, Table 10 lists largely standardized audio quality evaluation methodologies that are often used for quality assessments. This

Table 10. Evaluation of perceptibility in audio watermarking

Test Methods	Test Type	Description	Target Quality
BS.1116	Subj.	The ITU Recommendation BS.1116 assesses small impairments for high-quality audio material.	High
Pair Test	Subj.	This test assesses very small impairments for very high quality audio material. It can be used for proving audibility of impairments.	Very high
MUSHRA	Subj.	The ITU Recommendation ITU-R BS.1534 is for medium audio quality.	Medium
PEAQ	Obj.	Draft new Recommendation ITU-R BS.[10/20] assesses medium-quality audio material.	Medium–high
PAQM	Obj.	PAQM estimates the signals on the cochlea and compares the representation of the reference signal with that of the signal being tested. As such, the PAQM system tries to estimate test results on a scale used for BS.1116 tests.	High
NMR	Obj.	The interesting output value is the overall NMRtotal value expressed in dB to indicate the averaged energy ratio of the signal difference with respect to a just masked signal (masking threshold).	Medium–high

table distinguishes the test methods in terms of test types which include subjective and objective and target quality which is from very high to medium quality.

Selecting an appropriate body of test items is most important for all tests mentioned in the above table. Typically, items should not exceed 15–20 seconds in length and should be selected by a preselection test before the actual listening test. It is highly recommended to indicate audio signals that are known to be critical for audio coding since many watermarking schemes apply methods that are also used in the field of audio coding. The perceptibility evaluation methods of video watermarking have not yet been provided.

Evaluation of Payload Size

The payload size of a watermark is the amount of information that is carried by the watermark. Depending on the underlying media type, this amount may be most naturally measured in bits/second (audio or video) or bits/sample (audio, video images). There is a direct trade-off between payload size and other parameters, such as robustness, visibility, and error rates. For measuring the payload size, we need to distinguish three classes of watermarking systems:

- Watermarking systems with a fixed payload size
- Watermarking systems with a variable payload size
- Watermarking systems in which the payload size is determined by the embedder

Evaluation of Robustness

Robustness is the ability of a persistent association method to withstand signal modifications. These modifications, often called attacks, are divided into intentional and unintentional attacks. Several bodies, such as SDMI, EBU, and others, are specified in a list of standard attacks for audio signals that might degrade the watermark. Currently, the attack method of video watermarking is not provided, but will be specified in version 2. The attack methods of only audio watermarking are listed in Table 11.

Table 11. Attacks on audio watermarking systems

Impairment Class	Impairment Type	Parameter Types
Perceptual coding	ISO/MPEG Layer II as defined in ISO/IEC ISO/IEC 11172-3	
	ISO/MPEG Layer III as defined in ISO/IEC ISO/IEC 11172-3	At various bit rates
	ISO/MPEG-2/4 Advanced Audio Coding as defined in ISO/IEC 13818-7 and ISO/IEC 14496-3.	
	ISO/MPEG-4 High-Efficiency Advanced Audio Coding as defined in ISO/IEC 14496-3:2004	
	Commercial codecs such as Dolby AC-3, Dolby E, Microsoft WMA9	
Tandem coding		Using various perceptual coders and bit rates
DA/AD conversion		Several times
Filters	High pass	
	Low pass	Various frequencies and roll-off
	Band pass	
	All pass	
Down-mixing, up-mixing	Multichannel to stereo	
	Stereo to mono	
	Multichannel to Dolby Surround	
	Dolby Prologic	
Signal addition	Pink noise	dB levels relative to peak/average source level
	White noise	
	Voice-over	
Time scale modifications	Changing the sampling rate	
	Pitch-corrected time scaling	Various speeds
	Speed change (render items at non-nominal sampling frequency)	
Studio techniques	Pitch shifting	
	Multiband equalization	Various levels
	Echo addition	
Cropping or excerpting of content		Various lengths of excerpts
Combinations of the above		

Evaluation of Granularity

The term *granularity* describes the minimum consecutive amount of audio and/or video content that must be provided in order to retrieve the association bound to that content at a certain confidence level. For watermarking systems, this is related to the length and repetition cycle of the embedded message. The evaluation method of granularity of the watermarking system is to measure the amount of time of audio/video needed to detect the persistent associated data, that is, one mark within x% confidence.

Evaluation of Complexity

The work flow required to perform the PAT process should be described to allow the evaluation of complexity. This must include all steps in the process, including, if required, content decompression and remarking. The test methods of complexity for audio/video watermarking are embedding/remarking and extracting the payload.

Future Trends

The previously described MPEG IPMP is the international standard for DRM. Compared with the initial hook's approach of IPMP, IPMPX further enhanced interoperability of the IPMP system with more specific normative elements. Currently, broadcasting contents such as terrestrial, satellite, and cable TV, is carried over an MPEG-2 system. In the future, Web casting and mobile broadcasting contents will be transported over the MPEG-4 system. Therefore, MPEG-2/MPEG-4 IPMPXs will become an essential area for DRM development in various multimedia service systems. In the MPEG-21 multimedia framework, IPMP is only in the initial stages. However, MPEG-21 IPMP is also a vital area of the standards because MPEG-21 covers content distribution and transaction.

MPEG-21 Part 11, though, mainly deals with evaluation methods of audio watermarking, leaving video, text, and still image watermarking to version 2. In particular, broadcasting environments that are not considered in the current MPEG-21 PAT document must be included in upcoming versions. In actual broadcasting applications, video data is more important than audio data. Even

Table 12. Technical requirements in video watermarking for broadcasting application

Requirements	Description
Visibility	Perceptual degree of watermarks in video contents
	Subjective or objective test
Computational complexity	Computational load for embedding and detecting with computational amount, memory access speed, processor cycle, and so forth.
Implementation complexity	Designation one domain of spatial, frequency, and bitstream domains
Robustness	Survival for various attacks of watermark
Payload	Amount of payload with bits or bytes
Granularity	Minimum data segment for reliable detection
Reliability	Exact detection rate
Security	Watermarking security according to secret key or algorithm openness
Multiple duplication	Capability for detecting one of various technologies used
Time delay	Maximum time delay for embedding or detecting a watermark
Watermark detection	Blind or nonblind detection

though many reports and papers about video watermarking have been published, more evaluation tools to compare the performance of algorithms are needed. Furthermore, additional technical guidelines for the design of video watermarking systems are essential. Version 2 of MPEG-21 Part 11 must include video watermarking evaluation methods and technical requirements. Table 12 and Table 13 propose technical requirements and attack lists for robustness test in video watermarking for broadcasting application.

Figure 10 illustrates watermarking system development in broadcasting environments. At the watermark embedding stage, a watermark can be inserted in SDI input signal, MPEG-2 encoder, or compressed bitstream. Of course, watermark can be attacked on the same signal as the embedding format.

For robustness against compression, MJPEG, MPEG-2 4:2:2 50 Mbps and MPEG-2 4:2:0 2–6Mbps must be tested. Other commercial formats such as Panasonic/DV, JVC/Digital-S, Sony/DV, and Sony/Beta-SX, must also be considered. In the future, MPEG-4 video encoding may be tested. The above

Table 13. Attacks for robustness test in video watermarking

Impairment Class	Impairment Type	Parameter Types
Perceptual coding	MPEG-2	
	MPEG-4	
	MJPEG	At various bit rates
	Commercial codecs (Sony DV, Panasonic DV, JVD/Ditiala-S, Sony Beta-SX, etc.)	
Geometric	Rotation	Various angles and scaling ratio
	Scaling	
Filters	High pass	
	Low pass	Various frequencies and roll-off
	Band pass	
	Median	
Conversions	AD/DA	
	NTSC/PAL	
	Aspect ratio	Several times
	Frame rate	
	Line scan	
	Color space	
Signal addition	White noise	Various speeds
Cropping or excerpting of content		
Combinations of the above		

Figure 10. Watermarking system development in broadcasting environment

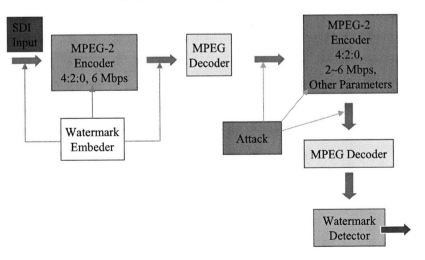

commercial format, MJPEG, and MPEG-2 4:2:2 50 Mbps are used in a production chain. For MPEG-2 4:2:0 2–6 Mbps, multiple times of compression must be declared with different GOP size. For digital and analog filtering, picture aspect-ratio conversion, frame-rate conversion, line-scan conversion, adding white noise, and color-space conversion tests are required. In the aspect-ratio conversion test, 4:3 and 16:9 conversions are examined. For frame-rate conversion, 24 Hz, 25 Hz, and 30 Hz are tested. In line-scan conversion, progressive and interlace tests are required. These filtering operations happen very often in the production chain of broadcasting environments. Geometric changes often occur in production chains. Cropping, shifting, and scaling tests are particularly important. Change rates in these operations, such as random and linear cropping, must be declared. Random cropping means cropping of the inner part of the contents, and linear cropping refers to the side of the contents. The above evaluation methods may be needed for a general test of PAT in broadcasting environments. These test methods are summarized in Table 13.

Of course, other evaluation methods must be specified for various applications in MPEG-21. The above-suggested evaluation methods of PAT often occur in a production chain of broadcasting environments. Thus, at least the above attack lists must be examined to measure the performance of video watermarking algorithms. The technical requirements and attack lists for robustness test will be a useful guideline for developing the second version of MPEG-21 Part 11 Evaluation Tools for Persistent Association Technologies.

Conclusions

Recent developments in IPMP and watermarking technologies are related to MPEG international standards. In particular, MPEG-2/MPEG-4 IPMP, its watermarking technology, and various evaluation methods of watermarking technology of MPEG-21 Part 11 are essential. In MPEG-2 Part 11 and MPEG-4 Part 13, watermarking technology may be used for intellectual property protection, and specific technical parameters, syntax, and corresponding semantics about audio and video watermarking. These watermarking parameters are used to extract the watermark payload from the contents and report results of watermark extraction. The watermarking technology in MPEG-2/4 IPMP as a normative standard may be an important tool for intellectual property protection in various applications.

Moreover, MPEG-21 Part 11 is a technical report and deals with technical requirements and evaluation methods of PATs including watermarking technology. The current version of MPEG-21 Part 11 covers only audio watermarking and fingerprinting, and may provide reliable evaluation methods for various audio watermarking technologies. Suggested technical requirements and evaluation methods for video watermarking technology may be an important basis for developing the version 2 of MPEG-21 Part 11 and testing various video watermarking technologies. Finally, watermarking technologies above MPEG-2/4/21 are still being developed and will affect the industrial world as intellectual property protection and reliable evaluation tools for various watermarking technologies

References

Bormans, J. (2003). *MPEG-21 requirements v.1.5, ISO/IEC JTC 1/SC 29/ WG 11/N5873*.

Bormans, J., & Hill, K. (2002). *MPEG-21 overview v.5, ISO/IEC JTC 1/SC 29/WG 11/N5231*.

Cox, I.J., Miller, M.L., & Bloom, J.A., (2002). *Digital watermarking*. Morgan Kaufmann.

ISO/IEC FDIS 13818-11: 2003 Part 11: IPMP on MPEG-2 systems. (2003).

Johnson, N.F., Duric, Z., & Jajodia, S. (2001). *Information hiding techniques for steganography and digital watermarking—Attacks and countermeasures*. Kluwer Academic.

Katzenbeisser, S., & Petitcolas, F.A.P. (2000). *Information hiding techniques for steganography and digital watermarking*. Artech House.

Koenen, R. (2001). *Intellectual property management and protection in MPEG standards, ISO/IEC JTC 1/SC 29/WG 11/N3943*.

Koenen, R. (2002). *Overview of the MPEG-4 standard, ISO/IEC JTC 1/ SC 29/WG 11/N4668*.

Lacy, J., Rump, N., & Kudumakis, P. (1998). *MPEG-4 intellectual property management and protection (IPMP) overview and applications document, ISO/IEC JTC 1/SC 29/WG 11/N2614*.

Ming, J., Chiariglione, F., Alberti, C., Kudumakis, P., Kaneko, I., & Schultz, C. (2003). *MPEG IPMP extensions FAQ WD 1.0, ISO/IEC JTC 1/SC 29/WG 11/N5790.*

Puri, A., & Chen, T. (2000). *Multimedia systems, standards, and networks.* Marcel Dekker.

Rump, N. (2002). *MPEG-21 MDS—Frequently Asked Questions (FAQ) v.5, ISO/IEC JTC 1/SC 29/WG 11/N5875.*

Rump. N., & Jessop, P. (2003). *Evaluation tools for persistent association technologies, ISO/IEC JTC 1/SC 29/WG 11/N5875.*

Schultz, C.A. (2002). *FPDAM ISO/IEC 14496-1:2001/AMD3, ISO/IEC JTC 1/SC 29/WG 11/N4701.*

Wang, Y., Ostermann, J., & Zhang, Y.Q. (2002). *Video processing and communications.* Prentice Hall.

Chapter VIII

Time-Variant Watermarks for Digital Videos:
An MPEG-Based Approach

Ernst L. Leiss[1]
University of Houston, USA

Abstract

Watermarks provide a means of embedding information into digital videos that can be used for a variety of purposes, such as establishing ownership, tracing origin of copies, and so forth. We outline an approach that permits a significant increase in the amount of information that can be accommodated in a watermark, namely time-variant watermarks. The approach is formulated assuming the video is represented in an MPEG format. Implementation issues of time-variant watermarks are discussed, as are their advantages over the usual time-invariant watermarks, with emphasis on defeating attacks using filtering, cropping, resizing, and other standard methods used to defeat watermarks, such as changing existing frames, as well as new attacks, such as removing, repeating, or permuting frames.

Introduction and Motivation

All digital information has the property that it can be copied perfectly (Leiss, 1982). The issue of perfect copies has a number of implications for data security and integrity. For example, it implies that it is impossible to distinguish a copy from the original; thus, if information is used to control access to resources, anyone who is able to copy the information will have access to those resources. Another implication is the difficulty of establishing true ownership; thus, two parties may each claim to be the legitimate owner of digital information.

Digital watermarks are an attempt to address the problem of perfect copies in digital data. While they are not foolproof, they are a workable approach provided a few conditions are satisfied. Briefly, when using a digital watermark additional information is embedded in or superimposed on the original images. As concerns about establishing ownership of digital media have escalated in recent years (witness the claims by the music industry blaming reduced sales of CDs on illicit file sharing), watermarks have attracted increased attention.

We may differentiate visible and invisible watermarks. Visible watermarks are most frequently used for video, TV transmissions, and similar media; in a fixed location in each image or frame, a small logo identifying the transmitter is inserted, obliterating, or obscuring that part of the image. Another type of visible watermark is provided by IBM's project watermarking a portion of the Vatican Libraries' holdings of images. Clearly, visible watermarks suffer from the fact that they can be easily removed, thereby removing (a portion of) the information contained in the watermark.[2] For this reason, invisible watermarks are preferred. Invisible watermarks change certain characteristics of the image, but this is done in a way that is not noticeable to the naked eye. In this chapter, we will consider exclusively invisible watermarks.

Depending on the objectives one wishes to accomplish, either robust or fragile watermarks are available. Robust watermarks are of interest if one wishes to attach an indelible stamp of ownership; clearly the methods employed must be robust, that is, impervious to various operations, such as rescaling, filtering, or superimposing an additional watermark. A variety of schemes designed to achieve these objectives have been proposed; see for example Barni, Bartolini, Cappellini, and Piva (1998), Bender, Gruhl, and Morimoto (1995), Berghel and O'Gorman (1997), Cox, Killian, Leighton, and Shamoon (1997), Duan, King, Chan, and Xu (1998), Lee, Oh, Baek, and Lee (1999), Matsui and

Tanaka (1994), and Tanaka, Nakamura, and Matsui (1990). Fragile watermarks, on the other hand, are designed to deteriorate after certain operations have been applied, including copying. While robust and fragile watermarks can be considered complementary, it is the robust ones that hold the promise of establishing ownership. In this chapter, we will consider exclusively robust watermarks.

One aspect that has not received much attention in the literature is the amount of information that can be encoded in a watermark. Clearly, robustness is directly correlated with the redundancy of the watermark; for example, if a certain small pattern is repeated many times in a watermark, the removal of the watermark through cropping an image is foiled. Similarly, the invisibility of a watermark is related to the extent of changes in the information that makes up the media. All this imposes certain limits on the amount of information that can be encoded in the watermark. To alleviate the problem of insufficient information available in the watermark, we propose the notion of time-variant watermarks. In this scheme, different frames of a video (or an audio) file will be tied to different watermarks. Not only does this make it much more difficult to defeat the watermark, it also lets one encode significantly more information in the watermark while permitting a great deal of redundancy and repetition. This redundancy in the watermark information can in turn be exploited to achieve increased protection of intellectual property.

All existing watermark schemes, visible and invisible, robust and fragile, are time invariant; this means that the embedded watermark is the same, independent of the frame in which it is embedded. In contrast, our time-variant watermark scheme permits the embedding of sequences of watermarks into the medium to be watermarked. Typically, the watermark will consist of a number of frames that may or may not be significantly smaller than the number of frames of the medium in which the watermark is embedded. If it is smaller, then as in time-invariant watermark schemes, the watermark sequence is repeated until the end of the medium in which it is embedded is reached. This allows one either to increase the amount of information that is encoded in the aggregate watermark or to reduce the amount of information that is contained in a single watermark frame. However, the case where the number of watermark frames is equal to the number of frames of the file to be watermarked is most interesting, as the watermark can then be used to insert sequencing information that is invisible to the viewer. This information can be used to detect, and demonstrate if required, whether original frames have been removed, permuted, or repeated.

We sketch our approach to time-variant, invisible, robust waterworks based on video media; an analogous approach can be formulated based on audio or similar media. An important aspect of any video is the amount of data required to represent it faithfully. Attempts to reduce the size of a video lead naturally to data compression techniques. Thus, we assume JPEG encoding for individual (still) images as well as intracoded frames. We assume a standard MPEG organization of the video sequence into I (intracoded), P (predictive-coded), and B (bidirectionally predictive-coded) frames. We outline our approach's advantages, in particular increased imperviousness against a variety of attempts to defeat the watermarking process, through filtering, cropping, resizing, and other operations, and quantify the increase in information content that can be accommodated in the new watermark.

We note that some of the objectives one pursues in using watermarks can be attained by other means, primarily encryption-based approaches (Leiss, 1982). For a discussion of these, see, for example, Chen (1995) and Chen and Leiss (1996). The current work is primarily based on research reported in two MS theses (Yang, 1999; Yang, 2001). The chapter will address some technical aspects of the proposed new scheme; however, it will also pay attention to the ultimate goal of protecting intellectual property.

The remainder of this chapter will provide a very brief review of what we expect of watermarks and what purposes we hope to achieve by using them. Then we give a thumbnail sketch of the MPEG organization of a video file, including the representation of color and the JPEG technique for still images, to the extent to which we need this information to explain some pertinent aspects of our approach. In the subsequent section, we outline the notion of time-variant watermarks and indicate the benefits obtained in this way. We conclude this chapter by summarizing the approach and its advantages and by giving some pointers for future work.

Requirements for Watermarks

We briefly review some aspects of watermarks pertinent to the work reported in this chapter (Bush, Funk, & Wolthusen, 1999; Chun, Hong, Oh, Shin, & Park, 1998; Cox et al., 1997; Hsu & Wu, 1998, 1999; Koch & Zhao, 1995). The overall objective is the protection of intellectual property (Berghel &

O'Gorman, 1997), in our case, the intellectual property contained in a digital video file.

As already stated, our interest is in invisible, robust watermarks. Robustness means that the watermark must be impervious to attempts at removing, destroying, obliterating, or overwriting it. Any attempt to do so should result in a severe and very noticeable degradation of the image before the watermark is lost. Given the environment in which the watermark is used, the process of embedding the watermark must be compatible with MPEG processes; more generally, watermarks must be able to survive both lossless and lossy compression techniques, as well as other common video processing techniques, such as scaling, cropping, resizing, and filtering (which in the case of color video includes changes in the color scheme, such as reducing the color palette [e.g., from 16 bit to 8 bit]).

The watermark should allow the owner to demonstrate ownership conclusively (for example, to a judge or adjudicator). This implies that sufficient information be present that can be used for this purpose. Below, we will argue that none of the existing watermark schemes fully attains this goal. The principal reason for this is the fact that within the context of MPEG-based compression, it is virtually impossible to guarantee that entire scenes have not been removed from the video nor that original scenes have been permuted or repeated.[3]

Finally, we mention three important practical aspects of any watermark; failure to satisfy any one of them will render the approach unacceptable in practice:

1. The insertion of the watermark must not affect the perceived quality of the video. While the watermark information is, of course, embedded in the signal, this must not affect the **perceived** quality of the signal.

2. The process of inserting the watermark must not substantially increase the overall complexity of generating and using the video, at least not significantly beyond what MPEG already requires.[4] This is the reason why certain cryptography-based signature schemes (see Chen, 1995; Chen & Leiss, 1996) are not acceptable in practice, even though they could be made arbitrarily secure.

3. It must be possible to demonstrate in a legal forum that only the true owner of a video is capable of embedding the watermark. If this is not possible in a legally binding way, the utility of a watermark for the protection of intellectual property is seriously compromised.

The Basic Organization of a Video File

We review the basic organization of video files, with special emphasis on compression aspects. We start with JPEG which forms the basis of MPEG, make a brief detour to color representation, and then outline the structure of a typical MPEG file which classifies each frame into one of three types.

MPEG is essentially a (family of) method(s) for compressing a video file. An ordinary 24-bit image with 640x480 pixels requires almost 1 MB of space (high-definition digital images would require even more). Since there are 30 frames per second in a typical digital video, a one-hour video amounts to about 100 GB of data. This amount of raw data contains, however, a great deal of (naturally occurring[5]) redundancy, the reduction of which is the goal of the use of (one of) the MPEG techniques.[6] All MPEG schemes are based on the JPEG technique, applied to (some of the) individual frames of the video.

JPEG (Wallace, 1992) is a standardized compression technique for full-color or gray-scale images of realistic digital images.[7] It is based on a lossy compression technique known as the baseline method; this is a scheme that employs the DCT.[8,9] It is not unusual to obtain a compression ratio (uncompressed file size compared with compressed file size) of 15 or more with excellent image quality[10]; this compression ratio can be even higher if some deterioration of the image quality is acceptable (Sonka, Hlavac, & Boyle, 1998). JPEG is considered a very popular and efficient coding scheme for continuous-tone still images. It also forms the basis of the MPEG family of approaches to encoding digital video. Before we describe MPEG-2 (which is at present the main representative of the MPEG schemes applicable to digital video), we provide a brief explanation of digital color and its representation.

Humans perceive colors as combinations of the primary colors red, blue, and yellow (the typical rainbow arrangement). Only slightly deviating from this, video hardware generally uses the RGB model (red, green, blue) wherein a pixel is associated with a triple (RGB) representing the color intensities; (000) represents black in this scheme (absence of everything), (kkk) white (presence of everything), (k00) pure red, and so on, where the value k is the quantization granularity for each primary color.[11] Thus, if k is 255 (a very common choice since it amounts to 8 bits or 1 byte), there are 2^{8+8+8} or 2^{24} different representable colors. Clearly, a smaller k will correspond to less faithfulness in the color scheme, and a larger value to greater faithfulness. With few exceptions (a contrary example might be a fairly uniform sky that continuously goes from light blue to gray), color schemes with more than 24 bits (eight for each of the three primaries) result in improvements in image quality that are virtually imperceptible to the naked human eye.

In practical applications, the RGB signal is usually transformed into one that is displayable without major artifacts on black-and-white devices (including printers!), namely the (Y, C_b, C_r) representation, where Y is the luminance, C_b is the blue chrominance, and C_r the red chrominance. (R, G, B) and (Y, C_b, C_r) correspond to each other linearly (Benoit, 1997):

$$Y = 0.587\ G + 0.299R + 0.114\ B$$

$$C_b = 0.564\ (B - Y)$$

$$C_r = 0.713\ (R - Y)$$

It is important for the designer of data compression techniques to understand that the human eye is less perceptive to color than to luminance. This implies for natural images that the chrominance component of a signal can tolerate a more reduced bandwidth than the luminance, without affecting significantly the perceived image quality. Typically, the bandwidth for chrominance may be chosen to be one half to one quarter that of luminance without affecting human perception (Benoit, 1997).

Lossy JPEG compression consists of six main steps (Wallace, 1992):

1. Decomposition of the image into blocks of size 8x8 pixels; each block can be viewed as a 64-point discrete signal which is a function of the two spatial dimensions.

2. The DCT is applied to each 8x8 matrix which generates a new 8x8 matrix consisting of the coefficients of increasing spatial frequency. These coefficients can be viewed as the relative amount of the two-dimensional spatial frequencies in the 64-point input signal. The coefficient with frequency 0 in both dimensions is referred to as the DC coefficient, while the other 63 are the AC coefficients.

3. Quantization (or discretization) is applied to the 64 DCT coefficients to yield an 8 x 8 quantization table $Q(u,v)$ consisting of integers. As a result of the DCT operation, the values in Q increase from left to right and from top to bottom. This takes into account the peculiarities of human vision,

in particular the fact that the human eye does not distinguish very fine details below a certain luminance level.

4.   The 63 AC coefficients in Q are concatenated into a zigzag scan; in terms of (u,v), this scan is

DC: 00
AC: 01   10
                                        20   11   02
                                    03   12   21   30
                                40   31   22   13   04
                            05   14   23   32   41   50
                        60   51   42   33   24   15   06
                    07   16   25   34   43   52   61   70
                        71   62   53   44   35   26   17
                            27   36   45   54   63   72
                                73   64   55   46   37
                                    47   56   65   74
                                        75   66   57
                                            67   76
                                                77

This helps in entropy coding by placing low-frequency coefficients, which are more important in perception, before high-frequency ones.

5.   Run-length coding replaces a sequence of identical values by one indica-tion of that value followed by the number of these values in the sequence. This is where major compression in JPEG occurs, since from a certain point p on in the sequence of the 63 AC coefficients of the zigzag scan, we can replace the remainder by zeroes without affecting the visual quality of the image. The value of p is a parameter in this process: if p is small, say 5, the image quality is reduced and the compression greatly improved; if p is large, say 30, the image quality is virtually unaffected but at the cost of reduced compression.[12]

6.   The final step consists of applying Huffman coding to the resulting sequences; this further reduces the amount of data to be transmitted.

MPEG is based on JPEG and attempts to remove temporal redundancies (redundancies that occur from one frame to the next) after JPEG has been applied to remove the spatial redundancies within each frame. Temporal redundancies are detected by motion estimation whereby portions of images in consecutive frames are matched up. There are three fundamental types of pictures that are distinguished in this process, namely, I-pictures, P-pictures, and B-pictures. Intra or I-pictures are encoded without any reference to other frames, while Predicted or P-pictures and Bi-directionally Predicted or B-pictures depend on other frames, in the case of a P-picture only on the preceding I- or P-picture, in the case of a B-picture on I- and P-pictures both preceding or following it. The number of P-pictures between two consecutive I-pictures is an important parameter: since much redundancy is detected (and removed!) between I-pictures, making this value large results in more savings. However, making it too large will affect the quality of the interpolated image frames. B-pictures fill in the gaps between I- (and P-) pictures and provide the largest savings. The objective is to have as few I- (and P-) pictures as possible without affecting the visual quality of the video. Since typically there are many more B-pictures than I- or P-pictures,[13] ratios of 200 can be achieved in video compression without sacrificing a great deal of quality (Sonka et al., 1998).[14]

Motion estimation involves defining a motion vector, which establishes the correlation between a "departure" zone in the first picture and an "arrival" zone in the second. This is done on the basis of macro blocks (blocks of size 16 x 16, or four 8 x 8 blocks of luminance, one 8 x 8 block for red chrominance, and one 8 x 8 block for blue chrominance[15]). This allocation of four times the amount of data for luminance than for each of the chrominance values reflects the differing levels of perception of the naked human eye.

Implementing Time-Variant Watermarks

First, we will briefly review the process of embedding a (time-invariant) watermark into an MPEG-2 digital video file. Then we will describe the differences between this classic approach and our time-variant method, outline the advantages of our approach, and indicate how it can be used to attain higher levels of protection of intellectual property.

Numerous approaches to embedding (time-invariant) watermarks into images have been described in the literature. They can be grouped into two major categories, namely, methods that embed the watermark by modifying directly the intensity of (some or all of) the pixels of an image (Bender et al., 1995; Nikolaidis & Pitas, 1998), and methods that act upon (some or all of) the coefficients of an underlying transform domain (most common are the discrete cosine transform or DCT and the discrete Fourier transform or DFT) (Barni et al., 1998; Boland, O Ruanaidh, & Dautzenberg, 1995; Cox et al., 1997; Duan et al., 1998; Koch, Rindfrey, & Zhao, 1994; Lee et al., 1999). While we concentrate on Yang (1999) and Yang (2001) for the method described in Cox et al. (1997), it should be clear that any of the domain-based approaches would do nicely in an MPEG environment. The underlying idea is the following notion known as spread spectrum technique: The frequency domain of the image to be watermarked is viewed as a communication channel and the watermark is viewed as a signal that is transmitted through it. Thus, the watermark is spread over many frequencies so that the energy change in any one frequency is small enough to render it imperceptible. The objective is, of course, that the embedded watermark survive common signal manipulations (such as lossy and lossless compression, filtering, conversions between digital and analog representation) and geometric manipulations (such as cropping, scaling, translation, and rotation). In addition to these, superposition of one or more additional watermarks should also be detectable. Finally, manipulations related to sequencing of pictures in a video are of concern; these include, in particular, adding new or removing original pictures. Another requirement relates to the ability to demonstrate conclusively to a judge one's ownership of the original video, that is, the owner, and only the owner, should be able to do this. We refer to the literature for the technical details of inserting the (time-invariant) watermark. For our purposes, it suffices to note that techniques exist which meet the stated requirements and which are sufficiently simple and efficient to permit their implementation within the context of an MPEG-2 video file without increasing the complexity of the operations involved in generating, viewing (or possibly removing the watermark), or adjudicating a watermarked video (Bush et al., 1999).

An important aspect of watermarking within an MPEG context is determining which pictures of a video file are to be watermarked. On the basis of our brief description, it is clear that the watermarking process involves individual frames or pictures which are subjected to JPEG compression. This implies that the watermark should be inserted into the AC coefficients that occur quite early in the zigzag scan, since later AC coefficients may simply be removed (set to 0) without affecting the visual quality of the image. There are different techniques that ensure that the injection of energy (that is, the embedding of the watermark) into these coefficients does not distort their values unduly. As noted in Benoit

(1997) and Katzenbeisser and Petitcolas (2000), this approach is robust and affects the visual quality only minimally. Given the process of MPEG compression, we have three types of pictures: I-, P-, and B-pictures. Since only I-pictures are independently encoded in MPEG, watermark insertion concentrates on I-pictures. However, this does not imply that P- or B-pictures are unaffected, in as much as they depend on (watermarked) I-pictures (as they are interpolated based on these pictures) and thus are indirectly watermarked.

Time-invariant watermarking schemes embed the same watermark picture[16] into all pictures that are explicitly watermarked (essentially all the I-pictures). In contrast, our approach to providing time-variant marking schemes takes a watermark *video* consisting of a number N_0 of pictures and embeds this video in the usual way, frame by frame.[17] This number N_0 is a parameter; clearly if $N_0 = 1$, then we have the ordinary, time-invariant watermarking scheme. If N_0 is greater than 1, the approach is time variant. A sensible upper limit for N_0 is the number of I-pictures in the original video; going beyond this value creates problems since in this case, the watermark video would have to be explicitly embedded not only in the I-pictures, but also in (some or all) P- or B-pictures.

The information contained in the N_0 frames of the watermark is entirely up to the user. It is, however, useful to provide some sequencing information in the watermark video because this will enable one to ensure that no original pictures had been removed from the watermarked video, especially if N_0 is equal to the total number of I-pictures in the video.[18] Note that it is this operation that traditional, time-invariant methods are entirely unable to detect since the removal of an entire scene (starting with an I-picture) is undetectable. Another subversion that time-invariant watermarks are unable to prevent, but that time-variant watermarking handles with ease, is given by the permutation and the repetition of scenes in the video.[19] Furthermore, while in traditional watermarking, information is injected into the signal corresponding to each of the watermarked pictures, the time invariance of this information is extremely wasteful. In contrast, although our approach will not inject any more energy into each of the watermarked images than the traditional methods, the information content our approach allows us to embed is dramatically greater, since it changes from one watermark frame to the next.

In summary, we present the following table which indicates in what way an attack against a watermark is foiled; here INV indicates that the traditional, time-invariant watermarking scheme will attain guarding against this attack or manipulation (preserving the watermark), while VAR indicates that this is achieved by time-variant watermarks.

lossless compression:	INV, VAR
lossy compression:	INV, VAR
filtering:	INV, VAR
conversion	
(digital <-> analog representation):	INV, VAR
cropping:	INV, VAR
scaling:	INV, VAR
translation:	INV, VAR
rotation:	INV, VAR
superposition of another watermark:	INV, VAR
adding new frames:	INV, VAR
removing original frames:	**VAR**
permuting original scenes:	**VAR**
repeating original scenes or frames:	**VAR**
legal demonstration of ownership:	INV, VAR

Conclusions and Future Work

We have outlined an approach to embedding time-variant watermarks in digital video files that permits a significant increase in the amount of information over conventional, time-invariant watermarks while retaining all the advantages of conventional watermarking. The approach was formulated assuming the video file is represented in an MPEG-2 format, involving I-pictures, P-pictures, and B-pictures. In view of the standard data compression algorithm underlying MPEG-2, frames of the watermark video are embedded in the I-pictures, that is, those pictures of the video that are encoded independently, using JPEG techniques. We discussed implementation issues of time-variant watermarks as well as their advantages over the usual time-invariant watermarks. In particular, this watermarking scheme permits one to defeat not just the usual attacks involving filtering, cropping, resizing, and changing color schemes, but also to guard against new attacks, such as removing or repeating frames as well as permuting scenes of the video. An important aspect of the technique is that the complexity of the operations of embedding the watermark, viewing the watermarked video, removing the watermark from the video, and the adjudication of the watermark remains unaffected by the watermark. Specifically, embedding of the watermark is incorporated in the MPEG-2 compression scheme and adds an insignificant amount of work; viewing the video is completely unaffected by the watermark, removing the watermark amount to MPEG-2 compression, and adjudication is essentially equivalent to extracting the watermark (which is, in turn, the same as removing it).

Future work on this topic involves the development of a prototype test bed for the study of time-variant watermarks. This test bed should be based on an open-source MPEG-2 implementation so that the integration of the watermarking process with the MPEG compression will be transparent. This should also permit a more detailed study of complexity issues that arise in this process; while the overall time complexity of embedding watermarks is dominated by the MPEG-2 process of data compression, it would be useful to be able to quantify this more precisely.

References

Barni, M., Bartolini, F., Cappellini, V., & Piva, A. (1998). A DCT-domain system for robust image watermarking. *Signal Processing, 66*, 357–372.

Bender, W., Gruhl, D., & Morimoto, N. (1995). Techniques for data hiding. *Proceedings of SPIE, 2420*, 164–173.

Benoit, H. (1997). *Digital television MPEG-1, MPEG-2 and principles of the DVB system*.

Berghel, H., & O'Gorman, L. (1997). Digital watermark. Retrieved from *www.acm.org/~hlb/publications/dig_wtr/dig_watr.html*

Boland, F.M., O Ruanaidh, J.J.K., & Dautzenberg, C. (1995). Watermarking digital images for copyright protection. *Image Processing and Its Applications*, 326–330.

Bush, C., Funk, W., & Wolthusen, S. (1999). Digital watermarking using DCT domain constraints. *Proceedings of the International Conference on Image Processing, 3*, 231–234.

Chen, F. (1995). *Multimedia authentication*. Unpublished MS Thesis, Department of Computer Science, University of Houston, Texas.

Chen, F., & Leiss, E.L. (1996). Authentication for multimedia documents. *Proceedings of CLEI PANEL'96–Conferencia Latinoamérica de Informática*, 613–624.

Chun, T., Hong, M., Oh, Y., Shin, D., & Park, S. (1998). Digital watermarking for copyright protection of MPEG2 compressed video. *IEEE Trans. Consumer Electronics, 44*(3).

Cox, I., Killian, J, Leighton, T., & Shamoon, T. (1997). Secure spread spectrum watermarking for multimedia. *IEEE Trans. Image Processing, 6*(12), 1673–1687.

Duan, F.Y., King, I., Chan, L.W., & Xu, L. (1998). Intra-block algorithm for digital watermarking. *IEEE Proc. Int'l Conf. Image Processing, 2*, 1589–1591.

Hsu, C., & Wu, J. (1998). DCT-based watermark for video. *IEEE Trans. Consumer Electronics, 44*, 206–216.

Hsu, C., & Wu, J. (1999). Hidden digital watermarks in images. *IEEE Trans. Image Processing, 8*(1), 58–68.

Katzenbeisser, S., & Petitcolas, F.A.P. (2000). *Information hiding techniques for steganography and digital watermarking*. Boston: Artech House.

Koch, E., & Zhao, Z. (1995). Toward robust and hidden image copyright labeling. *Proceedings of the IEEE Workshop on Nonlinear Signal and Image Processing*, 443–449.

Koch, E., Rindfrey, J., & Zhao, J. (1994). Copyright protection for multimedia data. *IEEE Proc. Int'l Conf. Digital Media and Electronic Publishing*, 203–213.

Lee, C.-H., Oh, H.-S., Baek, Y., & Lee, H.-K. (1999). Adaptive digital image watermarking using variable size of blocks in frequency domain. *Proceedings of the IEEE Region 10 Conference on TENCON, 1*, 702–705.

Leiss, E.L. (1982). *Principles of data security*. New York: Plenum.

Matsui, K., & Tanaka, K. (1994). Video steganography. *Journal of the Interactive Multimedia Association Intellectual Property Project, 1*(1), 187–206.

Nikolaidis, N., & Pitas, I. (1998). Robust image watermarking in the spatial domain. *Signal Processing, 66*(3), 385–403.

Sonka, M., Hlavac, V., & Boyle, R. (1998). *Image processing, analysis, and machine vision*. Pacific Grove, CA: PWS.

Tanaka, K., Nakamura, Y., & Matsui, K. (1999). Embedding secret information into a dithered multilevel image. *Proceedings of the 1990 IEEE Military Communications Conference*, 216–220.

Wallace, G.K. (1992). The JPEG still picture compressing standard. *IEEE Trans. Consumer Electronics, 38*(1), 18–35.

Yang, Q. (2001). *Time-variant watermarks in color digital video*. Unpublished MS Thesis, Department of Computer Science, University of Houston, Texas.

Yang, Z. (1999). *Time-variant watermarks in digital video*. Unpublished MS Thesis, Department of Computer Science, University of Houston, Texas.

Endnotes

[1]   Support of this work under NSF Grant SFS-0313880 is acknowledged.

[2]   It is, of course, true that this leaves one with the problem of what to put in the place of the removed visible watermark. This is important if the watermark is not added to the image but replaces it. If the watermark was added, subtracting it would restore the original image; however, if the watermark replaced the pixels of the image, it is not possible to restore the original image, leaving an "empty" spot in the image. This empty spot could be filled by interpolation but this will frequently provide unsatisfactory results. In many such cases, it will still be possible to discern the (rough) shape of the removed logo, even though information contained in the logo would no longer be accessible.

[3]   Briefly, a new scene in a video will almost certainly result in the use of an I-picture for the first frame of the scene. Since most of the watermark insertion concentrates on I-pictures, this implies that the removal of a group of frames (e.g., an entire scene) that begins with an I-picture would not be noticeable if all watermark images are identical, that is, if they are time invariant. While the running time of a video could of course be used to *detect* tampering in general, this technique would not allow one to determine *where* the tampering occurred—unless a time-variant watermark approach is employed.

4   Clearly, if the quality of the video images is visibly affected by the watermark insertion, users will refuse to accept the resulting lower quality of the images. On the other hand, no matter how well the image quality is preserved, if the process of inserting the watermark adds a significant amount of processing to the already somewhat time-consuming MPEG processing requirements, there may simply not be sufficient compute power to carry out the watermark *insertion* in real time. In most cases, the complexity of *using* (i.e., *viewing*) a watermarked video is not increased by the watermark, in contrast to encryption-based approaches.

5   It should be clear that in many videos, both individual frames and successive frames contain much overt redundancy. For example, the background of a scene will ordinarily not change from one frame to the next unless the camera moves; moreover, this background may be virtually featureless and constitute a relatively large percentage of the frame (e.g., when recording an interview), resulting in a large degree of redundancy. (This is, of course, amply borne out by the compression rates that are typically achieved by MPEG on video files.)

6   It is not only the storage of the data that is a concern; perhaps more important is the bandwidth requirement that results when transmitting a digital video file over a network. Were the file transmitted in its raw format, the minimum bandwidth necessary for sending a single digital video would be 240 megabits per second (without leaving bandwidth for anything else).

7   It is not designed for line drawings or lettering (although the presence of such features is not an impediment for JPEG). JPEG stands for Joint Photographic Experts Group, an ISO/CCITT committee.

8   A compression technique is called *lossless* if the information content of the original file can be retrieved from the compressed file in its entirety. A technique is called *lossy* if the compressed file loses some of the original information. While a lossless approach appears more attractive, it is typically the lossy techniques that are more interesting since they result in significantly larger savings. Moreover, the loss of information they suffer is typically imperceptible to the viewer.

9   DCT stands for discrete cosine transform (see Wallace, 1992).

10   JPEG, and consequently MPEG, allows one to specify the image quality in terms of rather intuitive parameters. Thus, the image quality can be varied, depending on the given application. For example, a major movie

may be encoded with greater faithfulness (and at greater cost in storage space or transmission bandwidth) than a video conference in a corporate setting.

11   There are k+1 possible values, from 0 to k.

12   Studies of typical images have conclusively demonstrated that even for relatively small values of p, say around 10, the perceived quality of the image is virtually unaffected. While the value at which people will notice a difference depends on the type of image, it is a very important aspect of JPEG to determine as small a value of p as acceptable from a visual perception point of view.

13   Let M (N) be number of pictures between two successive P-pictures (I-pictures). Typical values for (M,N) are (3,12). Thus, 1/12 of a group of pictures are I-pictures, 1/4 P-pictures, and 2/3 B-pictures.

14   This value of 200 is, of course, derived from the JPEG compression ratio and the removal of redundancy related to motion estimation, based on the I-, P-, and B-pictures.

15   The fact that luminance values (Y) are four times as frequent as either chrominance values (C_r, C_b) is directly related to the already-mentioned human perception of color.

16   This is frequently an image that is substantially smaller that the video image; for example, assuming a 640 x 480 pixel image, the watermark may be 80 x 60. (Also, it typically would be black-and-white in order to reduce the amount of information that must be accommodated in each video picture.) The watermark image might then be repeated 64 times to fill the entire image region.

17   Specifically, in the video frame number i to be watermarked, we embed the watermark frame number i, for i=1, 2, ..., N_0. If there are more than N_0 pictures in the video to be watermarked, the next batch of N_0 pictures get a second copy of the watermark video embedded, and so forth.

18   If N_0 is smaller than the total number of I-pictures, wraparound will occur. However, if an attacker wanted to delete pictures from the watermarked video, it would be necessary to remove as many as one or more complete copies of the watermark cover. If N_0 is not too small, the resulting shortening of the video should be an obvious giveaway. (Even if N_0 is rather small, information about the number of frames, or run-time of the video, could be part of the watermark information which would allow one to detect this type of tampering.) Finally, such an operation would require

a great deal of information about the MPEG structure of the video, which renders this attack even more difficult to carry out successfully.

[19]   While certain plays and operas (Büchner's *Wozzeck* is a particularly prominent example) are notorious for the fact that the author did not specify the order in which (certain) scenes are to be performed, this is not an argument for permitting the unauthorized permutation of scenes in a movie or video.

Chapter IX

Active Watermarking System:
Protection of Digital Media

Alexander P. Pons
University of Miami, USA

Hassan Aljifri
UAE Offsets Group, USA

Abstract

In the past decade, the business community has embraced the capabilities of the Internet to provide a multitude of services that involve access to data and information. Of particular concern to these businesses has been the protection and authentication of digital data as they are distributed electronically. We propose a novel approach that combines the reactive rule-based scheme of an active database management system (ADBMS) with the technology of digital watermarking to automatically protect digital data. The ADBMS technology facilitates the establishment of event-condition-action (ECA) rules that define the actions to be triggered by events under certain conditions. These actions are the generation of unique watermarks and the tagging of digital data with unique signatures. Watermarking is a technology that embeds, within the digital data's context, information identifying its owner. The integration of these two technologies provides a powerful mechanism for protecting digital data in a consistent and formal manner.

Introduction

The Internet has emerged as one of the most profound social, technical, and business phenomena in the history of humankind. It has allowed for a new model of business (e.g., e-commerce), altered the way individuals communicate (e.g., e-mail), and enabled organizations and individuals access to a wide spectrum and wealth of easily accessible digital data. E-businesses continue to develop and distribute a significant amount of digital data to vast audiences in the form of images, audio, and video. These digital items are referred to as objects. As the number of distributed digital objects has exploded, restrictions on an object's use, authenticity, and ownership have become highly desirable, and in some cases, necessary. Through the use of digital watermarking technology, a company can embed in an object a distinctive signature that uniquely identifies them. The embedded digital watermark can determine the veracity of the object's supposed owner or fingerprint the object and link it to a requestor. Additionally, a watermark can be used to detect any tampering of an object and hence validate its authenticity. Digital watermarking offers a way for a company to distinctively sign an object, indisputably verifying its ownership as well as the potential to identify violators, through the embedding of identifiable markings within the object. For example, when a company makes an object available on its Web site, Internet users can download the object to their local machines. These Web clients can use the object in any way they desire, including claiming ownership, altering its content, and/or passing the object to others. However, with digital watermarking, the company still would be able to claim ownership, verify the object's content, and determine a violator, since the object contains its identifiable markings.

Numerous areas of e-business have embraced database technology to organize and manage many of these objects. These passive databases function as large object repositories, which allow efficient access and management of these objects. Passive databases can be extended using rules and related procedures, which will execute once an object is stored, manipulated, or retrieved in order to watermark it in a dynamic and unique manner. These active databases respond to object manipulations in ways that enforce established business policies and procedures. The combination of these two technologies, active database and digital watermarking, enables the implementation of an active watermarking system (AWS) to protect, track, and authenticate digital data. The proposed AWS (Pons & Aljifri, 2003) automatically watermarks objects that are stored in the database in order to identify the object's owner. When the object is retrieved, it is also watermarked with the requestor's identity to track its release. In addition, the AWS extracts embedded watermarks from an object to authenticate its content and to determine the object's owner and possibly the object's requestor. Organizations and individuals that embrace e-business can greatly benefit from this type of data protection.

The protection of intellectual digital property has gained significant attention in recent years with the 1996 World Intellectual Property Organization (WIPO, 1996a) conference that revised the Bern Convention for the Protection of Literary and Artistic Works to include digital dissemination and use of literary and artistic properties. Provisions of the resulting WIPO Copyright Treaty include several important issues related to future expansion of the use of watermarking techniques. The ideal electronic copyright management system has been described by the writers to include several vital capabilities, including the detection, prevention, and tracking of a number of performed operational functions such as opening, printing, copying, or modifying of copyrighted properties (Burns, 1996; Smith & Webber, 1995; Stefik, 1996, 1997; WIPO, 1996b). The AWS supports many of these vital capabilities in a consistent and effective manner through the application of active rules.

The remainder of this chapter is organized as follows. The next two sections review the technologies of active database and digital watermarking, respectively. Then, we discuss the functionality and objectives of the AWS, and follow up with a section that focuses on AWS implementation issues. Next, the performance of the AWS under various workloads is discussed. Finally, we present a deployment strategy for AWS and concluding remarks.

Active Database Technology

Most business applications typically use conventional passive database management systems (DBMS) and function primarily as data repositories with querying tools to manipulate the stored data. These systems utilize a DBMS despite its inefficiencies and unreliability with regard to the enforcement and consistency of business rules, which reside in external components of the application outside of the database. The placement of business rule processing in external components severely limits their changeability, as all components that enforce the rules are affected, and must be updated individually in order to maintain appliance uniformity. An active DBMS (Widom & Ceri, 1996) provides all of the functionality associated with a passive DBMS and processes business rules in the DBMS by automatically responding to predefined situations or events (inserts, deletes, updates, and queries). When these events occur, conditions (object type, value ranges, etc.) are checked for relevance. If the condition is relevant, the DBMS triggers actions appropriate to the instigating situation or event. The inclusion of event-condition-action (ECA) rules in a passive database transfers data processing intelligence into the DBMS itself.

The AWS presented in this chapter employs an active database to enforce copyright protection and traitor tracking for digital media through the establishment execution of certain rules. Consider the following AWS rule:

Rule No: Rule Name	Event	Condition	Action
Rule 1: WM_Image	Inserts into table Object	If object is JPEG image with features $\{f_1, f_2 ...\}$	Executes image watermarking algorithm

On any insertion into the Object table, Rule 1: WM_Image is triggered. The rule determines the type and features of the object. If the object is a JPEG image with features $\{f_1, f_2, ...\}$, then the system watermarks the image using the appropriate algorithm. The placement of these rules in the DBMS guarantees that the rules and the data are consistent, since a rule is specified once and in one location, rather than several times in different applications. This method is ideal for e-business applications as it solves many rule consistency problems, while potentially increasing performance with the integration of data and rules. Furthermore, two advantages of active databases include (1) the reusability of rules which reduces the time necessary for the creation and maintenance of rules, and (2) the existence of rule development tools, available in several commercial databases that facilitate rule creation, debugging, and testing to expedite rule implementation.

Rule Enforcement

Organizations conduct business utilizing various types of rules that are enforced in different ways. In e-business, these anomalies cannot be tolerated, as business systems are extending beyond the boundaries of organizations to encompass much greater scopes. When rules are not consistently applied across applications, it can undermine the effectiveness of the rules' existence. In addition, organizations often change policies and procedures, which must be reflected in these rules. Having rules in various locations hinders an organization's flexibility in altering the manner that it conducts business reflected in these rules. The goal is a central location that affects all applications that supports rule consistency and maintenance.

The traditional approach to rule compliance has rules residing in the application programs that access the passive databases. The problem with this approach is that there is no guarantee that the rules and data are consistent, since the database can be updated with transactions that are independent of the application programs. Therefore, the database can be altered and become inconsistent when the established applications are not used. Apart from the potential of circumventing rule conformance, rules in an application are difficult to change, creating inconsistency problems. Bringing a database into conformity with new rules or changing an existing rule is difficult, since the rule may have to be created or updated in numerous places. Any application that is not properly adjusted can possibly lead to the user bypassing the new or changed rule. Furthermore, since the rule adjustment can occur in many applications that are programmed by several different programmers, there exists the possibility of deviant implementation affecting the effectiveness of the rule. As a result, embedding rules in application programs is cumbersome, erroneous, and can lead to variation in enforcement that cannot be tolerated in today's e-business environment.

The preferred approach is to have rules reside in the DBMS itself. In this case, the DBMS can guarantee that the rules and the data are consistent, as a rule is specified once and in one location instead of a rule in each application. This is the method that we encourage for e-business applications, as it solves many of the previously mentioned problems, while potentially increasing performance with the integration of data and rules. Additionally, two advantages of active databases include the reusability of rules and specialized tools for rule creation. Rule reusability is very attractive, since it reduces the time necessary for their creation and maintenance. While several commercial databases include triggers to realize rules, the proposed system is built on top of an Oracle database, which provides many development tools facilitating rule creation and testing. Finally, as discussed, using active database techniques in e-business applications has several inherent advantages over passive database techniques, while having the ability to simplify complex problems.

The Technology of Watermarking

Digital watermarking is a cutting-edge technology that combines traditional hardcopy watermarking techniques with digital representation. In this section, we begin with a survey of watermarking functionality and then discuss the implications for applications.

Proprietary digital media material are visually identified with the use of a visible watermark, an insertion or overlaying of a pattern, insignia, or some special identifying mark on or within an object. For example, the fictitious site name www.my-watermark.com might be overlaid on an image created for a Web site banner for marketing purposes, or the United Nations logo might be added to a picture taken at a conference and posted on the Web. The use of watermarks in the AWS focuses on watermarks that are not visually identifiable and are generally undetectable to the human eye. These watermarks are secret, allowing for a more security-oriented application of the technology. In addition, distinct from spread spectrum or other steganographic approaches, these watermarking techniques have greater robustness as the watermark is difficult to extract without altering or degrading the original object.

Watermarking Principles

Since the early 1990s, a variety of watermarking techniques and algorithms have been developed or proposed from a range of communities such as steganography, communications, and source coding. Watermarking systems contain two essential building blocks (Kutter & Petitcolas, 1999): a watermark embedding system and a watermark detection system. Figure 1 shows the general form of a watermarking system. The input to the embedding system consists of a watermark, an object, and a key. The watermark can be in the form of a number, text, or an image. The key enforces security through

Figure 1. Watermarking system

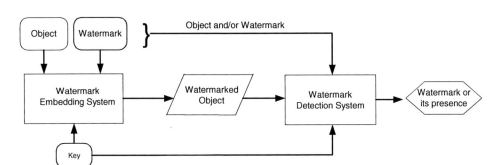

encryption, preventing unauthorized parties from recovering and manipulating the watermark. The output of the embedding system is the watermarked object.

The input to the watermarking detection system contains the watermarked object, the key, and depending on the watermarking methods, the original watermark or the original object. The output is the detected watermark or an indication of its presence.

Several aspects of an effective and relatively secure watermarking system must be considered: (1) the robustness of the watermark against attacks, (2) the degradation of the data itself in the watermarking process, and (3) the ratio between the host signal and watermark (Katzenbeisser & Petitcolas, 2000). These aspects bring to light perhaps the most important limitation of watermarking—that there is a general trade-off between robustness, perceptibility, and ratio, suggesting that algorithmic design should be highly dependent on the maximization of all three areas, measured independently and against one another.

Watermarking Applications

The requirements with which watermarking systems must comply are always based on the watermarking applications (Voyatzis & Pitas, 1999). It should be noted that there is no "global watermarking method." The work of Kutter and Hartung (2000) divides watermarking application into four categories: watermarking for copyright protection, fingerprinting for traitor tracking, watermarking for copy protection, and watermarking for image authentication.

Watermarking for Copyright Protection

The most vital application of watermarking today is the protection of one's intellectual property. The goal is to insert information about the source—the copyright owner—of the data in order to protect it from being claimed by others. Therefore, the purpose of watermarks is to establish rightful ownership. This application requires a high level of robustness. The focus of this application is the Web, which contains many images that the copyright owners wish to protect.

Fingerprinting for Traitor Tracking

Another type of application, "fingerprinting," is used to pass information about the legal recipient to identify single distributed copies of the data. This application requires the insertion of a different watermark into each copy distributed, a requirement that is helpful in tracing illegally produced copies of the data that may circulate. This method is equivalent to serial numbers in software products. Watermarks for fingerprinting applications require a high robustness against standard data processing, as well as attacks aimed at removing the watermark.

Watermarking for Copy Protection

The existence of a copy protection method to disallow unauthorized copying of media is a much-needed feature in a multimedia distribution system. Copy protection is not likely to be achieved in open systems; however, it is possible to use watermarks indicating the copy status of the data in closed systems. Consider DVD systems that embed copy information within the data as a watermark. The DVD player will contain copy control and copy protection mechanisms (Bloom et al., 1999; Linnartz, 1998) that use watermarking to signal the copy status of multimedia data, such as "copy once" or "copy never."

Watermarking for Image Authentication

In an authentication application, the objective is to detect modification of the data, to be achieved with so-called fragile watermarks. Fragile watermarks are watermarks that are used in authentication applications in order to detect modifications of the data rather than conveying un-erasable information. Fragile watermarks have limited robustness.

Active Watermarking System (AWS)

The Active Watermarking System (AWS) solves many of the concerns associated with the protection of digital intellectual property. The system addresses these concerns through the automatic insertion of hidden digital watermarks to establish copyright protection for ownership identification and fingerprinting for traitor tracking. In addition, the AWS maintains sufficient information to conduct digital data authentication, allowing content verification of a digital object using the embedded watermark. The basic functionality of AWS is supported using various components, including database tables, active rules, watermarking algorithms, and several user interfaces (owner registration, owner upload, requestor download, and authenticate). Prior to discussing these components, the different AWS user roles are presented and their responsibilities and actions defined. These users consist of object owners (O_O) seeking copyright protection, object requestors (O_R) accessing the digital data and being fingerprinted, and object authenticators (O_A) determining digital data trustworthiness.

Initially, the O_O must register with the AWS through the owner registration interface, which generates and assigns a unique owner identification number (O_{ID}) to the O_O. Subsequently, the AWS generates a unique owner watermark (O_{WM}) that is determined by the O_{ID} associated with the O_O. During O_O object submissions using the owner upload interface, each object is tagged with its owner's O_{WM}, thus copy protecting the object. Therefore, each object is stored with a hidden O_{WM} ready for O_R rendering. Any changes to the owner's information will not affect the O_{WM}, which remains valid for all past and future object uploads.

The O_R consists of Internet, intranet, and/or extranet users, depending on the AWS deployment strategy. When an O_R accesses the AWS through the requestor download interface, the system generates a unique requestor watermark (R_{WM}). The R_{WM} is composed of the requestor's IP address and the time/date of the request; this information allows the system to track objects. Each object made available to the requestor must be tagged (fingerprinted) with the hidden R_{WM}. Based on the intended user population, the IP address is typically sufficient to identify a particular O_R, but for public Internet users the AWS must require the O_R to register with the system to obtain more specific identifying information.

The role of the O_A is to receive an object and then determine either the object's owner or authenticity. The O_A could be any user of the AWS that has obtained a copy of the object, either directly from the system as an O_R, or indirectly from another O_R. Using the AWS authenticate interface, an object is supplied to the AWS, which extracts the embedded O_{WM} and R_{WM} to determine the O_O, O_R, and/or a statistical degree of confidence on the object's content.

In Figure 2, we depict the AWS work flow, its various interfaces, and information inter-exchanged for the normal usage of the system. An increasingly significant feature of the AWS in e-business is the ability to validate the contents of an object. Of concern to businesses is the possibility that a transmitted object could have been altered from the original object. In our system, an O_R obtains an object, changes its contents slightly, and sends it to a third party. Typically, it would be very difficult to verify the authenticity of the object's content. Using the AWS, the object's content is verifiable using its O_{WM}, which indicates whether any alterations have been performed on the object. Once tampering is detected, the AWS can provide the R_{WM} information that identifies the primary O_R.

When the O_O uploads an object, it is watermarked using the O_{WM} with an appropriate watermarking algorithm. The active component of our system automatically determines the watermarking algorithm based on the object's characteristics and O_{WM}. In this way, all objects stored within the context of the AWS are protected with the owner's watermark. In order to track object downloads, when an O_R accesses the AWS, a R_{WM} is produced in real time using information extracted from the current communication session. The active component in the AWS adds the R_{WM} in real time to each object supplied to the requestor. The manner in which each object is fingerprinted with the R_{WM} is based on the object type, its characteristics, and the properties of the R_{WM}. An object is only made available for downloading or viewing if it has been augmented with both the O_{WM} and R_{WM}, thereby uniquely identifying the owner and the requestor. The active rules in the AWS constitute the mechanism required to identify the object type, determine the object's characteristics, select a corresponding watermarking algorithm, and perform the watermarking off-line during object submission and in real time during object request. Further, the O_A can submit an object to the AWS, which will test the object's authenticity.

Figure 2. AWS and its user interfaces

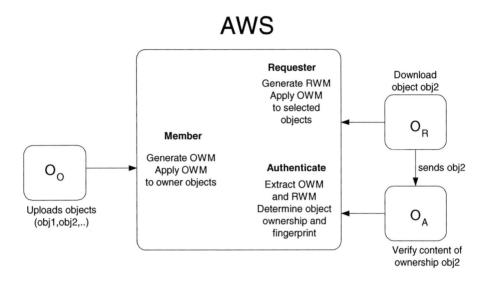

AWS Implementation

The AWS is a three-tiered Web application using various technologies at the respective processing sites—client side, Web server side, and data source. On the client side, there are static and dynamic Web pages comprising the various AWS user interfaces necessary for obtaining and viewing objects. Objects are uploaded using a form's "put" option and displayed by inserting the binary data comprising the object (image) into the Web pages. At the Web server side, Microsoft's Internet Information Server (IIS) provides the basic application logic to interact with an Oracle 9i enterprise database. At the data source, Oracle's PL/SQL language is employed to implement the system's triggers, which invoke calls to stored procedures and functions written in the Java programming language. These triggers and database executions constitute all processing necessary for object watermarking and authentication. Therefore, the AWS is execution intensive at the ADBMS and less so at the Web server and browser levels.

The handling of the digital data objects requires the storage and manipulation of binary large objects (BLOBs) in Oracle and Java. Oracle is an object relational database with active rule facilities, which allows the definition of user-defined data types that encapsulate attributes as well as behaviors. The user-defined Entity_Type contains a BLOB attribute named "item" used to hold the binary data in the database. The item attribute cannot be directly selected from the database through queries (though one can query the length of the item attribute). Consideration was given to alternative methods such as using tables of predefined Oracle data types to store BLOBs. These are easier to develop but do not apply the object-oriented concept that is sought for robustness and program logic. The Object table is created containing a column data of Entity_Type, which maintains the BLOB, other attributes, and several manipulation methods. The Oracle JDeveloper 9i was the selected tool used to map the Oracle user-defined type Entity_Type to the Java class. Once mapped to a Java class, the BLOB can be accessed and manipulated using Java code. These BLOBs are passed to the VB.net code as an intrinsic BLOB type for rendering at the client side.

While there is some research on watermarking video and audio, the majority of publications in the field of watermarking currently address the copyright of still images. Without significant loss of generality, we focus on watermarking still images. Therefore, the initial AWS implementation handles PGM images but can be expanded to other digital media with the incorporation of additional watermarking algorithms and the development of supporting Java classes through the use of inheritance.

Database Structure

The basic functionality of the AWS utilizes three tables: the Member, Object, and Session tables. These tables are sufficient to provide the essential tasks of copyrighting, fingerprinting, and authenticating protection of an owner's digital property.

We are able to store a watermark for each O_O that the system maintains, an impossible task for the O_R as the number of object requestors and selected objects can be prohibitively large. Data concerning the O_R and its computed R_{WM} is temporarily maintained in the Session table to avoid recalculation during the current communication session. Although the R_{WM} is not stored in the AWS beyond the current session, it is embedded in each O_R rendered object. The Member table stores O_O's registration information, which at the least consists of a record with an O_{ID}, the member's name, address, and affiliation. Inserting an owner record into the Member table triggers the Generate_OWM rule, which appends an AWS computed watermark to the member's information prior to adding the record to the table.

The objects submitted by AWS members are placed in the Object table. An Object table record consists of the owner's O_{ID} and the O_{WM} watermarked object. When an object is submitted, the Save_Object rule is triggered, which selects the most suitable watermarking algorithm and applies the owner's O_{WM} to the object, according to the object's type and characteristics. A second rule associated with the Object table is the Request_Object rule, which is triggered in response to the retrieval of an object, applying a generated R_{WM} to each object supplied to the particular requestor. To perform the necessary operations of an O_A, a set of DBMS stored procedures and functions are required. These stored modules process a submitted object for authentication by extracting its O_{WM} and subsequently searching the Member table for a matching O_{WM}. This process returns the object's O_{ID}, which can be used for further processing.

Active Rules

The following four basic rules comprise the core of our data protection system (see figure below). These rules take the form of ECA rules, which are supported in many commercial DBMS. Although not shown, there exist various versions of rules 2 and 4 in the system that handles the necessary watermarking task. These rules check the type of an object and its characteristics before executing a specific corresponding procedure and algorithm. For example, an object inserted into the Object table would trigger all rules associated with this

Rule Number: Rule Name	Event	Condition	Action
Rule 1: Generate_OWM	Inserts member data into Member table	Is member data unique	Processes member data and generates O_{WM} using O_{ID} to store along with the member data
Rule 2: Save_Object	Inserts object into Object table	Is it an image with dimensions less than 640 x 480	Processes image with corresponding watermarking algorithm with member's O_{WM}
Rule 3: Generate_RWM	Inserts requestor data into Session table	Is requestor data unique, obtain from communication link	Processes requestor data, generates and stores temporarily in the Session table the requestor's R_{WM}
Rule 4: Request_Object	Selects objects from the Object table	Is it an image with dimensions less than 640 x 480	Obtains the requestor's R_{WM} from the Session table and using a corresponding watermarking algorithm tag each object

event. The conditional part of each rule would check the object, identify a single rule from the triggered set to be used and process the object with the most effective watermarking approach. Rules 1 and 3 are responsible for augmenting inserted record data with a system-generated watermark. These rules are responsible for verifying the uniqueness of the computed watermark in order to guarantee distinct object ownership.

Java Class Hierarchy

The executable component of the AWS consists of the Java class hierarchy shown in Figure 3. The root and second-tier class are abstract classes, which mandate that certain behaviors be defined (and ultimately implemented) by inherited classes. In the figure, the JPEG and GIF classes are concrete, and map BLOB objects to their respective classes for subsequent manipulation. The AWSObj class defines the behavior for storing and conducting watermark embedding, extraction and detection, and other supporting methods. The second-tier media classes redefine abstract methods from the AWSObj class, while augmenting it capabilities with media-specific methods. The Audio, Image, Video, and Code classes, respectively, define the basic functionality to manipulate these types of media. The Code class is intended to support the watermarking of executable code, particularly Java code, which is widely deployed throughout the Internet. The copy protection of code is a vital issue for software modules deployed in distributed environments. The JPEG and GIF classes contain the specific watermarking manipulation algorithms for these two image formats. To expand the AWS for additional image formats requires the definition a new class that inherits from the Image class. To augment a class's watermarking algorithms, a new method would be defined that implements the

Figure 3. AWS class hierarchy

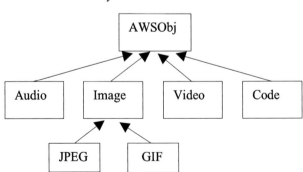

new algorithm. The method will share the same name (overloaded) as the other watermarking methods for the class, but it will be distinguishable according to the parameter passed (type and count).

Watermarking Techniques

The AWS is a copy protection scheme that provides reliable methods for efficiently watermarking an object and authenticating watermarked objects. The use of any of the methods of watermarking is application dependent. The design of AWS does not focus on supporting a single watermarking technique; however, it is flexible enough that any watermarking method can be used.

Watermarking techniques have emerged as the leading solution to protecting ownership and authenticating digital media documents. Watermarking algorithms must address the following issues:

- The ratio of the information contained in the watermark to that in the host object
- Image degradation due to watermarking
- Robustness of the watermark against object distortions caused during transmission

The ultimate watermarking method should resist any kind of distortion introduced by standard or malicious data processing. No perfect method has been developed yet; thus, practical systems must compromise between robustness and the competing requirements such as invisibility and information rate. For example, in image watermarking, if a method is needed that is resilient to JPEG compression with high compression factors, it is probably more efficient to employ a method that works in a transform domain rather than a spatial domain (Kutter & Petitcolas, 1999).

The watermarking algorithm consists of three stages: generating, embedding, and detecting. The generating stage is an off-line process (i.e., it is not performed in real time). There are two embedding stages: embedding the author's watermark, which is an off-line process, and labeling the requestor information, which is an online process (i.e., it is performed in real time). The most crucial stage is the detection stage, which is an online process. The detection technique is applied to a large set of images; therefore, a fast and efficient detection method is desirable. AWS adopts the detection algorithm D:

$$D(S,K,O_{WMi}) = \begin{cases} 1 \text{ if } W_E \approx O_{WMi} \\ 0 \text{ otherwise} \end{cases}$$

where S is the submitted object, K is the AWS key used to enforce security, W_E is the extracted watermark, and O_{WMi} is the watermark for owner i. The relation $\approx$ indicates that W_E is equal to O_{WMi} within some confidence measure that the given watermark O_{WMi} is present in S.

AWS Performance Evaluation

The AWS includes several key capabilities and features that have been described by researchers in the field of electronic copyright management systems. These features include the ability of the AWS to detect modification to copyrighted properties and the ability to identify the requestor of the materials and maintain records of users and their copyrighted materials. The AWS accomplishes these primary activities through processing conducted at the database shared among all AWS users. Therefore, performance analysis of the AWS is necessary to evaluate the cost of the watermarking process, the performance of the AWS under different loads, and the extra delays imposed on AWS users.

In order to determine the execution cost associated with watermarking and to obtain a baseline value to compare the operations of R_{WM}, images of various sizes (50K, 150K, 250K, and 1,000K) are retrieved without watermarks. Obtaining these values provides a reference to establish the percentage increase in execution time associated with watermarking. We focus on the embedding of R_{WM} and the detection of the watermark because they are real-time processes that significantly impact the system's performance, as opposed to examining the insertion of images and tagging them with an O_{WM}. The percentage increases associated with the R_{WM} images are attributed to the cumulative time required to generate and store the R_{WM}, identify a trigger, and watermark the image. The results in Table 1 indicate the percentage difference when a watermarked image is retrieved compared to its nonwatermarked form. For example, relative to an original image, it would take 7.89% more time to watermark and retrieve an image of size 250K. The percentage values of the extra time incurred increase with the image size, since the watermarking algorithm must process a larger image. This percentage increase reflects only the cost of watermarking, as trigger activation and R_{WM} production remain constant across the various image sizes.

The previous results focus on a single AWS user; in order to estimate the performance of the AWS under different loads, simultaneous object selects are performed to ascertain the system's response time compared to that for a single user. Table 2 contains the time increases of multiple users relative to a single user. The AWS being database-processing intensive does extend the system's response time according to the number of users (which necessitates our future research: developing a network of AWS nodes to distribute processing, and improve system performance). This is apparent from the higher values in the table, which indicate a user's mounting delay as numerous simultaneous transactions take place and stretch the resources of a single AWS installation. A user who accesses the AWS as the 30th active user would suffer a postponement of 26.4 times that of a single user in retrieving an image of size 250K.

An extra delay associated with the detection process during image authentication can be attributed to the identification of the original image. Currently, an extracted O_{WM} from a submitted image is used to find a match in the Member

Table 1. User percent increase

Image size	50K	150K	250K	1,000K
Increase time	5.49%	6.90%	7.89%	11.02%

Table 2. Number of simultaneous requests and image sizes

Image Size	10 Users	30 Users	50 Users	70 Users
50K	3.59	5.78	8.4	17.5
150K	4.56	7.3	10.9	30.3
250K	10.21	26.4	39.8	57.3
1,000K	16.23	32.8	45.8	60.2

table leading to the original image to conduct the process. As the number of O_O increases, the O_A performance degrades, because there is a corresponding increase in stored O_{WM} to match. A solution to this problem is to use a watermarked image histogram. This changes the detection process as follows:

- When the Object authenticator submits an image I, the histogram H_{OA} of that image is generated.
- The histograms H_i of the watermarked images stored in the database DB are generated and stored along with the images in the database. The matching algorithm M is performed to determine whether the supplied image has been watermarked by AWS.

$$M(H_{OA}, DB) = \begin{cases} 1 \text{ if } H_i \in DB \text{ and } H_i \approx H_{OA} \\ 0 \text{ otherwise} \end{cases}$$

The relation $\approx$ indicates perceptual similarity between the two histograms. H_i may not be equal to H_{OA} because of the R_{WM} embedding process, which tags an image with the IP address or personal information of an O_R. The use of the matching algorithm M and a multidimensional index, formed from the image's vector histogram, would reduce the number of images to consider. This would improve the authentication process as a result of increasing the storage capacity of the implementation and reduce the time required to detect a watermark in an image and related information. The addition of this capability forms part of our future work to improve AWS performance.

AWS Deployment Strategy

The proposed system can target users of intranet, extranet, and the Internet. An intranet deployment would consist of using the AWS within the boundaries of an organization, while an extranet deployment would extend the user base to consist of corporate partners that have access to an organization's information. In both scenarios, electronic documents can be registered, obtained, and authenticated for a limited set of users, augmenting an organization's document processing approach beyond a document repository. This provides a level of data protection that is often necessary in business-to-business transactions to remove any suspicions of improprieties. A single centralized AWS installation is sufficient to protect data within these e-business contexts, possibly housing the system at the organization's central office. Expanding the systems outside these constraints requires various deployments of the AWS in order to handle widespread use by the Internet population. This requires a network of AWS that communicate among themselves when a member registers or an object is authenticated. When a new member attempts to register with the systems, it is no longer valid to generate a unique watermark from the registering AWS. Rather, it must be a universal AWS watermark unique throughout all AWS installations. In addition, when an object is authenticated at an AWS, it must be checked at all AWS nodes that comprise the AWS network. Figure 4, depicts a network of AWS that collaborate using additional rules to provide these capabilities in a much greater scope.

The additional rules are triggered along with the respective functionality using lookup processes to communicate with the known AWS prior to acknowledging a user's request. Each AWS must maintain a directory of existing AWS that it uses to perform the generation of a universal O_{WM}. During object authentication, the information in the O_{WM} would identify the AWS that the object originated from, preventing unnecessary searching of unrelated AWS. When an object that is being authenticated has been changed, its O_{WM} could have been corrupted, requiring a universal check of all AWS, extending the object's validating time. In these circumstances, a statistical measure of the object alterations is rendered that provides an estimate of the degree of these changes.

Figure 4. Network of AWS exchanging member and authenticate information

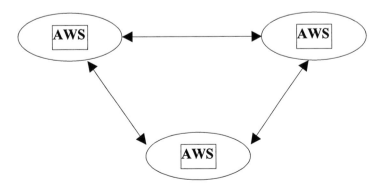

Conclusions

The digital world has brought about new protection requirements for proprietary information and data for businesses, individuals, owners, and creators of such valuable items. The ability to protect and authenticate the ownership of these electronic items will encourage an increase in e-business and enhance the Internet. The AWS proposed in this chapter addresses these issues of ownership and authentication, combining the technologies of watermarking and active database to establish the necessary protection requirements. The combination of these technologies establishes a powerful method for marking digital media to identify ownership and maintain data integrity and avoid potential misuse of the media. Furthermore, the AWS can fingerprint requested media to uniquely define when the data was tampered with and who the original requester was.

To date, the widespread use of watermarking as a tool has not been utilized in business. These systems are often developed in response to the unauthorized misuse of copyrighted materials over the Web (especially record labels and publishing companies). Although many watermark embedding and recovery systems are readily available, the standard is to develop custom-built applications that are specific to a watermarking technique. As the AWS demonstrates, the possibilities for the widespread use of more general applications utilizing watermarking of digital media are significant. The AWS has much to offer in protecting the intellectual and creative property of individuals and organizations in the digital age, while providing a flexible and scalable system that rapidly incorporates and manages new media types.

References

Bloom, J. et al. (1999). Copy protection for DVD video. *Proceedings of the IEEE, 87*(7), 1267–1276.

Burns, C. (1996). *Copyright management and the NII: Report to the Enabling Technologies Committee of the Association of American Publishers*. Washington, DC: Association of American Publishers.

Katzenbeisser, S., & Petitcolas, F. (2000). *Information hiding: Techniques for steganography and digital watermarking*. Artech House.

Kutter, M., & Hartung, F. (2000). Introduction to watermarking techniques. In S. Katzenbeisser & F. Petitcolas (Eds.), *Information hiding: Techniques for steganography and digital watermarking* (pp. 97–120). Artech House.

Kutter, M., & Petitcolas, F. (1999). Fair benchmarking for image watermarking systems. *Proceedings of Electronic Imaging '99 Security and Watermarking of Multimedia Contents, 3657*, 226–239.

Linnartz, J.P. (1998). The "ticket" concept for copy control based on embedded signaling. *Proceedings of the 5th European Symposium on Research in Computer Security, 1485*, 257–274.

Pons, A., & Aljifri, H. (2003). Data protection using watermarking in e-business. *Journal of Database Management, 14*(4), 1–13.

Smith, K., & Webber, F. (1995, November). A new set of rules for information commerce—Rights-protection technologies and personalized information commerce will affect all knowledge workers. *Commercial Week.*

Stefik, M. (1996). *Internet dreams: Archetypes, myths and metaphors.* Cambridge, MA: MIT Press.

Stefik, M. (1997). Shifting the possible: How digital property rights challenge us to rethink digital publishing. *Berkeley Technology Law Journal, 12*, 137–159.

Voyatzis, G., & Pitas, I. (1999). Protecting digital image copyright: A framework. *IEEE Journal Computer Graphics and Application, 19*(1), 18–24.

Widom, J., & Ceri, B. (1996). *Introduction to active database systems.* San Francisco: Morgan Kaufmann.

World Intellectual Property Organization (WIPO). (1996a). *Diplomatic conference on certain copyright and neighboring rights questions.* Geneva: WIPO.

World Intellectual Property Organization (WIPO). (1996b). *WIPO copyright treaty.* Geneva: WIPO.

About the Authors

Juergen Seitz received his diploma in business administration and information systems from the University of Cooperative Education, Stuttgart, Germany, and in economics from the University of Stuttgart–Hohenheim. He received his PhD from Viadrina European University, Frankfurt (Oder), Germany. He is professor for information systems and finance, and chair of information science, in particular e-commerce/e-business and m-business/telematics, at the University of Cooperative Education Heidenheim, Germany. Dr. Seitz is a member of the Executive Council of IRMA.

* * *

Byung-Ha Ahn earned a BS from the Korea Air Force Academy, Chongju, Korea (1965), and an MS and PhD in industrial engineering from Korea Advanced Institute of Science and Technology, Taejon, Korea (1977 and 1980, respectively). Since 1995, he has been a professor in the Department of Mechatronics, Gwangju Institute of Science and Technology, Gwangju, Korea. His research interests include system development and optimization, reliability analysis of large-scale systems, man–machine interfaces, and control for intelligent transportation systems.

Hassan Aljifri is an assistant professor in the Computer Information Systems Department at the University of Miami (USA). His research interest includes computer and network security, programming languages, and Internet technologies. He has published in several international journals and conferences. Most of Dr. Aljifri's recent research has been focused on methodology, framework, and techniques for designing secure systems.

Nedeljko Cvejic received a Dipl. Ing. degree in electrical engineering from the University of Belgrade, Serbia and Montenegro. Since 2001, he has been working toward a PhD at the University of Oulu, Finland. He is a research scientist with the MediaTeam Oulu, Information Processing Laboratory of the University of Oulu. His research interests include digital audio watermarking, steganography, information hiding, steganalysis, and audio compression.

Tino Jahnke received his diploma in business administration and information science from the University of Cooperative Education Heidenheim, Germany, and his bachelor's degree from Open University, London (2001). He is currently finishing his master's thesis in software technology at the University of Applied Science, Lueneburg, Germany and the University of Wolverhampton, UK. Apart from his teaching experience in universities and companies, Tino Jahnke has been appointed to examine students in their diploma exams. Since 2001, he has done research in digital watermarking technology, motion pictures, and audio signals.

Jong-Nam Kim earned an MS and PhD from the Gwangju Institute of Science and Technology (GIST), Korea (1997 and 2001, respectively). He worked in the Technical Research Institute (TRI) of the Korean Broadcasting System (KBS) from 2001 to 2003. Since 2004, he has been a professor in the Division of Electronic, Computer, and Telecommunication Engineering at Pukyong National University, Korea. His research interests include multimedia data processing, multimedia data compression, multimedia data watermarking, IPMP, MPEG, and VLSI design for video applications.

Sam Kwong received his BSc and MASc in electrical engineering from the State University of New York at Buffalo and the University of Waterloo, Canada. He later obtained his PhD from the University of Hagen, Germany. In 1990, he joined the City University of Hong Kong as a lecturer in the Department of Electronic Engineering. He is currently an associate professor in the Department of Computer Science. His research interests are evolutionary algorithms, signal processing, and intelligent computing.

Ernst Leiss is professor of computer science at the University of Houston (USA) where he has taught since 1979. He received an MMath in computer science from the University of Waterloo (1974) and a Dipl.-Ing. and a

Dr. Techn. degree from the Technical University of Vienna (1975 and 1976, respectively). He is the author of five books and over 130 peer-reviewed papers. He has supervised 13 PhD dissertations and approximately 100 MS theses. His research interests are in high-performance computing, security and integrity of data, and formal language theory. He lectures regularly worldwide in his areas of specialty.

Chang-Tsun Li received a BS in electrical engineering from the Chung-Cheng Institute of Technology (CCIT), National Defense University, Taiwan in 1987, an MS in computer science from the U.S. Naval Postgraduate School in 1992, and a PhD in computer science from the University of Warwick, UK in 1998. He was an associate professor from 1999 to 2002 in the Department of Electrical Engineering at CCIT and a visiting professor in the Department of Computer Science at the U.S. Naval Postgraduate School in the second half of 2001. He is currently a lecturer in the Department of Computer Science at the University of Warwick, UK. His research interests include image processing, pattern recognition, computer vision, multimedia security, and content-based image retrieval.

Zhang Li was born in Shan Dong province, China. She received a BS and MS in communication engineering from Ha er bin Institute of Technology and a PhD in communication theory from South China University of Technology. She was a research assistant in the Department of Computer Science at City University of Hong Kong from May 2001 to May 2002. Her research interests include digital watermarking, subliminal channel, image processing, and signal processing.

Alexander P. Pons is an assistant professor in the Computer Information Systems Department at the University of Miami, USA. He received his PhD from the University of Miami in electrical and computer engineering (1998). Dr. Pons has more than 15 years of industry and academic experience as an engineer, consultant, and professor. For the past several years, he has been involved in various aspects of real-time systems and databases as a researcher and developer. He has published in several international journals and conferences. His research interest includes real-time systems, programming languages, databases, and Internet technology.

Farook Sattar is an assistant professor in the Information Engineering Division of Nanyang Technological University, Singapore. He received his Technical Licentiate and PhD degrees in signal and image processing from Lund University, Sweden and his MEng from Bangladesh University of Technology. His current research interests include watermarking, blind signal separation, filter banks, wavelets, adaptive beamforming, 3D audio, speech/audio segmentation, speech enhancement, image feature extraction, and image enhancement. He has training in both signal and image processing and had been involved in a number of signal and image processing-related projects sponsored by the Swedish National Science and Technology Board (NUTEK) and by the Singapore Academic Research Funding (AcRF) Scheme. His research has been published in a number of leading journals and conferences.

Tapio Seppänen obtained his PhD (EE) from the University of Oulu, Finland in 1990. Currently, he is a professor of information engineering in the Department of Electrical and Information Engineering at the same university. His research topics include multimedia signal processing, digital watermarking, pattern recognition, information retrieval, language technology, and biomedical signal processing.

Eberhard Stickel studied mathematics and business mathematics at the University of Ulm, Germany and Syracuse University, New York, USA. He holds a PhD in mathematics from the University of Ulm. He is a full professor of Information Systems at Viadrina University, Frankfurt (Oder), Germany. Currently he is on leave and serves as founding president of the Hochschule der Sparkassen-Finanzgruppe, University of Applied Sciences, Bonn, Germany, a private university owned by a large German banking group. His research interests include cryptographic techniques as well as economic effects on data security and information systems in general.

Dan Yu received her BEng in communication with first-class honors from the School of Electrical and Electronic Engineering (EEE) at Nanyang Technological University (NTU), Singapore, in 2000. Having maintained an interest in multimedia information security, she started her PhD study at the School of EEE, NTU, supervised by Dr. Farook Sattar. Her PhD research concentrates on designing and developing information hiding and retrieval techniques as well as their applications to the intellectual property rights enforcement of the digital media. Since 2004, she has held a postdoctoral research position in the School of Computer Engineering, NTU. Her current research work is focused on software-defined radio, with special interests in filter bank design and optimization.

Index

A

active database management system (ADBMS) 233
active database technology 235
active watermarking system (AWS) 235, 241
affine transformation 104
asynchronous transfer mode (ATM) 186
audio watermarking 135
audio watermarking algorithms 137, 148
audio watermarking syntax 193
authenticate marking 58
authentication 9, 31, 101, 184

B

benchmarking 135
blind detection 102
blind watermark extraction 141
blind watermarking 59
broadcast monitoring 10

broadcasting 31

C

complexity 12
content authentication 54
content-targeting attack 35
copy protection 184, 240
Copy Protection Technical Working Group 7
copyright 1
copyright protection 9, 101, 184, 240
cryptography 5, 55

D

data hiding 3
data payload 12
data protection 102
database management systems (DBMS) 235
decryption 103
Diffie-Hellman problem 91
digital age 2